WITHDRAWN

CREATIVE TEACHING OF READING
IN THE
ELEMENTARY SCHOOL

All reading is not creative reading.

Creative Teaching
of
Reading
in the
Elementary School
2nd Edition

JAMES A. SMITH

State University College
Oswego, New York

Allyn and Bacon, Inc.
Boston, London, and Sydney

Library of Congress Cataloging in Publication Data

Smith, James A
    Creative teaching of reading in the elementary school.

    First ed. published in 1967 under title: Creative teaching of reading and literature in the elementary school.
    Includes bibliographies and index.
    1. Creative thinking (Education) 2. Reading (Elementary) 3. Literature—Study and teaching—United States. I. Title.
LB1573.S756   1975   372.4'1   74-23955

ISBN 0-205-04687-8 (Hardbound).
ISBN 0-205-04688-6 (Paperbound).

CONTENTS

PART TWO: THE NURTURE OF CREATIVITY THROUGH READING AND LITERATURE

Contents

FOREWORD

In the Foreword of the first editions of the books in the Creative Teaching series, E. Paul Torrance said that many exciting, meaningful, and potentially important ideas have died because no one has translated them into practical methods, and he expressed concern that this could be the fate of the creative movement. Fortunately, this concern has not been realized. In the past ten years, educational literature has been flooded with reports of research studies, theories, and experimental programs that focus on the creative development of each child as a goal in modern education.

Including the developing of creativity in each child as an educational objective is a staggering challenge for all school personnel. It calls for the invention of new materials and tools, the development of new time schedules and new patterns of organization, the use of a new approach to child study, the invention of new testing methods, the devising of unique evaluation processes, and the creation of new textbooks and teaching procedures. And, most of all, the task calls for the commitment and dedication of many people to take risks, to make choices and decisions, and to push their own creative potential to new limits.

This has been done! In the past ten years, the creative spark has caught fire. In the creative movement, thousands of people in all walks of life have found self-realization and the challenge of making life meaningful for others. The educational scene in America has become peppered with experimental projects in the development of creative thinking.

No other movement in education has swept the world as the creative movement has. Today, the need for creative people is tremendous. Developing the creative potential of each child has become an educational objective in all corners of the world. The authors of the Creative Teaching series hope these volumes will contribute in some bold measure to the changes necessary in teaching methods in the elementary school to realize this objective.

James A. Smith
State University College
Oswego, New York

PREFACE

This is a revised edition of *Creative Teaching of Reading and Literature in the Elementary School,* one of the books in the Allyn and Bacon Creative Teaching series. The main objective of the book is to translate into methodology those principles of creative thinking and creative development that I have culled from reading research done in the past ten years. This book will be most effective if it is read in combination with the first book of the series, *Setting Conditions for Creative Teaching in the Elementary School.*

Since reading has a definite place in the logical sequence of development of the language skills, the reader will also benefit by reading *Creative Teaching of the Language Arts in the Elementary School,* 2nd ed. All the material discussed in that book is pertinent to the creative teaching of reading, and some of it is essential. The basic material from *Setting Conditions for Creative Teaching* and *Creative Teaching of the Language Arts* is summarized in Chapters 1 and 2 of this volume.

Both reading and creativity are precious commodities. In the past decade, more research has been done in these two areas than in any other areas of the elementary school curriculum. But, in spite of the new knowledge about reading that has resulted from this research, reading problems in our schools seem to mount, and concern over the lack of specific reading skills in our elementary school children grows. This dilemma may be due in part to the fact that the pseudoscientific focus on reading has made teaching it a dull—often dead—communication process. But language is not dull or dead. It is dynamic, powerful, and constantly changing. Language is the tool of communication, and printed language must be read to fulfill its communicative function. Reading can be vibrant and exciting to children *if* it is taught in a vibrant, exciting way.

The key to effective teaching lies in combining the knowledge gleaned from research in the area of reading with that in the area of *creativity*. *Changing* teaching is *creative* teaching. Creative teaching employs certain principles unique to creative development. Creativity in children can be developed in the teaching of reading, and, conversely, reading can be taught just as well and with more positive gains when taught creatively than when taught through the more conventional systems.

The material in this book is geared to two groups of people: teachers-in-training and teachers-in-practice. Parents also will enjoy its many illustrations of creative teaching and its philosophy. That philosophy promotes the concept that the great creative potential inherent in all humans at birth can be developed through all areas of the elementary school curriculum. The remaining books in this series illustrate how creativity can be developed through teaching in the social studies, the fine arts, mathematics, and science.

Readers of the first edition of *Creative Teaching of Reading* have asked for more material in almost all areas covered by the book. I have attempted in the revised edition to expand many of the areas most often suggested by readers.

The material presented here is intended to spark the creative thinking of each reader so he can devise his own creative ways of teaching reading and literature. Each chapter is introduced by a quotation or a description of an observed experience in some type of reading situation. Each chapter is followed by three sets of exercises. The first is designed for the student in teacher training; the second is for the classroom teacher; and the third is for members of a graduate class that includes both teachers-in-training and experienced classroom teachers.

The chapters themselves present new ideas and principles based on tapes made by the author in his own classroom or in visits to the classrooms of his colleagues and students. It is hoped that accounts narrated here will substitute in a small way for direct classroom observations.

Some of my readers will dislike the use of the personal pronoun "she," which I employ throughout the book when I refer to the teacher. In many instances, I refer to a specific person and, wherever possible, use names, both male and female. In spite of the fact that I observed many creative males at work, the vast majority of the teachers with whom I worked were women, and I justify the use of "she" in referring to them simply because I had a specific person in mind and it was more comfortable writing that way.

I am indebted to many people for the material in these books. First of all, I must thank the children with whom I worked and the cooperative teachers who allowed me to use their classes to try out many new and creative ideas, or who tried their own ideas and permitted me to observe the creative process that developed. I am grateful to my student teachers, who were often uninhibited and daring in their work with children. They were a source of inspiration.

Special thanks must be given to Joseph Pittarelli, principal of the Brewerton Elementary School, and his colleagues Maureen Davison and Kathleen Brown for their help in getting pictures of actual classroom happenings. Special thanks must also be given to Mary Dixon, Holly Weller, and Kathy King, of the Palmer Elementary School, in Baldwinsville, for other pictures of creative experiences.

James A. Smith
Oswego, New York

CREATIVE TEACHING OF READING
IN THE
ELEMENTARY SCHOOL

PART 1

The Nature of
Creative Teaching

CHAPTER I

Basic Principles

TO THE READER

This chapter presents a review of *Setting Conditions for Creative Teaching in the Elementary School,* the first book of the Creative Teaching series. If you have not already done so, examine that volume before reading the material presented here. Even if you have read that book, you will want to read the first part of this chapter, which describes how the basic principles of creative teaching were applied in the beginning class of a British Open School.

ALL ABOUT CHARLIE

England was damp and gloomy that March—but only out of doors. Inside it was a different story: the warm voices, the happy laughter, the sparkling eyes, and the red cheeks of the children generated a sunshine akin to nothing in nature.

I was there to study the British Open Schools. It turned out to be a joyous experience, especially my meeting with Charlie.

Charlie was six, and it was his first day in school. He came to a new school, built on land that had once been cluttered with slum homes. Now there were high-rise apartments surrounding a beautiful building with green grass and a playing field.

Charlie came to school for the first time in March because the headmaster had four entrance dates for children: September, November, January, and March. Charlie had turned six the middle of February, so now he was eligible to leave the kinder-garten and come to the "big school."

He came with his brother, Alan, who took him to meet Miss Douglas at once. Miss Douglas was one of the teachers in the infant group, and Alan liked her.

"Well, good morning, Charlie," said Miss Douglas cheer-fully. "And are you glad to come to school?"

"Yes," said Charlie, "and I want my book!"

"Good boy," said Miss Douglas. "Come right along and we'll fetch it!"

She took Charlie by the hand and led him to a desk in a large cubicle. She handed Charlie a simple book made of some sheets of newsprint stapled together. It had a bright wallpaper cover.

"Here you are, Charlie," said Miss Douglas. "You do what you want in it and bring it to me when you're finished. Now, would you like Alan to show you around?"

Charlie clutched his book to his chest. It was his—all his. Miss Douglas had printed his name on it. Alan read it to him. "It says 'Charlie's Book,'" he said.

Alan fetched Charlie a box of crayons. Then he took him around to meet other children. Charlie was comfortable because many of the children were his neighbors.

There was lots to see in the room. All the children were working at many things. Charlie watched, but after awhile he found a table with an empty place, sat down, and drew in his book with the colored crayons. On the first page he drew his school. Then he drew his brother showing him around.

As he went through the day he drew other pictures: the children eating at lunch time; an illustration for a story Miss Douglas read; Mr. Stonebridge, the headmaster, who came to see if he was getting along all right; and, finally, a new little girl (who also had a new book) whom he liked.

Then he went to look for Miss Douglas. She was helping other boys and girls, so he waited, but she spotted him. "Why, hello there Charlie, how are you getting on?"

"I've done my book," he said.

"Good boy!" she said. "Bring it here."

So Charlie showed Miss Douglas his pictures. She liked them. "What do you want to say about them?" she asked, and he told her.

"This is my new school," said Charlie, pointing to the first picture.

"Good," said Miss Douglas. "And I'll write it under the

picture: 'This is my new school.'" She printed it with a thick, black flo-pen. "Read it to me, Charlie." And he did.

"Now what?" asked Miss Douglas.

"This is Alan showing me around," said Charlie.

"Right!" said Miss Douglas. "We'll write: 'Alan is showing me around my new school.'"

The next page read, "We are having lunch," and the next, "This is a picture of Frederick the mouse." Then came, "This is Mr. Stonebridge, our headmaster." The last page said, "Shelly is my new friend."

"It's a fine book," said Miss Douglas. "Let me read it to you, and then we'll see if you can read it back to me." So she did, and Charlie read it back to her page by page.

"I'm going to write something on the last page," said Miss Douglas, "and you can draw a picture to go with it." She wrote, "Miss Douglas is my new teacher," and they read it together.

It was that afternoon that I met Charlie, just before school let out. "That's Charlie," Miss Douglas pointed out. "He's new today, and he already has a book."

"May I see your book, Charlie?" I asked.

"I'll read it to you," he said, and he wiggled a place between my knees and proudly read to me page by page. I saw him later talking to everyone who would listen. "Want me to read my book?" he asked, and in most instances they did.

FIGURE 1-1. *Creative readers write their own books.*

For Charlie, on the very first day of school, reading had begun.

This is one form of creative teaching. Creative teaching catches the magic within children and turns it on so that they learn; it brings the magic out in the open so that you can get at it and work with it. Creative teaching is different from other kinds of teaching. In *Setting Conditions for Creative Teaching* I showed how such teaching is different by extracting from current research those facts we know to be true of creativity and by compiling a set of principles about creative teaching. Before we can fully understand what creative teaching is, we will need to review the knowledge and principles behind creative teaching.

CREATIVITY: A DEFINITION

Although a more detailed definition is needed for creativity in some instances, a simple one will do for our purposes: Creativity is examining past experiences, rearranging them into new relationships, and coming up with something new. This something new need not be new to the world, but it must be new to the individual. Something that is new to the world is high-level creativity.

BASIC PRINCIPLES OF CREATIVITY

Researchers have come to accept the following statements about creativity as basic to our understanding of it:

1. All children are born creative.
2. There is a relationship between creativity and intelligence; highly creative people are always highly intelligent, though highly intelligent people are not always creative. But all children can create to some degree.
3. Creativity is a form of giftedness that is not measured by current intelligence tests.
4. All areas of the curriculum may be used to develop creativity.
5. Creativity is a process and a product.
6. Creativity is developed by focusing on those processes of the intellect that fall within the general area of divergent thinking. This area of the intellect has been greatly neglected in our teaching up to this point.

7. All creative processes cannot always be developed at one time or in one lesson. Lessons must be planned to focus on each process.

8. We cannot teach creativity; we can only set conditions in which it can happen and insure its reappearance through reinforcement, although direct teaching to develop the components of creativity appears to raise children's scores on tests measuring creativity.

9. In order to be able to create (especially on high levels of creativity) teachers *and* pupils need knowledge about any particular subject, many facts about that subject, and a cluster of skills that are unique for any creative act.

10. The theories of creative development lead us to believe that children must be able to tap all of life's experiences in order to become truly creative; unnecessary rules and actions may force much of their experience into the preconscious or subconscious where it cannot be readily used.

11. Excessive conformity and rigidity are true enemies of creativity.

12. Children go through definite steps in the creative process.

13. Creative teaching and creative learning can be more effective than other types of teaching and learning.

14. Children who have lost much of their creativity may be helped to regain it by special methods of teaching.

BASIC PRINCIPLES OF CREATIVE TEACHING

From the statements above and from other studies in creativity, Smith developed the following principles for creative teaching.[1] Specific principles for creative teaching of reading will be found in Chapter 3.

In creative teaching something new, different or unique results. For example, Charlie went home from school on his first day with a new reading book of his own creation.

Divergent thinking processes are stressed. Divergent thinking, the opposite of *convergent* thinking, is the basis of all creative thinking. To teach for divergent thinking, the teacher places the child in a situation that is open-ended—where many answers are possible—and challenges the child to present a logical, creative solution to a problem. Miss Douglas gave Charlie an empty book—an open-ended situation. Charlie decided what

1. James A. Smith, *Setting Conditions for Creative Teaching in the Elementary School* (Boston: Allyn and Bacon, 1966), pp. 151–169.

FIGURE 1–2. *In creative teaching something new results: a creative reading chart composed and decorated by first-graders.*

he should put in it. Miss Douglas then used his answers to teach.

A convergent approach would be to introduce Charlie to an experience chart made by the teacher—to teach him the words and have him parrot them back to the teacher. In convergent thinking there is generally one answer already known by someone, usually the teacher.

Motivational tensions are a prerequisite to the creative process; the process serves as a tension-relieving agent. Charlie was motivated by a desire to fulfill what he considered to be expected behavior at school. Some children are not so easily motivated. They come to school with social-emotional problems or extremely negative attitudes. When such children appear, the teacher is challenged to find creative ways to motivate them. Some writers insist that little creativity takes place unless the creator is driven by a passion to solve a problem. Using natural or contrived motivation is a necessary first step in teaching for creativity.   An example of contrived motivation is given in the story at the beginning of the next chapter.

Open-ended situations are employed in creative teaching to foster divergent thinking.   Miss Douglas used open-endedness in the approach to reading described above.   Let's compare a traditional teaching procedure with another example of open-endedness.   In one methods course I visited in a neighboring college the students were learning how to teach reading.   They had been discussing phonetics and their importance in teaching reading.

"Here are some ways we can introduce beginning consonant sounds to children," the instructor said, and he proceeded to show three techniques that he had culled from current reading workbooks.   The students took notes and wrote down addresses from sample work books as they were passed around. The students left the class without understanding the reason for teaching beginning consonants, and all felt there were only a few proper ways to do it.

In another methods course that I visited, the instructor and the students discussed the principles behind the learning of phonetics.   The instructor brought out the fact that children often focus on the first part of the word when they do not know it; he reviewed the characteristics of the five-year-old and the six-year-old with some clever anecdotes and slides; and then he said, "Knowing that the sounding of letters at the beginning of words is one key to unlocking the pronunciation of the word, and taking what you know about five- and six-year-olds, let's see all the ways you can think of to teach beginning consonant sounds to children."

For the next ten minutes the ideas poured forth until twenty-five were listed on the chalkboard.   The students then evaluated the ideas.   These students left the class understanding the basic problem and principles of teaching beginning consonants, and each had a headful of creative ways to do it.   They also knew that there were other, unexplored ways—as many as their own minds could conjure.

Open-ended teaching not only results in creative individual responses but also trains students to use their own resources.

There comes a time in the creative teaching act when the teacher withdraws and the children face the unknown themselves.   Miss Douglas didn't hover over Charlie; she presented him with a challenging problem and let him take off.   The instructor of the second methods class gave the students some background material and then let them find their own answers. Creative teaching and creative learning involve risk-taking. Teacher and children must be adventurous—willing to try new things, to take a chance, and to fail. Learning is always trial and error mixed with a generous dose of discovery.

In creative teaching the outcomes are unpredictable. Miss Douglas knew that Charlie was interested in starting his book, but she had absolutely no way of knowing what he would put in it. He may have done the whole book about his dog, his mother, his father, or his kindergarten teacher. The methods-class instructor knew he would get *some* ideas for teaching beginning consonants, but he didn't know *how many* or *what* they *would be*. To a great degree, creative products are unpredictable. That's what makes them creative. To create means to be adventurous. And an adventure is, according to Webster, "a dangerous or risky undertaking: an enterprise or performance involving the uncertain or unknown . . . the encountering of risks: hazardous or exciting enterprise or experience."

The concept of unpredictable outcomes of teaching leads to some questions when we try to write behavioral objectives. How can terminal behavior be stated as part of an objective when the behavior to be elicited is unpredictable? It can't. For a discussion on this aspect of creativity see page 116.

Creative teaching sets conditions that make preconscious thinking possible. Much of creative ability depends on the accessibility of material that the child can mentally reassemble into new relationships. A creative person must have on tap a great reservoir of remembered facts and experiences and a large background of skills and techniques that he can draw upon freely and with little inhibition. Classrooms where children are discouraged from using out-of-classroom experiences shut off each child's creative potential considerably. Often the teacher's own values clog the thinking ability of the children when she refuses to allow them to discuss certain topics, such as drugs, sex, race, and religion. Integration of subject matter helps the children sense the relatedness of life and encourages them to draw upon all their experiences to create. How important this background of experience is as a reservoir from which to draw when learning to read!

In creative teaching, students are encouraged to generate and develop their own ideas. Differences, uniqueness, individuality, and originality are stressed and rewarded. Miss Douglas praised Charlie's book. Such statements as "I like your book. It is different from everyone else's," put value on individuality and uniqueness. Once children sense that the teacher values individuality, they tend to become more original and more individual. Creativity is individuality. In a democratic society individuals are important, but they never become outstandingly important unless they remain individual.

Because children are individuals, no one learns, reacts, or behaves, the same as another. Because children are individuals, no single reading method, or system, is going to teach all children, not *even all the creative ones*. Some children have problems that are unique, and others have special interests. The way to handle the highly diversified differences is to have a highly individualized reading instructional program.

The process of creativity is as important as the product. The sparking of ideas comes from interaction with others. Ideas are sometimes forced into new relationships, and creative ideas are born. Some of the ideas resulting from interaction in the college class mentioned in item 4 were the following:

a. Take child sounds heard on the playground, print them on cards under a picture symbol, and then make lists of all the words beginning with the consonant sound or blend. *Example:* Boys playing tiger on the playground said, "Gr-r-r." Draw a tiger on a card, print *Gr-r-r* under it, and then make lists of words beginning with the /gr/ sound, such as *grass, grow, growl, gray, grunt, green, grand, grit, grind, grid, grill, grim, grin, grip*.

b. Give the children a sound to go with a letter, such as /p/. Have them lip it and give you as many words as they can think of beginning with the /p/ sound, such as *pow, pan, park, pair, pin, pen, pep*, and *pet*. Write the first letter with magic chalk. After the list is compiled, put on the blue light and allow the children to discover that this particular beginning sound belongs to the letter *p* and that it looks and sounds alike in all the listed words.

Certain conditions must be set to permit creativity to appear. Inasmuch as creativity, as such, cannot be taught, an environment must be established that encourages its appearance and reinforces the feelings of success a child has when he creates. Special items should appear in such an environment to foster the teaching of reading. A suggested environment is described on page 126.

Creative teaching is success-oriented rather than failure-oriented. No child should leave school any day without feeling

FIGURE 1–3. *The process is as important as the product: pages from a homemade first-grade reading book.*

he has been successful. Activities in reading can be planned so that each child is successful in something. In the college class described above, no idea was ridiculed, negated, or rejected. All were put on the chalkboard so that the students felt that each idea was worthy. Later, each was evaluated, and some were rejected as impractical, too expensive, uneconomical in terms of time, etc. In each instance, however, the idea was given proper consideration, and the student knew *why* his idea was not applied. And the ideas were evaluated by the group, not the teacher. Accepting all ideas at first and evaluating them after all ideas are listed is called *deferred judgment*. The technique helps a great deal in making creative ideation successful for all participants.

Creative teaching not only teaches knowledges and skills but also encourages students to apply them to new problem-solving situations. Creative teaching is not laissez-faire teaching; it is the opposite. The more knowledge a person has, the more skills he can master, the more techniques he can use, the better able he is to form new relationships. There is a place for learning facts and skills convergently. The main difference between creative teaching and more traditional types of teaching is that creative teaching provides the student with the opportunity to put a new skill directly to work.

Once a week, the students in the methods class mentioned above had the opportunity to try some of the ideas listed in the class. Each student went into the campus school and worked with children in reading groups. Learning takes on meaning when it is immediately applied.

Self-initiated learning is encouraged. The second day of school, Charlie made another book and again went to the teacher for help when it was finished. Helping children to draw on their own resources encourages them to learn by themselves. Many new and creative materials in reading are designed so that chil-

FIGURE 1–4. *Self-initiated reading is encouraged.*

dren can learn skills and can have a great deal of reading practice on their own.

Skills of constructive criticism and evaluation are developed. Evaluation is closely embedded in the creative process. The principle of deferred judgment develops evaluation skills. People who create are constantly forced to make large and small decisions and to pass judgments—the author seeks the proper word, the painter seeks the proper color, the architect searches for the proper stone, the composer wants the proper note. Children learn to assess their own work in relation to others' when creative teaching takes place. In reading, a system should be devised that encourages the child to keep records of his own progress and to understand his growth in terms of his ability.

Ideas and objects are manipulated and explored. A high correlation has been identified in research studies between adults who are highly creative and the degree to which they were allowed to manipulate and explore materials as young children.

Creative teaching employs democratic processes. Creativity is highly individual. Children help plan their own learnings and take part in evaluating these learnings. They take part in discussion and learn how and when they must conform and how and when they may act as individuals. Each child is respected as an individual, and his program in reading is built around his own interests and needs. The children learn to work together, they develop values of living together, they learn aesthetic values, and they become concerned about each other and respectful of each other's abilities. Creative teaching is humanistic teaching.

Some methods used in creative teaching are unique to the development of creativity. These methods have been tried in many situations, and some have proven successful in the teaching of reading. *Brainstorming* and *deferred judgment* were used in the college class mentioned above.

Dewey Chambers summarizes the qualifications for creative teaching in an article in *The Instructor*.[2] He lists these factors as the variables within the educational environment that are most likely to promote the growth of creative behavior: less emphasis on conformity, flexible scheduling, provision of enough time, less emphasis on group work, less dependence on panaceas, wise use of tests, less stress on the sex role, reasonable use of the closed question (with more use of the open question implied),

2. Dewey Chambers, "Signposts for Creative Teaching," *The Instructor*, Oct., 1968, p. 57.

responsive school policy and administration (encouragement of creativity by administrators), and flexible teacher attitudes (with a value placed on creative production).

SUMMARY

Creative teaching is a special method of teaching. Although it uses many of the principles of all good teaching, it is attainable only when teachers understand those factors that make it different from other types of teaching. Every area of the curriculum can be a tool for developing creativity if the basic principles stated in this chapter are understood and applied. We have seen how, through creative teaching, a teacher can develop creativity *while* he is developing basic reading skills. The teaching of reading can indeed be a highly creative process.

TO THE COLLEGE STUDENT

1. Read *Spinster,* by Sylvia Ashton-Warner, and discuss it in class. Then read *Teacher,* by the same author.
2. In a classroom I visited, the teacher placed new words on a chart in front of the room only when *every* child in the room knew the word. Discuss this statement: *Using a chart of "Words We Know" is a good technique for building reading vocabulary.*
3. Choose any reading manual in your curriculum library and select from it one story to teach to the children. Rewrite it so that you develop as many as possible of the creative principles mentioned in this chapter.
4. In 1964, Sylvia Ashton-Warner wrote *Teacher,* in which she described her teaching strategies as *organic teaching.* I believe she was talking about the same thing that I call creative teaching. Following is a quote from her book. Apply it to "All About Charlie." Do you think Miss Ashton-Warner's writings had an effect on English education?

It's a sad thing to say of the vocabulary of any set of reading books for an infant room that it must necessarily be a dead vocabulary. Yet I say it. For although the first quality of life is change, these vocabularies never change. Winter and summer, for brown race or white, through loud mood or quiet, the next group of words, related or not to the current temper of the room, inexorably moves into place for the day's study.

I tried to make this division between the climate of a room and an imposed reading book by making another set of books from the immediate material, but all I did was to compose another dead vocabulary. For although they are closer to the Maori children than the books of the English upper-middle class, their vocabulary is static too, and it is not the answer to the question I have asked myself for years: What is the organic reading vocabulary?

At last I know: Primer children write their own books.[3]

5. Study some current textbooks for children with the accompanying hardware and software. Also read some acclaimed children's books (the Newbery Award books, for instance). Children are taught to read so that they can enjoy books like those. How closely are they woven into the general reading program? Can you develop a reading program built around the material children will read?

6. Read the two quotations below and then decide which is open-ended.
   a. "Now you may go to your seats and do the exercises on page 26 of your workbook. You will find the same words we learned today on this page. You will draw a line from the picture to the word."
   b. "On these cards I have printed our new words. Read the word and use it somehow in a picture."

7. Ask everyone in class to write a detailed definition of creativity. Collect them and read some at random. Everyone will probably have some different ideas, but it is highly likely that everyone will also have many ideas in common. Remember, unless someone in your class is a student of creativity these definitions are just unsubstantiated opinions. To discuss creativity meaningfully, we must turn to the work of the scholars of creativity. Some members of the class may be assigned the job of bringing in some of the definitions of such experts as E. Paul Torrance, J. P. Guilford, Donald McKennon, Sidney Parnes, and Frank Barron.

TO THE CLASSROOM TEACHER

1. Watch your pupils carefully while you are teaching reading and ask yourself these questions:
   a. Are they really interested?
   b. Are they bored?
   c. Do they see the purpose behind what I am doing?

3. Sylvia Ashton-Warner. *Teacher* (New York: Simon and Schuster, 1964), p. 54. Copyright © 1963 by Sylvia Ashton-Warner. Reprinted by permission of Simon and Schuster.

    d. Is reading a discovery time, a highly exciting and strongly motivating time?

    e. Do the children love books and clamor for them outside of reading periods?

    f. How many of my lessons this week helped children to be creative?

2. How many of the principles of creative teaching listed in this chapter are applicable to your reading lessons?

3. How might you apply the principles of creative teaching to each of the following areas of reading:

    a. The teaching of phonics.

    b. The teaching of reading comprehension.

    c. The teaching of structural analysis.

    d. The teaching of map reading.

4. Take from your teacher's manual a lesson that you will teach in the next few days and make it as creative as possible by applying as many as possible of the principles mentioned in this chapter.

5. From reading the small example of the British open school presented in the beginning of this chapter, how do you think Miss Douglas will develop Charlie's reading program? Is this an open-ended question?

6. Can you predict what kind of a creative reading program will be presented in the following chapters? How will reading experiences for children need to change in order to be creative? What is creative reading?

TO THE COLLEGE STUDENT
AND THE CLASSROOM TEACHER

1. Examine each of the principles of creative teaching summarized in this chapter and apply them to the reading lesson at the beginning of the chapter. How many of the principles were apparent in the lesson? Were there some that were not?

2. Examine each of the principles of creativity. Which ones did Miss Douglas apply in her lesson?

3. Examine a teacher's manual for a reading series. How many lessons might be classified as creative? As criteria for making your judgment, use the principles stated in this chapter.

4. Take any lesson from a teacher's manual and rewrite it so that it employs the principles of creative teaching *and* develops creativity in the children.

5. Three days after my first visit, I returned to Charlie's school. Charlie grabbed me by the hand and dragged me to a reading

center, where he showed me how he was reconstructing his book stories on a folding pocket chart. While I was there, he got another "book" and drew some pictures of me. Then he asked me to print beneath the pictures such statements as:

This is Mr. Smith.
He is my friend.
He came to visit my school.
I made a book for him.
This is it.

Discuss this incident from the standpoint of creative teaching.

6. Using the principles of creativity listed in this chapter, assess the reading practices you experienced as a child, especially the following:
   a. Reading a certain number of assigned pages aloud each day
   b. All children reading the same material even though it was sometimes read on different days
   c. Grouping by ability
   d. Using a textbook for reading lessons
   e. Reading by phonic and structural analysis
   f. Following the teacher's manual page by page
   g. Filling dittoed pages in workbooks

7. Take the list of qualifications suggested by Dewey Chambers (see page 14) and add to them other environmental factors you feel are necessary to develop creativity in your classroom, especially through the reading program.

8. The open classroom is currently very popular in the United States. However, I have found that many of the main ingredients of the British Open School are often missing in the American Open School; namely, the children's strong desire to learn, the children's natural happiness, the teachers' commitment to teach for individual growth, and the administrators' lack of concern about tests and set curriculum content. How do you explain these differences?

SELECTED BIBLIOGRAPHY

Anderson, H. E. (ed.). *Creativity and Its Cultivation.* New York: Harper and Row, 1959.

Ashton-Warner, Sylvia. *Spinster.* New York: Simon and Schuster, 1959.

————. *Teacher.* New York: Simon and Schuster, 1964.

Cobb, Stanwood. *The Importance of Creativity.* New York: The Scarecrow Press, 1968.

Eisner, Elliot. *Think With Me About Creativity: Ten Essays on Creativity.* Dansville, N.Y.: F. A. Owen Publishing Co., 1964.

Evans, William (ed.). *The Creative Teacher.* New York: Bantam Books, 1971.

Getzels, Jacob W., and Phillip W. Jackson. *Creativity and Intelligence.* New York: John Wiley & Sons, 1962.

Ghiselin, Brewster (ed.). *The Creative Process.* New York: Mentor Books, 1955.

Gowan, John Curtis, George D. Demos, and E. Paul Torrance (eds.). *Creativity: Its Educational Implications.* New York: John Wiley & Sons, 1967.

Guilford, J. P. *Intelligence, Creativity and Their Educational Implications.* San Diego: R. R. Knapp, 1968.

————. "The Structure of the Intellect." *Psychological Bulletin* 53 (1956): 277–295.

Kagan, Jerome. *Creativity and Learning.* Boston: Houghton Mifflin, 1967.

Kneller, George. *The Art and Science of Creativity.* New York: Holt, Rinehart and Winston, 1965.

Kohl, Herbert R. *The Open Classroom.* New York: Random House, 1970.

Kornbluth, Frances S. *Creativity and the Teacher.* Chicago: American Federation of Teachers, 1966.

MacKinnon, Donald W. "What Makes a Person Creative?" *Saturday Review* (February 10, 1962) p. 15.

McMahan, R. H., Jr. "What GE Has Learned about Brainstorming." *Sales Management* 81 (1958): 97–101.

Marksberry, Mary Lee. *Foundation of Creativity.* New York: Harper and Row, 1963.

Mars, David. *Organizational Climate for Creativity.* Buffalo, N.Y.: The Creative Education Foundation, 1969.

Massialas, B. G., and Jack Zevin. *Creative Encounters in the Classroom: Teaching and Learning through Discovery.* New York: John Wiley & Sons, 1967.

Michael, William (ed.). *Teaching for Creative Endeavor: Bold New Venture.* Bloomington: Indiana University Press, 1968.

Miel, Alice. *Creativity in Teaching: Invitations and Instances.* Belmont, Calif.: Wadsworth Publishing Co., 1961.

Muenzinger, Karl F. *Contemporary Approaches to Creative Thinking.* New York: Atherton Press, 1967.

Osborn, Alex F. *Applied Imagination.* New York: Charles Scribners, 1963.

Parnes, Sidney. "The Need for Developing Creative Behavior." *Viewpoint* 19, no. 3 (1964): 2.

Razik, Tahir (comp.). *Bibliography of Creativity Studies.* Buffalo: Creative Education Foundation, 1965.

Reed, E. G. *Developing Creative Talent.* New York: Vantage Press, 1962.

Rosner, Stanley (ed.). *The Creative Experience.* New York: Grossman Publishers, 1970.

Rubin, L. J. "Creativity and the Curriculum." *Phi Delta Kappan* 44 (1963): 438–440.

Rugg, Harold. *Imagination: An Inquiry into the Sources and Conditions that Stimulate Creativity.* New York: Harper and Row, 1963.

Shumsky, Abraham. *Creative Teaching.* New York: Appleton-Century-Crofts, 1965.

Smith, James A. *Setting Conditions for Creative Teaching in the Elementary School.* Boston: Allyn and Bacon, 1966.

Taylor, Calvin W. *Creativity: Progress and Potential.* New York: McGraw Hill, 1964.

———. *Widening Horizons in Creativity.* New York: John Wiley & Sons, 1964.

Torrance, E. Paul. "The Creative Personality and the Ideal Pupil." *Teachers College Review, 1963–65,* pp. 220–226.

——— (ed.). *Creativity.* Minneapolis: University of Minnesota, Center for Continuation Study of the General Extension Division, 1959.

———. *Education and the Creative Potential.* Minneapolis: University of Minnesota Press, 1963, pp. 103–118.

———. *Encouraging Creativity in the Classroom.* Dubuque, Iowa: William C. Brown Co., 1970.

———. *Guiding Creative Talent.* Englewood Cliffs, N.J.: Prentice-Hall, 1962.

———. *Rewarding Creative Behavior.* Englewood Cliffs, N.J.: Prentice-Hall, 1959.

Torrance, E. Paul, and R. E. Myers. *Creative Learning and Teaching.* New York: Dodd, Mead & Co., 1970.

———. *Learning and Teaching.* New York: Dodd, Mead & Co., 1971.

CHAPTER II

The Nature of Reading

I see the mind of a five-year-old as a volcano with two vents: destructiveness and creativeness. And I see that to the extent that we widen the creative channel, we atrophy the destructive one. And it seems to me that since these words of the key vocabulary are no less than the captions of the dynamic life itself, they course out through the creative channel, making their contribution to the drying up of the destructive vent. From all of which I am constrained to see it as creative reading and to count it among the arts.

> *First words must mean something to a child.*
> *First words must have intense meaning for a child. They must be part of his being.*[1]

SYLVIA ASHTON-WARNER

TO THE READER

This chapter describes the reading process and the reading program. The seasoned teacher may want to omit this chapter and look at the ideas for creative teaching in Chapter 3. The teacher-in-training will need to read the whole chapter and think through the experiences suggested.

The story included in the following introduction is reprinted from the first edition of this book by request. It describes one of my teaching experiences in a culturally disadvantaged school. When it was known that *Creative Teaching of Reading*

1. Sylvia Ashton-Warner, *Teacher* (New York: Bantam Books, 1964), pp. 29–30. Copyright © 1963 by Sylvia Ashton-Warner. Reprinted by permission of Simon and Schuster.

and Literature was to be revised, instructors sent me many letters and some helpful reviews that said, "My students love the story of Kevin.   Please don't cut it out."   So, here it is.   It is an example of a creative reading lesson.

INTRODUCTION

"They are *such* slow learners," the teacher tells me as I survey the group of six-, seven- and eight-year-olds.   "I don't believe any of them has an IQ above ninety.   And with their poor backgrounds and all added to that, I don't think they are *ever* going to read," she adds, almost in despair.

"Well," I ask, watching the children who stare at me dull eyed but with a certain spark of curiosity, "just what *can* they read?"

"Oh, they *all* know the twenty words on this chart," she says, pointing to a chart labeled "Words We Know."   "When *everyone* knows a word we put it up here.   A few of them can read in the preprimers, but that's all."

I turn to the chart and read *I, them, they, book, see, run, mother, father, it, me, my, to, the, see, baby, dog, walk, in, oh, book.*

"May I watch for a while?" I ask.

And I do.   Three children go to a corner of the room and play some commercial readiness games with the teacher while the rest work on some dittoed readiness sheets at their desks.   For two hours there is a shifting of groups as children come to work with the teacher.   Little by little, the children at their desks become bored and restless; more and more, the teacher interrupts her group work with such remarks as "Daniel, you are not cooperating," "Maria, I know you have work to do," and "Kevin, why are you out of your seat?"

What work Maria is supposed to be doing is difficult to discern.   Christmas is only a week away, yet the room is barren of things for the children to do.   In the back of the room three small bulletin boards are fastened to the cloak closets.   On one there is a commercial cutout of a Christmas tree; on another, a commercial cutout of a reindeer; and on the third, a commercial cutout of a Santa Claus.   Along the window sill sit a row of scrawny plants.   On a table in the front of the room stand piles of books—old, worn, faded, unattractive books.   Over the chart, "Words We Know," is a shelf on which there is a box with SUR-PRISE printed on it, but it is out of reach, and in all the days of my visit I never see it used. And that is all, except for thirty-five screwed-down desks and twenty dull, apathetic faces that steal timid glances at me from time to time.

And this is reading! Slow-learning indeed! "Culturally deprived," they say. "Educationally deprived," I say—and by people who should know better. How I long to get at them, to erase that dull apathetic look from their faces, to make them come alive!

I get my chance the next day, after I have learned a little about the children. And little by little they become human beings, lovely human beings, *creative* human beings. Kevin, supposed to be the slowest in the room, falls in love with me—and I with him. Kevin has no father, and I become the substitute. Kevin couldn't read anything, the teacher had told me, not even all twenty words on the chart, but she had to make exceptions— it wasn't totally fair to the other children not to!

I bring in a tape recorder before school starts that day. "What is it?" they ask, crowding around.

"Haven't you ever seen one before?" I ask.

"No—no—what is it?"

How do you explain a tape recorder? "Well," I say, "it is really called a tape recorder, but I call it my magic box. Do you know what *magic* is?"

"No—what is it?"

"Haven't you ever seen a magician on television or at the movies?" I ask.

"Maybe," says Thomas. "I think I saw one once. He had two big rings and he went like this and they were together and no one could pull them apart. I think they said he was a magician."

"He *was* a magician," I say. "A magician does tricks."

"Oh," says Peggy with the apathy leaving her eyes, "I think I saw one on TV too. He pulled a rabbit out of a hat!"

"Now you've got it!" I encouraged. "Anyone else—"

Words, words, words—they spill out, fill the very corners of the dull room with color and action, and I listen. With such a wealth of spoken words, why no reading words? We would see.

"O.K. Now listen and I'll tell you about the magic box." Dead silence.

"It's magic because, when we talk into this little box, these wheels go round and our voice goes on this tape here. After we talk I can push this button and you can hear your own voice saying exactly what you said into the box."

"Can we try it? Oh, let us try it, please!"

"Of course, we've got to try it, but first we have to make sure everyone gets a chance. Why don't you make a line here and then listen to me once more."

Shoving and pushing and laughing eagerness, but only for a minute. Then Margaret says, "Sh! Be quiet! Mr. Smith wants to talk."

More silence.

"Thank you, Margaret. What I wanted to say was this: Sometimes we can't think of anything to say when it's our turn. So you say anything you want to, but if you can't think of anything, tell me about you—where you live, how many there are in your family, about your pet or favorite toy, what you do after school—or tell me about Christmas. Think about it for a minute. What are you going to say?"

Dead silence—eyes rolling, fingers tapping foreheads, the wheels grinding.

"Well, Charlie, you seem to be first in line. Are you ready?"

Push the button—hand the mike to Charlie, who is all grins. "My name is Charlie Martin and I go to Maple Street School. I live at twelve Pine Avenue, I have a mother, a father, three sisters, and four brothers in my family—"

I nod encouragement. Charlie finishes and passes the mike to Owen. One by one they speak. Soon it is all over. I stop the tape and rewind it. The suspense in the air is thick. "Now for the magic!" Each child leans forward in his seat. The tape talks. "My name is Charlie Martin—" Giggling, hiding of faces in folded arms on the desk, an occasional guffaw of laughter, squeals of delight. And, after it is over, chatter, chatter. The magic box is a hit!

"Let's do it again!"

"Later," I say. "That's why I wanted you to try it out now so you will know how to use it later."

It is now school time. Everyone in his seat, hands folded, but no apathy now. A sea of faces (Caucasian, Negro, Oriental) so far below me, all chins turned up, all faces smiling.

"I think we'll have some fun together this afternoon with many kinds of magic," I say, "and we'll start by making sure you can tell that wonderful word when you *see* it as well as when you *hear* it. This is how it looks." Dare I put it on the coveted list of "Words We Know"? No, better not! So I print it on the chalkboard. "Read it to me," I say, and they all shout, "Magic!"

"Good!" I say. "We have learned to read a new word.

Now we're going to make some magic—would you like that?"

A chorus of "Yes—how?"

"Watch me carefully," I say, "for I'm going to draw something on the board and you're going to help me. And after a while you'll make some magic with what I am putting on the board."

They lean forward as I draw. "Two Christmas trees," they say when I have finished.

"Right," I say, "two Christmas trees, but I must tell you something about them. They're very, very sad Christmas trees. Could you guess why they're so sad?"

No response.

"Well," I go on, "just imagine you were a Christmas tree and it was only one week before Christmas—why would *you* be sad?"

Hands pop up.

"Lucy?"

"They haven't got any decorations," says Lucy.

"Well, I guess that would make any Christmas tree sad," I comment. "No decorations. Now that's a big word. I wonder if we could read it?" And I print it under the word *magic* on the chalkboard.

"That's a big word, all right," volunteers Jonah. "I bet that's a *fifth-grade* word."

"It is, indeed," I say, "and now you can read a fifth-grade word. Well, now, I don't like to think of Christmas trees feeling sad around Christmas. What can we do about it?"

Kevin shouts, "Decorate them!"

"A good idea," I agree. "Let's do that. Kevin, you pass this box of chalk around and let everyone take a piece. Now the people in these two rows can work on this Christmas tree and the people in these two rows can work on this one. Each one of you draw one thing on the tree—you can draw it more than once if you like, but each draw *one* thing and then everyone will get a chance. O.K., let's see how many *different* things we can draw!"

Four children go to the board and begin to draw, two to a tree, then four more. While they are drawing, I put some chart paper on the chalkboard.

"I'd like to do something else while those people are working at the board," I remark. "I'd like to write a story on these papers about our Christmas tree. Do you think those of you who are finished drawing could help me?"

Eyes are now torn between the drawers and the teacher.

"Watch if you like," I say, "or help me if you like. Does anyone have a name for our story?"

Arthur—sensitive, shy Arthur—says, "The Sad Christmas Tree." I tell him I like it and print it with red flo-pen across the top of the chart paper.

"And how shall we begin our story?" I ask.

"Once there was a Christmas tree," says Lucy. Of course, how else? The joy of storytelling. Once there was . . . I print it on the chart.

"And what about the Christmas tree?"

"It was sad." (Arthur again.) I print it.

"So what did we do?" I ask.

"We decorated it," says Nancy.

I print that too.

"Let's see how we decorated it," I say. "Charlie, what did you draw on the Christmas tree?"

"Stars."

"And Melba?"

"Candy canes."

"Kevin?"

"Candles."

"Let's put it in our story." And I print, "Charlie drew stars. Melba drew candy canes. Kevin drew candles."

Before long the trees are decorated; beautiful, childish, and creative, they cover the chalkboard. And the story is finished, too. Well, almost. . . .

The Sad Christmas Tree

Once there was a Christmas tree.
It was sad.
We decorated it.
Charlie drew stars.
Melba drew candy canes.
Kevin drew candles.
Daniel drew tinsel.
Maria and Jimmy put presents at the bottom.
Thomas drew snowflakes.
Peggy and Walter drew Christmas balls.
Owen and Willard drew bells.
Lucy drew strings of beads.
Jonah drew wreaths.
Arthur drew holly.
Nancy and Sarah drew lights.
Peter drew a Santa Claus.
June put a star on top.

Ellen wrote "Merry Christmas" over it.
Harry drew a manger.

I read it to them, using a liner.   "My, that's a good story," I say.   "And now how shall we end it?"

June's hand is up.   I nod to her.   "We could put 'So, it was glad!'" she says.

"Perfect," I say.   "Now listen once again while I read it, and this time will you each try to remember the line that tells what *you* did?"   So I read it again—and the next time each reads his own line.   Harry draws my attention to the fact that we have used the big word from the chalkboard in our story, so we spend some time talking about the difference between the word *decorations* and the word *decorated*.   They discover that it sounds different at the end—and looks different, too.

"I've got a good idea!" I exclaim.   "Let's read our story like we just did and we will put it on the magic box.   Let's all read the first three lines together, then each person will read his line alone.   Then we can all read the last line together.   Shall we try it once before we put it on the tape?"

We try it, and it is good.   But there is a problem where two people's names appear on one line.   Daniel resolves this by suggesting that both people read the line together.   Good!   It adds variety and music to the tape.   They clap after the playback.

"Play it again," they beg.

"All right, but only once because we have something else to do.   Did you forget about the magic?   We're going to make magic, remember?"

They have forgotten, so we listen to the tape once more and Jonah says, "Now, what about the magic?"

"Well," I say, "the Christmas trees you drew are beautiful, but they're not like the Christmas trees I see when I walk along Genesee Street where all the store decorations are.   How are they different?"

We have a discussion about that, and Walter suggests they are only black and white chalk.

"I feel like Walter does," I agree.   "Christmas trees generally have a lot of color.   Let's do some magic.   Kevin and Charlie, you pull down the shades; Jonah, you stand by the light switch and wait until I tell you what to do."

I have snapped a black light on a table, which I slide under the chalkboard.   The children do not know that I have given them fluorescent chalk with which to draw.   When the shades are down

I tell all the children to say "Let there be magic" with me.   I print
the phrase on the chalkboard and ask if anyone can read it.   They
figure it out, and we say it together.   Jonah snaps out the lights
on the word *Magic,* and the Christmas trees burst into color.
Gasps of delight!   "We made magic!"

We write a story then about the Magic Christmas Tree.
We have to find good words to describe it, and we have to find
words to tell how we felt when the magic came.   It goes like this:

> ### The Magic Christmas Trees
> *Once there were two Christmas trees.*
> *They were on the chalkboard.*
> *They were sad.*
> *They had no decorations*
> *So we decorated them.*
> *And we said,*
> *"Let there be magic!"*
> *There was magic.*
> *Suddenly they were all in colors.*
> *Beautiful, wonderful, happy trees*
> *All tinsel, stars, and colored toys.*
> *We were surprised and happy.*
> *Happy girls and boys!*

Such a sense of achievement!   So many "fifth-grade"
words, and even some poetry in it (that was Lucy's idea).   We
have to put it on tape, too, and so we work out a pattern for saying it.

"Play it again—play both our stories."   So we play it
again while they read the words from the charts at the front of
the room.

The afternoon is over.   Where did the two hours go?
"Will you come back tomorrow?"   They help me pack my things
and take them to my car.

"Keep reading the stories," I comment.   "I'll be back tomorrow, and I'd like to hear each one of you read them to me.
I'll leave the magic box so you can listen and get help with the
words you forget.   So many good words—and such big ones!   I
don't know how many you will remember.   Try and see."

Kevin is waiting at the door.   "Do you want me to read
you the big words now?" he asks.

"Indeed I do."

We turn back to the charts.   I hand him a pointer—he is
so small!   Meticulously, he points first to the word on the board.
"It says 'magic,'" he says.

"Yes," I answer quietly, "it certainly does."

He points to the first chart. "That says 'Christmas,' " he says, pointing to it twice, "and that says 'decorated'—and this says 'Kevin made candles.' "

"You are so right!" I exclaim. Such big words you learned today. Can you read any of these?" We look at the other chart.

"That says 'magic' too," he says, pointing, "and that says 'Christmas tree' and that says 'Christmas tree,' and that says 'magic' and here is 'decorations' again."

They all want to read the words to me but it is time for the bus. We all hate to go. It is such fun making magic!

"And with their poor backgrounds added to that I don't think they are ever going to read," the teacher had said. "Twenty words we know . . . Kevin is the slowest; he doesn't even know all the words on the chart. . . ."

But Kevin had read the fifth-grade words. All told, the whole afternoon had been one of magic.

Reading falls into the natural sequence of language development after good listening and oral expression skills have been developed (see *Creative Teaching of the Language Arts*).[2] When a child is speaking many words and using them as an integral part of his personality, he is ready to read them. In teaching reading to young children, word selection is often the first place where we go wrong: we pull words from thin air and try to put them into the child. Often we make matters worse by putting these strange words into printed context outside the realm of the child's experience and expecting him to read—and he cannot.

Children can learn to read any word they speak. One of the greatest hoaxes in all of educational pedagogy is that which says that reading vocabulary must be developed in a predetermined logical sequence. It just isn't so. Linguists tell us that when a child comes to school he has all the language equipment he needs in order to learn reading and all the other skills of language. The trouble is that we don't use his equipment. We contrive artificial systems of language development and methods of teaching reading, and we impose them on children. It is almost as though the child has to learn two languages in order to be able to read—one for communication and one to "get through" his reading books.

2. James A. Smith, *Creative Teaching of the Language Arts in the Elementary School*, 2nd ed. (Boston: Allyn and Bacon, Inc., 1973).

More research has been done in the area of reading than in any other area of the elementary school curriculum.   This is justifiable because reading is an important skill needed for learning.   But is is not the most important method of communication. It is important only to the degree that it *communicates!*

Much confusion exists about this research.   It is the second place where we go wrong.   We have built up a vast storehouse of knowledge about reading, but *all* the needed knowledge is not yet known.   And, because there are great gaps in that knowledge, we have turned to the next best source—the opinion of the experts in the reading field.   Many experts have advocated their "systems" of teaching reading, basing them on known truths but filling in the gaps with their own ideas.   When gaps in knowledge are filled in with opinions, we often confuse the two. As a result, schools have often adopted a reading system so wholeheartedly that teachers are not permitted to skip one page of a basal reading book or omit one single exercise in the reading manual that accompanies the text.   Many teachers have simply become middlemen, transmitting the ideas of the authors of a basal series to the children and not daring to use their own ideas to teach reading as a communication skill.   This procedure takes all the sense out of language skill development and reduces the role of the teacher to that of a puppet.   Certainly no creativity can break through such rigid conformity.

Teachers are *teaching* experts.   Their training has made them this.   Reading experts can help with a multitude of ideas, but they cannot possibly know the problems of any *one* teacher with any *one* group of children.   Basal readers and teachers' manuals work *only* if they are adapted to the group of children using them; they can be invaluable when used this way but are almost worthless when they are not.

The children in Kevin's class are a case in point.   All the children were from culturally deprived areas.   In the basal pre-primers and primers of the series that the teacher was using *not one single* story (if we can call them that!) had any relationship to the experiences of these children.   The children in the primer have pets; these city children are not allowed to have pets. The children in the series are all Caucasian; only five children in the class are Caucasian.   The grandmother in the series is a little, old, white-haired lady who wears a shawl, lives on a farm, and doles out goodies.   Most of these children never see their grandmothers, and those that do never see one like the one described in the text.   The "basal" children live in the suburbs; these children live in the slums of the city.   No wonder they do not identify with these books! They are, indeed, learning another language in order to be able to read.

Most of the reading books on the market today are written by the experts, and these experts are all concerned with making a living. Consequently, they plug their reading systems. One reading expert recently told me he was almost frightened by the dogmatic way in which his reading series was being used by school people. He has a good basic series, and in the introduction of the teacher's manual he clearly states that the series must be adapted to the children and makes many logical suggestions for this adaptation. Apparently some teachers do not read introductions to teachers' manuals; they plunge into Lesson I without first learning the primary objectives of the series and its basic philosophy.

We teach *children,* not reading. Any system of reading that does not consider the *particular* group of children and *each child in that group* first is pseudoscientific in its approach. And only a teacher can know the children she teaches—and know them she *must* before any significant gains can be accomplished.

Reading becomes vital only when the teacher becomes the source of the plan of the teaching and when she is able to utilize the experts' books, materials, gimmicks, devices, and ideas to help her develop her *own* plan for her *own* particular group of children. Teaching is a creative role, not a mimetic one, and the teaching of reading must be a creative process.

Linguistic research of the past ten years has provided us with more implications as to how reading should be taught than has any other source. Two books published in the past decade have contributed significantly to the creative approach to the teaching of reading: Sylvia Ashton-Warner's *Spinster*[3] and *Teacher.*[4] Miss Ashton-Warner calls her pedagogy "organic reading." I call it the creative teaching of reading. Miss Ashton-Warner knows how to teach reading creatively; more important, she knows how the reading process takes place.

WHAT IS READING?

Reading is the ability to recognize and understand the printed symbols of the child's spoken vocabulary. Printed words, as well

3. Sylvia Ashton-Warner, *Spinster* (New York: Simon and Schuster, 1959).
4. Sylvia Ashton-Warner, *Teacher* (New York: Bantam Books, 1964).

as spoken ones, are meaningful to the young child only insofar as his field of experience overlaps that of the author of the printed text. The old cliché "You can take from a book only what you bring to it" is, in essence, true. The reader learns from a book only if he is able to understand the printed symbols and rearrange them into vicarious experiences in his mind. His ability to think, to reason, and to conceptualize makes it possible for him to receive new ideas from a printed page without actually experiencing the new idea, *but he must have experienced each symbol that helps make up the new idea!*

This is illustrated by an incident in a typical first-grade room. A city child told of a trip he took in the summer to an animal farm, where, among other things, he saw a kangaroo. None of the other city children had ever seen a kangaroo. Ideally, the teacher would show a picture of a kangaroo and, through discussion, build the understandings necessary to give children a correct visual image of a kangaroo. But there was no picture available at the moment, so the teacher resorted to the use of word symbols. She printed the idea on the board:

Tommy went to the game farm.
He saw a kangaroo.

Because of the unusual shape of the word *kangaroo* children memorized it quickly, but they learned nothing until the word took on meaning. The teacher gave the word meaning by using the children's past experiences. Every child in the room had experienced size and variances in height, so when Tommy said, "The kangaroo is as tall as my Daddy," an image formed in each child's mind. If the children did not know Tommy's daddy, this image varied among them as they compared it to their own daddies. In the early part of the year, a rabbit had been brought to the classroom, so each child had experienced "hopping," "softness," and various concepts about the rabbit. Consequently, when the teacher added, "The kangaroo is soft. He hops. His back legs are much bigger than his forelegs," the children projected their past experiences into the new experience and gradually the blurred image of the kangaroo became more clear. Experience combined with the power of imagery made it possible for the children to gain new understandings, concepts, and learnings from their reading of the new word.

The sentence below may or may not communicate meaning:

John drove into the megalopolis each Saturday and took a class in origami.

Immediately we know that John went somewhere and took a course in something. But only those who have experienced and labeled a city or chain of cities as a *megalopolis,* and only those who have seen the art of Japanese paper-folding and have used the label *origami* to define it, will know the entire meaning of the sentence.

Read the sentences below:

1. *The sentinent walked down the street with a pogo.*
2. *The coult walked down the street with a jeliet in his hand. Along came a magpiet.*
3. *The sentinent barep denred his oastes.*

In each of these situations, you can probably read each sentence perfectly. But can you? Can you read or can you simply figure out sounds and words? Your knowledge of phonics and the skills in attacking new words that you learned in grade school have all been summoned up and put to use—but to what avail? Do you yet know the meaning of the sentences? You may be able to guess the meaning of numbers 1 and 2, but with number 3 you are completely lost. This is so because number 3 contains so many words unrelated to your field of experience that all your reading skills are still not adequate to give meaning to the sentence. It is beyond your reading level because it is beyond your experience level (both direct and symbolic).

Think back on how you read these sentences. You probably sounded out the unfamiliar words or associated them with similar words in order to put sense into the sentence. Look at sentence 1. What is a *sentinent*? You probably are thinking, "A guard or a soldier." What is a *pogo*? You are probably thinking, "A pogo stick." Why did you think that? You are trying very hard to put sense into the sentence—to tie it in with your experience, which was your first criterion in reading it. Then you used other criteria, but all directed toward the first: *to make it make sense!* Here are some of the things you probably did:

1. You sounded out the unfamiliar words and said them two or three different ways, trying to associate them with some spoken symbol within your own experience. *Children learning to read do this also. They try to apply phonics skills to new words and then associate them with some word in their oral vocabulary.*

2. You probably then associated the word *sentinent* with the word *sentinel* because they look alike and the sentence makes sense when you use this particular word. *In learning to read,*

children, too, associate words with other, familiar words in their visual vocabulary if they make sense.

3. You probably then related the word *pogo* to a *pogo stick* because it, too, *looks like* the word *pogo* and it, too, *makes some sense. Children, in learning to read, learn meanings of words by the way they are used in context.*

In sentence 2 you probably thought of *coult* as a young horse because you associated it with the word *colt*. The word *jeliet* probably was difficult because, even though you could pronounce it, you could associate it with no word looking like it that could be effectively substituted in this particular context to give it meaning. Then you came to the word *hand,* and the meaning you had been able to build up in the sentence to this point was immediately shattered because young horses do not have hands. You hastened on to try to find a context clue but did not get much help. You probably read the last sentence as, "Along came a bird," associating *magpiet* with *magpie*.

Sentence 3 is completely lost to you; it is no more than jargon. Can you, then, read the sentence? No, you cannot. Because reading is not word-calling; it is getting the meaning of the printed word from the page. The teaching of reading means simply helping children acquire those skills needed to get the meaning of the printed word from the page. But we have seen that the acquisition of all the skills is of little or no value without the ingredient basic to all reading—experience with the words to make them meaningful.

Now it is easy to understand why young children, before they can really learn to read, must have a wide range of experiences to which they have attached a multitude of oral symbols. We can see, too, why the primary program in reading must be loaded with experiences to which children and teachers apply symbolic expression. Thus, the children are constantly building up new words in their speaking vocabulary so that they will be able to read them.

Reading is the ability to recognize and understand the printed symbols on a page. The readers' ability to read is a skill or tool that makes it possible for an author to communicate with them. Children read because they want to know what is on the page. The reading itself is not sacred. It is what the reading *tells* the child that is important. Reading is an important means of communication but it is not the only one, nor is it the best. To insure the development of a good primary reading program, children must have (1) a large background of experiences, (2) the ability to listen well, and (3) a good oral vocabulary that labels their experiences meaningfully. With this background, almost every child can be taught to read, provided, of course, he also has the required intelligence and has no serious physical, social, or emotional problem.

Teaching reading as a subject rather than a means for communication can be deadly for children. No one reads *reading*. He reads *something*—letters, books, poems, stories, newspapers—and he reads with a purpose. Each reading experience with children should have meaningful content, obvious purpose, and pleasant associations.

Not all children are ready to read at the same time. The wide socioeconomic and experiential backgrounds of children, combined with their physical development and intellectual ability, will determine the points at which children are able to begin the formal reading process effectively. The teacher is responsible for the continued development of the child as a whole, and to deprive him of a rich variety of experiences so that he may spend time reading from books is the quickest way to insure reading difficulty among children, both in ability and attitude. School personnel have been guilty of spending long hours having children read laboriously from good books that the children soon come to hate. The biology of the child is violated in long, tedious, uncomfortable sitting periods, in tiresome repetition, and in meaningless or dull stories.

When a first-grade teacher sees the teaching of reading as her major objective and consumes a major part of the child's day with reading, she is capitalizing on the excellent experiences the home and the kindergarten have provided for the child. For, after all, these give meaning to his reading stories, which, at the first-grade level, are based on his first-hand home and school experiences. She may flatter herself on the excellent reading ability of her children and be smug in her knowledge that she can teach any child to read! What she fails to realize is this: unless she continues to provide suitable additional experiences in social studies, community contacts, literature, music, and so forth, she is depriving succeeding teachers of their privilege of doing a good job in teaching reading. This explains why, too often, children start out as good readers but experience reading difficulty by the time they reach third grade. They lose meaning in their reading because planned background experience stops when formal reading begins.

A little girl in the first grade came home from school one day and announced to her parents that the children were to have two friends in school, and she named the two main characters in a popular reading series.   For the next few days the child was enthusiastic over the motivation the teacher was giving them for the basic preprimers.   Little by little, however, the enthusiasm died, and the two characters were not mentioned for quite some time.   Finally, one evening, her father asked her if she was reading about her two friends.   Picking up a book, she opened to the page the children were reading and said, "Listen, Daddy!" and she read one of her preprimer stories.

Closing her book with an emphatic bang she looked up at her father and said disgustedly, "That's what we read today.   Now, Daddy, I ask you, isn't that the dumbest story you ever heard!"

To children of the Space Age, who have radio, television, automobiles, fine recordings, and lovely books, primer stories must seem insipid and cannot be expected to hold their attention long.   Their real first interest in reading lies in their joy at discovering they *can* read.   To exploit this joy, and to use it for needless repetition, means to soon destroy the only motivation children have.   The subject-matter of a primer does not hold them; we cannot, as a rule, expect them to be interested in these first "stories" for long.   In the average classroom, children not only hear these stories read and reread by every member of their group but also hear them read dozens of times by preceding and succeeding groups working at various ability levels.

HOW DOES A CHILD LEARN TO READ?

To understand how a child learns to read, one must first understand how he learns anything, especially how he learns to apply symbols to the world around him.   It is a well-known fact that children the world over are born with the same physical equipment for producing sound.   M. M. Lewis has shown that all children make the same initial sounds in crying, babbling and gurgling.[5]   But children in different cultures *hear* different sounds; at a very early age children begin to listen and to imitate those sounds that they hear and are able to reproduce and that meet their personal needs.   The first sounds they are able to make require little tongue or lip agility and no teeth; the sounds are made largely by blowing air through the lips with variance in the force of the air and differences in the shape of the lips.   Thus

5. M. M. Lewis, *How Children Learn to Speak* (New York: Basic Books, 1959).

"mama," "papa," and "nana" (for grandmother) are often among the first sounds American babies imitate.

Soon children repeat other sounds, and then, with the development of the tongue, lips, and teeth, and with repeated experience, the children realize that all objects in their life can be identified with a verbal label. They soon learn that all actions also can be labeled, and before long they are chattering words over and over—testing their ability to label those things with which they are familiar.

Children must memorize a word for every object in their environment and for every action they perform, and they must also learn the words that tie actions and objects together to make sensible sentences. This means they must recognize actions (such as walk, dance, run, jump, and crawl) and label them. It also means they must learn the shape of every object in their environment and remember it so they can label it. They must remember what a chair looks like, what a stove looks like, what a spoon looks like. Recognizing the shape, they can say the symbol that identifies it.

Children understand several verbal symbols on the conceptual level from the first time they speak them. The word *table* is not only a label for a specific table; it is a concept because it is a generalization from several experiences with many different kinds of tables. The children have learned that tables are objects with a flat top and four legs, which look somewhat alike, although there can be variances in size and shape.

In a college class the author attended, several different kinds of tables were set about the room. A four-year-old from the campus nursery school was brought in to visit. Each time she was asked to identify one of the tables by the question, "What is this?" she said, "Table," even though the tables varied in size, shape, and adornment. The next day, when she was returned to the room, the tables were dismantled—legs had been removed, cloths folded up, and the parts set about on the floor. When asked what each object was, she said, "Iron," "Wood," "Table-cloth," "A stick," "A plank" (for a piece of the picnic bench), "A board," and "A leg, I think." When asked if she knew what they could make, she suggested many things—but not a table.

A metal chair belonging to a kindergarten class had been left outdoors and was run over by a truck. When the chair was brought into the room, it was interesting to see that one child said, "What is that?" while another in the same room said, "What happened to the chair?" One child was able to visualize the original shape of the smashed chair, but to the other child, once it lost its shape, it lost its identity. So it was with the four-year-old from the nursery school. And so it is with most little children —a table is only a table when it is assembled as such; when ripped apart it is something else.

Children learn to recognize the symbols for objects in the same way they memorize the object—by its shape. At the beginning of the learning experience the word *table* is easily read because of its shape. Children do not need to know the phonetic sounds of the letters or the names of the letters themselves. To introduce these skills may slow the beginning reading power of some children, because then they have many things to learn and apply, and they do not need some of these things yet. Just as they learned to identify the table by seeing its shape, they will learn to read "table" most quickly by recognizing its shape. Most children pick up a wealth of words by recognizing their shapes (*sight* vocabulary).

Acquiring a sight vocabulary has its complexities. So many words are so nearly alike in shape that they become confusing, especially if they are also rather abstract in meaning. Study the words below:

1. *on   no*
2. *saw   was*
3. *then   there*
4. *grandmother*
5. *hippopotamus*
6. *submarine*

It is easy to see how a child can become very confused by the first three sets of words in this group. They are much alike in shape. A beginning reader often has difficulty developing a left-to-right concept because he has learned to recognize objects whether he sees them frontwards or backwards; he does not always look at a word from left to right and often calls *on, no* and *no, on.* Simple words, therefore, often create more reading difficulty in a child than the more complex words, 4, 5 and 6, above. Each of these words has an unusual shape, as well as emotional or physical associations. Grandmother is very dear to most children, and the smaller word *mother* may be familiar to them. Therefore, the word *grandmother* has many pleasant associations and is easily remembered. All the circles (o's) in *hippopotamus* may help the child remember it is about the big, fat animal the teacher showed them in a film. The shape of the word *submarine* even looks like a submarine, which may enable some child to remember the word after very few exposures to it.

A child learns to read his first words mainly by recognizing their shapes. After he is using many words fluently in his speech (sound images) and has many words in his sight vocabulary (visual images), skills are developed from these sight *and* sound images that help him to read all other words as well as to read independently. These skills include phonetic application, word analysis, and structural analysis.

STAGES OF READING DEVELOPMENT

There are basically four recognizable stages in the normal development of reading:

1. The readiness stage
2. The beginning reading stage
3. The stage of rapid growth
4. The stage of reading power

The first three stages generally constitute the normal growth pattern of the primary-grade child. The stage of reading power is developed, as a rule, in the intermediate grades.

The Readiness Stage

The four stages of reading help to define the instructional jobs of the primary teacher. In the teaching of reading the first instructional job is to *provide a sound reading readiness program.*

Preparing Children for Reading. A major part of any sound readiness program is the setting of certain conditions that will *prepare* children for reading. Although these conditions do not necessarily deal with the decoding of symbols in books or with books themselves, they are a part of a plan that paves the way for the child to become involved in the reading act.

First, the child must have a wide *experiential* background. Reading is the visual presentation of an oral vocabulary derived from experience. As stated above, to be able to understand the visual symbols, the child must have a direct or vicarious experience to back them up.

Consequently, a primary teacher preparing children to read must provide the class with many common experiences that can be meaningfully verbalized. She must also be aware of common out-of-school experiences that the children have that can be used to build an oral vocabulary to be transferred to printed symbols later.

Second, the child must be developmentally ready to read. This means he must be physically, socially, and emotionally mature enough to read. Physical readiness means that his eyes must be developed enough so that they can focus properly on print about twelve inches from his face. It means that he must be able to hold a book and sit fairly quiet, and his attention span must be long enough so that he can concentrate for ten or fifteen minutes on a single thing. Physical readiness means that he has enough eye-hand coordination to react to printed symbols and handle reading materials automatically. His fine finger muscles must have matured to the point where he is not clumsy in his use of reading materials. And he must have developed certain physical skills, such as auditory and visual discrimination ability (see page 177).

Recently, a great deal of emphasis has been placed on the relationship between children's motor coordination and their success in reading. Children may have such poor eye-hand coordination or such poor motor control of their bodies, for instance, that they do not learn to read properly. Some children who have experienced great difficulty in learning to read have been experimentally placed in situations where their basic motor movements have been reestablished and practiced (crawling, creeping, dancing, balancing, and the like). The result has been exceptional improvement in reading in those skills that require motor coordination.

Bentley says that children experiencing difficulty in learning to read have made great strides after the origin of their difficulty was located and then remedied by work in basic movement fundamentals.[6] And Dr. Joseph Gruber says, "Those coordinated movements that require a child to think through the performance patterns before execution are the same type of activities that tap the same learning mechanisms that are utilized when learning to read and write."[7]

Studies in the area of creativity indicate that creative youths remembered having had many experiences, as children, in manipulating and exploring. It appears that exploring and ma-

6. William G. Bentley, *Learning to Move and Moving to Learn* (New York: Citation Press, 1970), p. 15.
7. "Exercise and Mental Performance." Address to the American Association for the Advancement of Science, Dallas, Texas, Sept. 27, 1968.

FIGURE 2–1.   *This is reading readiness.*

FIGURE 2–2. *And this is reading readiness.*

FIGURE 2–3. *And this.*

nipulating the body not only develops creative skill but reading skill as well.

Social and emotional maturity mean the child must be psychologically ready—he must have the correct attitude toward reading. He must feel emotionally secure and socially at ease; he must have status as an accepted member of a congenial group. Emotional disorders can provide blocks in the reading process. The child must feel accepted by his teacher and be comfortably at ease with reading materials. He must also feel challenged and motivated by the reading experience.

Also, the child must be intellectually ready to read. He must be able to conceptualize, to recognize symbols, and to understand the meaning of reading. Very intelligent children may be ready at an earlier age than normal children. Since intelligence and reading ability are highly correlated, there will be vast differences in the reading abilities of children within any given grade.

The job of the primary teacher, then, is to get to know

FIGURE 2–4. *And this is reading readiness.*

each child well and to keep records of him that will help her to decide if he is developmentally ready to read.   In his folder, if possible, a teacher should include information about the child's home and parents: is he, for instance, often read to?   How many books are in the home?   Is he taken on trips with his parents? Does he have many and varied experiences in a family setting?

The teacher will also want to know how the child performs in school activities other than those carried out in the classroom.   Is he creative, for instance?   Does he have good coordination in Physical Education classes?

In addition to experiential, psychological, and intellectual readiness, certain skills must be developed in each child before he is able to read.   The development of the following skills constitutes the main thrust of the Reading Readiness Program (suggestions for their development are incorporated on pages 166–204):

1. He must have a desire to read.
2. He must develop the ability to listen.
3. He must develop a good oral vocabulary.
4. He must develop the left-to-right progression concept and the ability to read on a line.
5. He must develop audio acuity.
6. He must develop a keen sense of visual discrimination.
7. He must develop the ability to comprehend.
8. He must develop skill in oral communication (speech).
9. He must develop skill in concept formation.
10. He must develop a knowledge of the alphabet.
11. He must learn how to handle books.

Determining Whether a Child Is Ready to Read.   How does a teacher know when a child is ready for a formal reading program?   Basically, when he begins to read!   A child brings material to the teacher to read.   He may pick out phrases or words with his fingers and read them.   He seems to have a high motivation toward figuring out the printed symbols.   He sees differences in words and shapes.   He has a good sense of audio discrimination.   He talks freely and expresses himself well.   He is physically mature.   And at this psychological time, he should be taught to read.   Grade level has nothing to do with it.

There are many ways a teacher may determine whether or not a child is ready for formal reading.   Careful observation is the first.   In observing each child, the teacher may note countless clues that will indicate whether or not the child is ready to read. As the children work and play at kindergarten and first-grade activities, the observing teacher notes that George cannot put simple puzzles together; he has no concept of the relatedness of shapes.   At clean-up time Ellen persistently tries to put a long block back on a short shelf.   Alice tries to shove a large doll carriage through a smaller doorway.   Marcia cannot tell one note from another.   Jerry cannot sit with the group for a discussion.

All these children show a need for more reading preparation.   George, Ellen, and Alice need more direct experience in developing visual acuity; Marcia needs more direct experience in audio discrimination; Jerry is too immature to concentrate.   The teacher will provide more direct experiences for these children to prepare them to read.

Many checklists are available to help teachers determine a child's readiness.   Checklists serve the purpose of directing the teacher's observation to specific acts in the child's daily routine that indicate whether or not he has mastered certain readiness skills.

Teachers may also give reading readiness tests to help determine whether their interpretation of a child's behavior is logical.   Has he mastered the fundamentals prerequisite for success in formal reading?

Much research has been conducted to identify the effectiveness of readiness tests in predicting children's later success in reading.   The predictive value of most readiness tests for reading success in first grade has been quite moderate, as has the use of the IQ test as a predictor.[8]

Harris states, "It would appear that as beginning-reading programs become more diversified in nature, the predictive value of existing measures may need to be reevaluated."[9]

A teacher who understands the reading process and the necessary components of a good reading program can probably predict the success of her children in reading as effectively as most tests do.

Many workbooks are geared to checking reading readiness, but a wise and observant teacher can determine readiness without printed devices, which do not appeal to all children.   Workbooks used as a check for readiness are justifiable, but, when used as instructional material at this stage, they often create

8. Alfred C. Senour, "A Comparison of Two Instruments for Measuring Reading Readiness," in *The Roles of Research in Educational Progress.* AERA, 1937, p. 178–83.
9. Theodore L. Harris, "Reading," in *Encyclopedia of Educational Research,* 4th ed., edited by Robert L. Ebel (London: Macmillan & Co., 1969), p. 1088.

more problems than they solve. Overuse of the workbook may mean that children are not getting the meaningful experience background necessary to understand the material to which they will later be exposed. Workbooks can deal only with printed symbols; they do not replace direct experience in any way.

The teaching of reading must be individualized. While much reading can be taught by group work, time should be allotted each day for personal instruction for those children who need it. Often the whole class may read together, as illustrated by the lesson in this chapter. But no teacher can teach a child to read without knowing a great deal about him, his likes, dislikes, home life, neighborhood experiences, and level of experiences from day to day.

The best teaching of reading requires *both* group and individual work in the classroom. Each child is ready to read at a different time, and because each child is unique he may need a different approach or different techniques when he reaches the formal reading stage. The large classes confronting elementary teachers in our classrooms today prohibit to some extent this kind of teaching, though more of it could be done. The use of groups has been developed, and children are organized into areas of "like" problems that facilitate the teaching of reading, or any other subject for that matter. Some ideas concerning grouping and individual teaching will be discussed later in this book. (See pages 102 and 208.)

Probably the first sign of a child's readiness to read is his ability to read pictures, which are often his first symbolic experiences. In our culture the use of picture symbolism has reached such proportions that we cannot conceive of a child who does not understand its use to some degree by the time he comes to school. Yet not so many years ago in a little rural school, a teacher showed a young child of Polish descent the picture of a cow and the child said: "What is that?" "Why, it's a cow," the surprised teacher said. And the child smiled wisely and answered, "Naw, this no cow! The cow—she's big, she's fat, she's round and soft . . ." and in his broken English he proceeded to describe the cow with the aid of his waving hands.

This child, of limited experience, could not identify the very first step in symbolism: the picture of the actual object. It is difficult for us to imagine children today with so little background and experience that they have never before seen a picture! Somewhere (incidentally, perhaps, but certainly at an early age), every child comes to recognize a picture of an object, and that is the first time he understands the meaning of symbolic representation. It is another step, and sometimes a difficult one, for him to recognize the printed words as symbols representing the pictures. In our modern books, pictures provide a bridge for the gap in the reader's understanding of written symbols. Many adults still find that pictures are easier to read than printed words, and many modern magazines capitalize on this knowledge and tell their stories in pictures to a wide reading audience.

The concept of symbolism develops within a child as he matures. At first it is difficult for him to associate the noisy, screaming, racy, bright red object that tears down the street with the dull, inactive symbol *fire engine*. As he learns that everything can be represented symbolically and then remembers best the names of unusual objects, he remembers best the unusual words. The shape and contour of a word helps the child to retain its visual image, as was shown on page 37.

The Beginning Reading Stage

The second instructional job of the early primary teacher is to design a beginning program in reading that involves the following tasks:

1. Developing a basic sight vocabulary.
2. Developing good reading habits, including correct eye movement.
3. Developing reading skills that include an understanding of basic word structure, appropriate speed patterns, and comprehension of what is read.
4. Developing the child's ability to read independently.
5. Developing the child's creative reading abilities.

Developing a Basic Sight Vocabulary. Developing a sight vocabulary in children means exposing them to phrases and words used in many different contexts so that they remember their shapes and recognize them at sight. The creative teacher will find many ways to do this.

The Experience Chart. The most common way to build a sight vocabulary is the experience chart. It is a logical method because it follows what we know to be sound in the development of language. The teacher takes the children on a trip (common experience) to a farm. There they talk about what they see (listening and then oral labeling). "What is the man riding, Miss Allen?" "It's a tractor, Bill." "What is that tall thing?" "That's a silo." "What is it for?" "They store ensilage in it," and so on. The teacher and children return to the classroom and record their experiences on a series of simple charts.

> *Our Trip*
> *We went to the farm.*
> *We saw a barn.*
> *We saw a silo.*
> *Ensilage was in the silo.*
> *We saw the cows.*
> *They ate the ensilage.*
> *We like the farm.*

First they learn to read the chart in whole sentences or phrases. The teacher helps them to recognize and remember the words by making a duplicate chart and cutting it into strips. Children match the sentence on the strips with the original chart by reconstructing the story on a pocket chart. The children may then have fun mixing the sentences and creating a new story with them.

Obviously, work with the first reading charts is largely memorization. Children have memorized whole stories long before they come to school. Every parent has had the experience of reading "The Three Bears" to his three- or four-year-old only to find that, in attempting to omit a line or two, he was prompted by the child, who knew every word by heart.

The purpose of beginning reading charts must be kept clearly in mind: to memorize words and phrases to build a sight vocabulary. Memorization of the entire chart is necessary before memorization of the individual words is very logical.

After the teacher has developed a visual sensitivity to any particular chart, she can then cut it up into logical phrases and words, and the children can work with them in reconstructing the original story or creating new ones.

Caution must be exercised not to overuse a chart. As soon as the children seem to have memorized the phrases and words on one chart, more charts can appear using those words and introducing new ones. Charts can be embellished with pictures to make them more attractive.

Miss Holmes, in constructing her first reading chart with the children, had used the school bus as a common experience. The chart read like this:

Our School Bus

We have a school bus.
It is big.
It is yellow.
It is noisy.
It bounces.
We all ride it.
Mr. Ames is the driver.

The children memorized the story and had fun reconstructing it on a pocket chart. The day after the original chart
had been made, Miss Holmes introduced the same words in a
different context. On the pocket chart, she had inserted a picture
of a school bus clipped from a magazine cover. Under it she had
printed on strips of cardboard:

What Is It?

It is big.
It is yellow.
It is noisy.
It bounces.
We all ride it.
What is it?

On the third day, Miss Holmes introduced a new chart,
which said, "Who is he?" Under it she constructed this story,
using again the words from the old reading chart.

Who Is He

He is a driver.
He drives a bus.
It is big.
It is noisy.
It is yellow.
It bounces.
We all ride with him.
Who is he?

Quickly the children learned to read about Mr. Ames. By
this time they had memorized the words well enough so that
Miss Holmes was able to construct another reading chart with
the children at the next meeting of her beginning reading group.

If reading charts really originate in the oral vocabulary of
children, they will differ greatly in context from school to school.

My Older Sister

My older sister is a drag.
She is always fixing herself up.
She uses perfume.
I like it.
It smells nice.
She uses perfume when she goes on a date.
Her boyfriend is handsome.
I like him.
I don't like my older sister.

The Playground

Every Saturday we go to the playground.
Tommy's sister takes us.
We slide the slides. Wheeee!
We ride the merry-go-round. Boom-pa-pa!
We use the see-saws. Up, down, up down.
We play ball. Thump, thump, thump.
We make things with a pretty girl.
We have a good time.
Playgrounds are fun!

Careful guidance in constructing reading charts is essential so that old words appear repeatedly in new context and new words are introduced at a rate of speed commensurate with the child's ability to memorize them. Any defect in the use of reading charts is due largely to the inability of the teacher to find exciting, new, and interesting ways to use the constantly developing sight vocabulary of the children.

Charts need not all be *experience* charts—though they should obviously use words that children are using orally and that are based on their own experiences. As soon as a few words are known, they can be used in many ways on different kinds of charts. Thus, children may have the opportunity to read them over and over in new situations.

Creative ideas for the development of reading charts are further developed in Chapter 5.

The Use of the Basic Text. A creative teacher will make a careful study of the reading books she intends to use with her class so that she becomes very familiar with their content. The story about the element of discovery told on page 82 illustrates how the introduction of the preprimer can be a highly motivating experience if the teacher is so aware of the vocabulary the child will encounter there that she has helped him to learn many of the words by including them in his experience charts beforehand.

The introduction of any reading book should be an exciting experience for every child.

Once a child begins to read in books, his chart experiences should not cease. Chart-making may shift from story charts to those concerned with gleaning information (planning charts, vocabulary charts, evaluation charts, and such), but charts still play an important role in having the reading experiences of the young child grow out of his spoken experiences.

There are two points of view regarding the use of a basic text in developing a sound reading program. Some teachers avoid the use of the basic text until very late in the reading program because they feel it does not have meaning for many children.

Not long ago, beginning basal readers were written about a Caucasian boy and girl, their parents, and their pets. They did not present the lives of children in subcultures or in mixed racial groups. Nor did these basals represent children in low socioeconomic groups. Consequently, to some children these basic texts were as much outside the realm of their experiences as were the ancient fairytales.

Great strides have been made in changing the pictorial and verbal content of the basal text in the past few years. A more democratic, realistic text is presented in stories about children of all races and of varying socioeconomic levels. The life of a democratic society is more truly represented. However, the teacher may become a victim of the same mistakes made in the past in the use of the primers and succeeding basals if she does not understand the place they play in the beginning reading program. A primer or basal that introduces children to a mixture of races or to a socioeconomic level different than their own may cause confusion and lack of comprehension if no preparation is made on the *experience* level before the text is introduced. The old basals were written about the life of children in the suburbs. They are still useful for children in the suburbs providing, of course, that they have kept abreast of suburban life. Because beginning basal readers cannot include all social situations in the life of all children, the teacher will want to select those texts that most nearly represent life of the children in her classroom. *She will need to prepare the children on the experience level for any text she uses.* This is done by having an introductory *experience* with the words in the text and making certain that these words become a common part of each child's oral vocabulary.

Non-educators do not always interpret this phase of a reading program properly. Often they criticize the schools for the limitations placed on children by selecting material that only reflects life experiences.   These critics go to great length to tell how modern schools limit the child's horizons by giving him such restricted material to read rather than the great pieces of literature they had when they were children.   Such critics have long forgotten the manner by which they were *taught* to read and confuse the method with *what* they read.   Generally, once a child begins to read, he can then begin to reassemble his reading thoughts into new concepts and is ready for material outside the realm of his experience.   When a child reads, "The Martian looked like a robot.   He had no face, only two large eyes similar to those of a frog and like a frog, he was green," he is obviously reading something he has never experienced, but he has experienced *each word* so that he can reassemble the meanings of each word into a whole new concept.   He has experienced the word *Martian* and *robot* somewhere.   He knows about face, eyes, large, frogs and green.   Consequently, he can get new meaning from the words.   The ability to put old experiences into new concepts is one of the creative aspects of reading.

Generally, when children have developed a large sight vocabulary and have learned skills in order to attack new words, they are able to read comfortably outside the realm of their own experiences, and it is at that time that works of literature are most effectively introduced.   Picture books and books of simple print help the child to make the transition.   This phase of the reading program generally designates the beginning of a period of rapid growth (see below).

Some teachers also feel that the manuals that accompany basic texts give the impression that unless they are followed page by page the children will not develop good reading ability.   They also feel that the stories in some of the primers (for all their changes) are still contrived, insipid, uninteresting, and, consequently, very disappointing to children who have been making their own exciting charts.   These teachers often use a basic text as a supplement to a well-developed reading program for the purpose of teaching skills, evaluating pupil growth, and securing material for a variety of purposes very quickly.

On the other hand, other teachers feel the basic text has been prepared by experts and the step-by-step guidance offered in the teacher's manual is the most scientific way of teaching reading known to man.

Actually, a combination of the two points of view probably produces the best program in reading instruction.   In teaching reading, as in all other teaching, the variable that makes the difference is the teacher. The creative teacher will use all materials and will make them work for her.

Often the child is introduced to books through the use of the "big book" used at the front of the room. This is a natural transition for him, because the big book resembles the charts his teacher has made. After the big book has been read by the class, each child will be happy to discover that he can read the small copy of the same material in his own hands.

Time should be taken at this point to help children understand the difference between the basic texts and the books they have been looking at and trying to read. If children understand clearly that a basic text is designed to help them *learn* to read, they will realize that it performs a different function for them than books of children's literature that they *want* to read. (See Chapters 4 and 8.)

Some children develop such a rich sight vocabulary that they literally breeze through preprimers and primers. Contrary to popular belief, every page of a reader does not have to be covered. The one best guide for the development of a reading vocabulary is to listen to the words the children are *speaking* with meaning. If these words are the same as those used in the basic text, the children are ready for it. But the basic text should not constitute the total reading program of any classroom.

Easy Books for Beginners. Lately, the reading program of many classrooms has been enriched by the introduction of easy beginning books written especially for beginning readers. These books often do what the beginning readers do not. In a simple, direct way, they tell a sensible, exciting story that rewards the children by making the reading of the story worthwhile.

Along with the easy beginning books has come much criticism of their literary value. Literary value or not, they are far superior to the beginning stories in many basic text series. A visit to any classroom where these easy books are being used will show how eagerly they are accepted by children. Words are repeated over and over to help the child develop a broad sight vocabulary. Various root words, beginning word sounds, word endings, prefixes, and suffixes are so simply introduced and so often repeated that children often begin to use phonetic and word analysis skills to figure out the new words for themselves, thereby enabling the teacher to launch into a sound word-attack program at the time the child is most ready for it.

Many bright children have taught themselves to read with the "easy books," and many other children have delighted in their ability to read these books after one or two readings by the teacher.

Criticism or not, the "easy books" have made their way into the reading programs of most children, at least out of school, where parents have seen these books as one means to satisfy the hunger of the highly motivated beginning reader. The books can be put to profitable use within the school program if they are carefully integrated into the total reading program.

Developing Good Reading Habits. Good reading habits are developed at the onset of the reading experience if the teacher introduces reading to the children in the ways mentioned in previous sections of this chapter. Children develop good eye movement across a page because they are taught to see and read for ideas rather than words.

Physical conditions must be appropriate for developing good reading habits. The presence of books, bulletin boards, daily stories, and all the other motivational devices previously mentioned is necessary. One part of the room should be set aside for quiet reading time. Distractions should be removed. Simple rules for reading time should be established. Above all, reading should be enjoyable.

Reading is a tool or a skill to be used in many ways and for many purposes. Therefore, reading goes on all day—not just during a reading period. The children plan their day together and teacher prints their plans on the board. The children read these plans as soon as they are able, along with their individual notes and directions for finding special surprises (see page 208). The teacher writes the news on the board when they "share and tell" and thus provides another chart. Billy and the others read their surprise charts to the group after the surprise is known; the class writes a chart of Billy's experience. Teacher reads stories to the children. Long-term plans for a puppet show are printed on a chart. A list of "Things We Want to Know" constitutes another chart of questions the class will ask on their train trip. And at some specified time during the day, teacher meets with groups or individuals for individual reading experiences or help in techniques.

Such a program shows the need for reading to the children and places reading in its proper place meaningfully. Children do not read just for the sake of reading; they do it to communicate, to hear what others have to say.   Reading can be established as a habit for communicating when the skills taught during the reading period are put to use all during the school day.

Developing Reading Skills.   As soon as a basic sight vocabulary has been learned, the reading habit has been established, and children are reading charts or books, the teacher must begin to build skills that will lead the child into independent reading ability.   All these skills center around developing techniques in word recognition.   These techniques may be listed as follows:

1. The use of picture clues to identify words
2. The use of verbal context clues
3. The use of word-form clues
4. The use of phonics analysis
5. The use of structural analysis

One instructional job of the teacher in developing independent reading skills is to provide independent seat work.   She must also be concerned with expanding the children's reading range through the introduction of new topics and supplementary reading materials.

Using Picture Clues to Identify Words.   On page 46 an example of a child who had not learned to read pictures was given.   This almost never occurs in our classroom today, when books, magazines, billboards, posters, television, and other forms of communication media introduce the children to their first basic printed symbol for a real life experience: the picture.

When children have had extensive work with pictures, such as the activities suggested in *Creative Teachings of the Language Arts in the Elementary School*, 2nd ed., they develop the ability to study pictures closely and to be sensitive to many of their component parts.   Ability to read a picture well will ultimately help a child to read the printed symbols that appear under it.   In his desire to make his reading have sense, his eyes wander back to the picture to find the pictorial image of the word.

One picture in a primer shows two children pulling a third child in a red cart.   The child reader does not have the word *cart* in his sight vocabulary.   Being a rural child, he reads one of the sentences under the picture as follows: "Ted and Alice pull Sally in the wagon." *Wagon* is his word for the object in the picture as obviously the only word that makes sense.

The child's teacher will accept the word *wagon* until the child finishes the page, so as not to destroy the meaning of the story. As soon as the child finishes reading, she may ask him to look at the picture and the word he read as *wagon* and will ask if he knows another word that can be used as a substitute for wagon.   If he does not, she introduces the word *cart* by printing it on the chalkboard.   Often, 3 x 5 cards can help the child note the different configurations between the words *cart* and *wagon*.   The teacher cuts slits in the card with a razor blade so that only a word or phrase is exposed when the card is laid on a page of reading material.   This has the advantage of blotting out the words immediately surrounding the troublesome word while allowing the child to see it used in context as soon as the card is removed.

Once the teacher is certain the word is in the child's vocabulary, she will correct it when he is reading to her if he mispronounces it.   When children are reading so that their stories make sense, they are probably using picture clues to identify unknown words.   Other skills will be needed to remedy mistakes, but for the time being the child is using well the resources at his command.

Using Verbal Context Clues.   While pictures may help children in reading many beginning stories, there are some instances when they do not. Then the child resorts to searching for clues in the context of the story itself.   In the reading readiness program, he developed many verbal context skills in the work with audio discrimination, visual discrimination, listening, and oral expression.

Context clues, like picture clues, are often obtained by simply using the word that makes sense in the sentence.   When the boy who read the word *cart* as *wagon* has more context clues at his command, he will look at the beginning letter of the new word and realize it could not be *wagon* because it begins with a /k/ sound.

Suggestions for developing context clues follow in Chapter 3, along with suggestions for the development of phonetic clues and word-structure clues.

Using Word-Form Clues.   Word-form clues deal with the outward appearance of the word.   Recognizing likenesses and differences in words, recognizing beginning sounds and endings, and noting the lengths of words are the first kinds of word-form clues that a child uses to figure out the pronunciation of a word. The phonics program expands this ability, and a program in structural analysis tends to complete it.

In developing a sight vocabulary, children build a base

for skill in using word-form clues. Continued work in oral vocabulary building as described on pages 177 and 196 is necessary
so that the spoken words of the child may be meaningfully recognized in print.

Using Phonics Analysis. Phonetics is the branch of linguistics that deals with *speech* sounds and the art of pronunciation. Phonetics is concerned with the production of these
speech sounds by the articulating organs of the speaker, the
sound waves in which they result, and the auditory effect they
produce on the hearer.

Phonics is simplified phonetics for the teaching of reading.
It is the practice of using sounds as an aid to word recognition
and writing. It is one element in the total field of phonetic
analysis. Phonics plays an important part in the teaching of
reading. In the reading readiness program, phonics sounds are
often used to refine audio discrimination. Children learn the
consonant sounds such as /m/ and the vowel sounds such as
/a/, the speech consonants and consonant blends such as /ch/
and /br/, and so on, less as a technique for teaching them to read
than as a technique to help them hear and see minute differences
in sounds and shapes. When these exercises are taught as games,
or in meaningful ways, they are fun. It has been pointed out
that children create sounds and use them in their speech and
early writing. Teachers can capitalize on the "ch-ch-ch" for *train*
and have the children reproduce this sound to accomplish the
same ends as the more formal lessons in the manual. There is
the "sh" sound when rocking baby to sleep; the "da-da-da-dat"
sounds of playing at shooting machine guns, the "whrr-whrr" for
the airplanes, the "z-z-z-z" sound of an automobile, and a multitude of others.

Learning sounds in the readiness stage of reading does not
insure the child the ability to read by using phonics, however, for
that is not the purpose of sound consciousness at that stage.
Many children do carry over this knowledge later into their reading but they should not necessarily be expected to. Most children learn to read initially by recognizing the *shapes* of words
because they learn about people, animals, and things by *their*
shapes. To a little child, all men may be classified as "Daddy"
because they have a similar shape. Dogs soon become "bow-wow"
regardless of size, because the shapes are similar; coffee tables,
end tables, dining-room tables, and bridge tables are all "tables"
at first due to their similarity of shape. It is later that the details
of shapes within the shapes begin to make for discrimination.

The child notices the unusual parts of objects and sees differences. Thus, the tail of the dog, which is always moving, and the head, which is always barking, eating, or licking, come to his attention; differences are noted, and a more definite classification results. "Dog" becomes "cocker," "dalmatian," "collie." "Daddy" becomes "man," or "grandpa," or "Mr. Jones." "Table" becomes "coffee table" or "dining-room table."

So the child learns to identify words by shape, and then the peculiarities within the words draw his attention. He sees wiggly /g's/ and tall /T's/ and when he notes differences within shapes he is also ready to notice they stand for the differences within the sounds he is making. This is the time when phonics should be taught as a reading aid and a step toward independent reading. Now the child needs techniques for attacking new words so that he may eventually read independently. Again, the element of discovery can provide an excellent motivating force if the teacher teaches phonics skillfully enough so the child discovers new words through sounds. Many teachers prefer to begin phonics apart from the reading groups themselves, through word games. This is perhaps wise in that it does not interfere with the child's eye-span or slow up his reading when he is in the initial stages of establishing the reading habit. After a series of sound games have been played and the basic consonant and vowel sounds and consonant blends have been established, the teacher naturally makes the transfer to the reading situation by having the children sound some of the words they do not know in their reading books. This can be discovery, it can be fun, and children can spend time sounding out new words they meet daily.

It must be remembered, however, that phonics is but one way to recognize new words and is no more important than a number of other contextual clues.

Using Structural Analysis. Almost as soon as he begins to read, the pupil will find likenesses in words. First he will notice a familiar base word with a new consonant beginning, such as *night* and *sight*. Often he will recognize small words in compound ones, as *mother* in *grandmother*. When this begins to take place, children are capable of understanding the structure of words; now they may be taught the variations and deviations of words, which will help them in developing independent reading. A study of structure of words involves an ability to:

1. *Recognize base words in derived words.* A child reads: Helen was *reporting* to the class. He recognizes the word *port* and is able to apply his knowledge of prefixes and suffixes to "sound

out" the word.   Once he says the word to himself, he recognizes it as one he already uses orally and he has brought meaning to the sentence.

2. *Omit first or last letters to make a word.*   The child substitutes a /p/ for the /j/ in jump, or drops the /e/ from rote.   He applies his knowledge of consonant sounds in the first instance, his knowledge of vowel sounds and their changes in the second instance.

3. *Recognize compound words.*   Knowing the words *rain* and *fall,* he quickly recognizes a new word, *rainfall.*

4. *Divide words into syllables.*   Knowing that each sound syllable contains a vowel helps the child to properly pronounce the word *at-ten-tion.*

5. *Recognize contractions.*   (See *Creative Teaching of the Language Arts in the Elementary School,* Chapter 8.)

Developing Independent Reading.   The development of good reading habits and basic reading skills should place the child well along the road toward independent reading.   Most children enter the stage of rapid growth (see page 62) in reading as soon as they begin to read independently.   The main jobs of the teacher at this point are to continue to develop those skills that will give the child independent reading power and to supply a wealth of material geared to the reading ability level of each pupil.   In addition to the reading act, there are certain mechanics of reading that greatly aid the child in the use of books and increase his power to work with books by himself.

Developing Mechanics for Independent Use of Books in the Primary Grades.   The primary teacher must accomplish the

FIGURE 2–5. *Primary children write their autobiographies and draw self-portraits to go with them.*

following instructional tasks to develop the mechanics necessary for independent use of books:

1. Teach the alphabet names (very soon after the reading act is established).
2. Teach the order of the letters of the alphabet through:
   a. Arranging children's names in alphabetical order.
   b. Using the picture dictionary to find words the children wish to use in sentence- or story-writing.
   c. Making a spelling booklet, using a page for each letter of the alphabet and then alphabetizing weekly lessons.
   d. Singing alphabet songs.
   e. Grouping words with same initial blends, same vowel sounds, or same endings.
   f. Finding names in telephone books.
   g. Alphabetically classifying words encountered in social studies such as names of countries, cities, occupations, seaports, and rivers.
   h. Words where first and second letters are the same.
3. Teach the mechanical features of a book by:
   a. Using table of contents to—
      (1) Locate new stories.
      (2) Find stories children wish to reread.
      (3) Find material for research in Citizenship Education, Science, etc.
      (4) Select favorite story.
   b. Using title page.
   c. Using index to—
      (1) Locate specific subjects.
      (2) Locate songs.
   d. Recognizing statements, questions, and quotations.
   e. Understanding that the book is divided into units according to various topics, such as animals and seasons.
   f. Reading a double-column page through use of *Weekly Reader*, etc.
   g. Understanding relationship of page numbers to place in book, page 10 near front of book; page 150 in or near back of book).
4. Teach care and handling of books.
5. Use alphabetical skills in other books such as:
   a. Dictionary (picture and others).
   b. Telephone book.
   c. Address books (make some).
   d. Reference materials in children's encyclopedias.
6. Develop an interest in authors and publishers.
7. Develop library skills by:
   a. Learning that the card catalogue in library is in *a-b-c* order.
   b. Learning that encyclopedias are in *a-b-c* order.

    c. Looking for pictures on given topic.
    d. Locating materials on library shelf.

These skills may be further developed through a variety of activities such as the following:

1. Organize a Reading Club composed of children interested in helping locate books and caring for them. They meet once a week to locate books and stories about two or three topics of particular interest to the class and their studies.
2. Make booklets using table of contents, title page, etc., for Citizenship Education.
3. Put words on chalk tray and have children select words alphabetically.
4. Fish for words in alphabetical order.
5. Play various games whereby children put words in boxes with letters on them.
6. Make booklets in correlation with Citizenship Education, Science, etc., making use of the mechanics of reading.
7. Prepare cards upon which a number of related words are printed. In an envelope, place smaller cards that contain words to classify the groups. Child picks a card from the envelope and matches it with the appropriate set of words on the larger cards:

> *People*
> girl
> man
> boy

8. Use two sets of alphabet letters—one of capital letters and one of small letters. Mix them up and pass to class. Match pairs.
9. Write words in large letters on cards and put the cards in a box. Each child takes one card. One child calls out the letter that begins a word on one of the cards, the child holding that card stands in position in an alphabetical line.
10. Divide alphabet into three parts (a-g) (h-p) (q-z). Have children tell you in which part of alphabet a certain word is found.
11. In the library corner have a reading tree. Children can make their own creative symbols to put on the tree every time they read a book. A key to the symbols could be close by for quick interpretation.
12. Have a reading league in the spring or summer. Baseball mitts cut from paper could hold the individual child's book record.

13. Refer to *Creative Teaching of the Language Arts,* Chapter 8, for other suggestions for the creative teaching of the above mechanics of reading.[10]

Developing Creative Thinking Abilities.   Since the development of creative thinking through reading is an area that has not been explored very deeply in reading programs in this country, Chapter 3 is devoted to a discussion of the creative reading concept. The creativity of children can be developed through each stage of the reading program if the teacher will keep in mind the principles stated in Chapter 3 and will recall the principles basic to creative teaching as stated in Chapter 1.   The story of Kevin, which opened this chapter, is an example of the manner by which one teacher taught many of the skills mentioned in this chapter in a meaningful and creative experience.

The Stage of Rapid Growth

Some children learn to read before they come to school.   Others have had little experience with books or with the types of readiness materials mentioned above.   In some families, it is a custom for the parent to read a story to the child each evening at bedtime.   In other families, children have no books to handle or study.

Children come to school, then, in various stages of reading readiness and with various reading skills.   Therefore, individualization of the reading program is necessary.   All children will not need instruction in all the skills.   The teacher will need to make certain, however, that the children have mastered the skills even if they were not learned in school.

Students of childrens' reading behavior have observed that almost all children go through *a period of rapid growth.* This stage occurs at different ages for different children, often depending on the experiential background of the child when he comes to school.   Some children from disadvantaged homes, for instance, struggle through a beginning reading program, seeming to make some progress in skill attainment and reading ability but in a plodding, often discouraging, manner.   But at some point in their exposure to reading materials the *concept* of reading seems to become clear to them and they develop enough confidence in themselves and acquire enough skills to suddenly be able to read

10. Smith, James A., *Creative Teaching of the Language Arts,* 2nd ed., Boston: Allyn and Bacon, 1973.

at a much higher level of speed and comprehension than they did the previous week.

Children who come to school from a background of rich experiences and many reading exposures also appear to go through such a stage, only they do it earlier than children of different backgrounds.

A period of rapid growth is a natural stage in the development of most children, and it often marks the beginning of a great spurt in independence in reading. The challenge to the teacher at this time is to make the skills program interesting and absorbing to the child so that he will continue to develop needed skills, and to supply him with a wealth of material to read on his independent reading level.

The Stage of Reading Power

From the examples of creative teaching described in this book, we can see that reading is used in the primary grades largely for enjoyment, for information-gathering, for recording class activities, and for planning purposes (using references).

But reading is also a tool to be used for many other purposes, and the intermediate grade program should basically develop the child's power to use reading to serve his needs in his daily living as well as for enjoyment.

The intermediate grade program in reading is often misunderstood or neglected because it is interpreted as a continuation of the primary program. Some of the instructional tasks of the intermediate grade teacher may be the same as the primary teacher's, but others go far and above those tasks developed in the primary grades.

Reading power is developed in the intermediate grades. When analyzed into its many parts, reading power is seen to come from the acquisition of many necessary skills. Developing these skills is the job of the intermediate grade teacher. She must concentrate on the following tasks:

1. Continuing development and expansion of primary reading skills
2. Continuing independent reading
3. Expanding the vocabulary and range of materials
4. Developing more refined techniques of comprehension
5. Developing the techniques of critical thinking
6. Developing techniques for effective reading rates

7. Developing the skill of reading carefully for directions and details
8. Developing skill in oral or audience-type situations
9. Developing more skilled approaches to word study and word attack, such as:
   a. Building word meanings
   b. Using mature techniques of word recognition
   c. Using advanced word-analysis skills
   d. Using the dictionary
10. Teaching the efficient use of reference techniques:
    a. Locating information
    b. Note-taking
    c. Outlining
    d. Summarizing
    e. Using library resources
11. Teaching how to apply reading skills in these ways:
    a. Using the dictionary
    b. Proper care and handling of books
    c. Locating information
    d. Selecting main ideas
    e. Skimming
    f. Reading for beauty—interpretative and appreciative
    g. Reading for detail
    h. Reading dialects
    i. Reading charts, maps, and graphs
12. Developing organizational skills

Something needs to be said about grouping and its direct relation to reading in the intermediate grades. One common conception of grouping is that the class is divided into three or four groups—the fast readers, the average readers, and the slow readers. This type of grouping implies that we are primarily concerned with reading rate and comprehension: the best (fastest and with greatest comprehension, generally above grade level); the average (about where they should be in terms of rate, comprehension, and grade level); and the poorest (slow reader, below grade level). Speed and comprehension (the acquisition of the thought the author is attempting to communicate) are related, but they must be taught separately. There are important skills involved in the reading process that children will need help in developing. Vocabulary building is one. The ability to select the main ideas from different selections, to skim and to read differently for different material, to attack and discover meanings for new words, to summarize, to outline, to read for information, to read poetry—these and a host of other skills must be acquired by children if they are to be effective readers.

FIGURE 2–6. *Intermediate children continue to develop visual acuity by creating new shapes.*

Teachers can discover who needs help in these areas and *group the children according to similar problems.* This is possible at any level once the reading act has been efficiently established. At the beginning of this chapter you saw how vocabulary building may be developed with any group regardless of speed in reading. In a like manner, the creative teacher can work up a series of lessons to help children gain skill in selecting the main ideas from stories or paragraphs regardless of their reading ability level. She may, for instance, run off on a ditto machine a story aimed at the poorest reader; her purpose is to teach a skill, not to worry over the reading matter itself. Everyone reads the story, and through discussion they select the main ideas and may even outline the story on the board. The teacher then gives each child a book to read on his own reading level, and he practices with a story from the book. There are advantages in this heterogeneous grouping in that children who read well can help those who do not. Good social relationships are developed in this process, and the sights are raised for the slow child while the quick child gains status in the group.   The slower child also stands a stronger chance of responding to and discovering answers so that he, too, gains status in the group.

Ability grouping is necessary to some extent.   The problem the teacher confronts here is raising the ability in reading, if possible.   But this is not the only reason for grouping.   It is important that teachers remember that the best way to help children become better readers is to teach them the skills that will help them read independently.   Fast readers as well as slow ones often have difficulty selecting main ideas, attacking new words, or understanding what they have read.   When children are grouped to work on problems, the groups constantly change, and the stigma attached to a slow reading group dissolves.   Real ability grouping implies flexibility.   The grouping described above is really *content* grouping although it is often misnamed *ability* grouping.

Another logical way to keep children reading independently at the peak point of their ability level is through the personalized reading program described on page 102.   In this type of reading program the major portion of the child's time is spent reading as an individual, not as a member of a reading group. Inasmuch as this is the way most people read in life, it seems to be a rewarding and practical way to teach children to read.

In the past few years many systems (each with a variety of hardware and software) have been designed to help each child progress at his own speed and in keeping with his own interests and ideas.   Some of these systems, such as the Personalized Reading Center produced by Xerox Education Center,[11] are dedicated to developing children's creativity as well as their personal reading skills.   These programs often use machines, cards, and other devices, singly or in combination, to teach children basic phonics skills or structural analysis skills and to provide practice in developing them.   Some materials then encourage the children to view filmstrips that show scenes from suggested supplemental books, which they may read and to which they may apply their new learnings.   This process allows the child options, and he is almost certain to find something that kindles his interest.

11. Personalized Reading Center (Columbus, Ohio: Xerox Education Center, 1973).   The complete individualized reading program for each grade level includes books, cards, check forms, records, etc.

Many other systems, or programs, offer a variety of materials to keep reading on an independent level. Science Research Associates are pioneers in this field. Some creative devices, such as the language machines, make it possible for children to study phonics with a minimum of aid from the teacher. The machines are equipped with cards on which are printed letters or combinations of letters and pictures. Putting the card in a designated track in the machine and pulling it across the track creates a voice that speaks to the children and articulates the sounds. Many such creative inventions can be of excellent value when used wisely with children.

Organizational plans in a classroom can develop or hinder independent reading. The open classroom situation described at the beginning of this book encourages independent learning and independent reading. The independent reading program described on page 102 emphasizes a classroom organization that recognizes the need for a variety of materials to suit the diversity of reading skills. Such programs also recognize the need for accessibility to a school library or a classroom library with many books written on many levels of reading ability and on many topics. Scheduling is an important consideration if children are to use the school library effectively.

Success in obtaining independence in reading is based largely on the conditions set in each classroom for making reading an integrated, useful skill to be used throughout the school day. When children are successful in applying skills, they hunger to master more skills to attain more success. Success at each step of reading development is necessary to produce the psychological atmosphere in which achievement can develop.

SUMMARY

To understand how the basic principles of creative teaching may be applied to the teaching of reading, one must understand the process of reading and know which skills to develop. This chapter has explained the process involved in the reading act and has defined the skills that must be developed in order to produce good readers.

In the next chapter we will discuss creative reading and the methods and organization plans for teaching reading that are currently popular in our elementary schools. Each method will be evaluated according to the extent to which it is adaptable to the principles of creative teaching.

TO THE COLLEGE STUDENT

1. This chapter has given you an overall picture of the reading process and some ways you might teach this process. You will need to read in more detail about other reading topics. Some are listed below. Assign topics to various classmates and ask them to read up on their topics and report to the class. The bibliography at the end of this chapter will be of help to you.
   a. The Pre-School Reading Readiness Program
   b. Remedial Reading and Corrective Reading
   c. Evaluation in Primary Reading
   d. The Role of the Reading Consultant in the Elementary School
   e. The Place of Workbooks in the Primary Reading Program: Can They Be Used Creatively?
   f. Worthwhile Independent Reading Activities
   g. The Diagnosis of Reading Difficulties
   h. Establishing an Individualized Reading Program
   i. Organizational Plans for Teaching Reading
   j. A Study of the State of Reading in the United States Today Compared to Fifty Years Ago
   k. Supplementary Reading Materials
   l. Reading Tests
2. Using what you have read in this chapter, defend or refute this statement: Television harms children's reading habits.
3. Make a list of all the creative ways you can think of to motivate children to read for a variety of purposes.
4. Take any reading manual you have in your classroom and rewrite several of the lessons to present a more creative approach to the lessons than the one used in the manual.
5. Take some children to the library and allow them to choose any books they like. Make note of the range in interests and abilities. Discuss ways to meet the difference in interests and abilities in the classroom.
6. Chapter 8 contains suggestions for motivating children to read books. After you read that chapter, come back and review this one with this question in mind: How does a good literature program fit into the primary reading program?
7. Visit the poorest socioeconomic level of your community. Then examine the reading texts in the schools that the children from this section of town attend. Do the stories reflect the experiences of the children you visited? How might a teacher in such a section begin to teach reading?

TO THE CLASSROOM TEACHER

Examine your own reading program in respect to these questions:

1. Is my reading program a challenge to each child?
2. Do I have a plan for grouping that makes it possible for me to meet the individual needs of each child?
3. Are the books in my classroom and in the school library being constantly used by my children?
4. Does every child know why he comes to meet with a reading group each time we meet?
5. Do I use the manual and textbook as an *aid* or do I follow it slavishly?

   If the answer to any one of these questions is no, you have an indication that a part of your program needs strengthening. Try one new thing each day to improve your reading program.

TO THE COLLEGE STUDENT
AND THE CLASSROOM TEACHER

1. In the reading lesson described in this chapter, the children spent the entire afternoon developing language skills. Tell how the teacher taught good listening skills. How did he foster skills in effective oral expression? In reading? Is this total blend of teaching without specific class periods a good idea? Justify your reasoning.
2. Discuss the following statements:
   a. Mr. Smith used the logical, sequential development of language skills while teaching his lesson.
   b. Mr. Smith considered the biology of the children while teaching his lesson.
   c. Mr. Smith used "contrived" teaching techniques to develop his lesson.
   d. Mr. Smith used "normal" teaching techniques to develop his lesson.
3. What should have been done on the day following Mr. Smith's lesson to insure the fixation of vocabulary and its further development?

SELECTED BIBLIOGRAPHY

Anderson, Verna Dieckman. *Reading and Young Children.* New York: Macmillan, 1968.

Aukerman, R. C. *Approaches to Beginning Reading*. New York: John Wiley and Sons, 1972.

Austin, Mary, and Coleman Morrison. *The First R: The Harvard Report on Reading in the Elementary Schools*. New York: Macmillan, 1963.

Bagford, Jack. *Phonics: Its Role in Teaching Reading*. Iowa City, Ia.: Sernoll, 1967.

Burron, Arnold. *Basic Concepts of Reading Instruction: A Programmed Approach*. Columbus, O.: Charles E. Merrill Co., 1972.

Bush, Clifford L., and Mildred H. Huebner. *Strategies for Reading in the Elementary School*. New York: Macmillan, 1970.

Chall, Jeanne S. *Learning To Read: The Great Debate*. New York: McGraw-Hill, 1967.

Dawson, Mildred A., Henry A. Bamman, and James J. McGovern. *Fundamentals of Basic Reading Instruction*. New York: David McKay Co., 1973.

DeBoer, John, Martha Dallmann, and Walter J. Moore. *The Teaching of Reading*. 3rd ed. New York: Holt, Rinehart and Winston, 1970.

Dechant, Emerald. *Improving the Teaching of Reading*. 2nd ed. Englewood Cliffs, N.J.: Prentice-Hall, 1970.

Durkin, Dolores. *Teaching Them to Read*. 2nd ed. Boston: Allyn and Bacon, 1974.

Frey, Sherman H. "The Case against Programmed Instruction." *Clearing House* 40 (September 1965): 27–29.

Fry, Edward. *Teaching Machines and Programmed Instruction*. New York: McGraw-Hill, 1963.

Gans, Roma. *Common Sense in Teaching Reading*. New York: Bobbs-Merrill, 1963.

Goodacre, Elizabeth J. *Children and Learning to Read*. Boston: Routledge and Kegan Paul, 1972.

Hall, Mary Anne. *Teaching Reading as a Language Experience*. Columbus, O.: Charles E. Merrill Co., 1970.

Harris, Albert J., and Edward R. Sipay. *Effective Teaching of Reading*. New York: David McKay Co., 1971.

Heilman, Arthur W. *Principles and Practices of Teaching Reading*. 3rd ed. Columbus, Ohio: Charles E. Merrill Co., 1972.

Hester, Kathleen B. *Teaching Every Child to Read*. 2nd ed. New York: Harper and Row, 1964.

Hildreth, Gertrude. *Teaching Reading*. New York: Holt, Rinehart and Winston, 1968.

Hughes, John. *Linguistics and Language Teaching*. New York: Random House, 1968.

Jones, Daisy Marvel. *Teaching Children to Read.* New York: Harper and Row, 1971.

Karlin, Robert. *Teaching Elementary Reading: Principles and Strategies.* New York: Harcourt Brace Jovanovich, 1972.

LeFevre, Carl A. *Linguistics and the Teaching of Reading.* New York: McGraw-Hill, 1964.

McKee, Paul, and William K. Durr. *Reading: A Program of Instruction for Elementary School.* New York: Houghton Mifflin, 1966.

McKeown, Pamela. *Reading.* Boston: Routledge and Kegan Paul, 1973.

McKim, Margaret G., and Helen Caskey. *Guiding Growth in Reading.* New York: Macmillan, 1963.

Morrison, Ida E. *Teaching Reading in the Elementary School.* New York: The Ronald Press, 1968.

Smith, Frank. *Understanding Reading: A Psycholinguistic Analysis of Reading and Learning to Read.* New York: Holt, Rinehart and Winston, 1971.

Spache, George. *The Teaching of Reading.* Bloomington, Ind.: Phi Delta Kappa, 1972.

————, and Spache, Evelyn. *Reading in the Elementary School.* 3rd ed. Boston: Allyn and Bacon, 1973.

Stauffer, Russell G. *The Language-Experience Approach to the Teaching of Reading.* New York: Harper and Row, 1970.

Strang, Ruth. *Diagnostic Teaching of Reading.* 2nd ed. New York: McGraw-Hill, 1969.

Veatch, Jeannette. *Reading in the Elementary School.* New York: The Ronald Press, 1966.

Wallen, Carl J. *Competency in Teaching Reading.* Chicago: Science Research Associates, 1972.

Wardaugh, Ronald. *Reading: A Linguistic Perspective.* New York: Harcourt, Brace Jovanovitch, 1969.

Zintz, Miles V. *The Reading Process: The Teacher and the Learner.* Dubuque, Ia.: William C. Brown & Co., 1971.

CHAPTER III

The Creative Teaching
of Reading

Great progress has been made in developing helpful techniques and materials for teaching reading, but no packaged process will ever meet the wide variety of personalities faced by teachers in classrooms and looked after by parents at home. This is especially true if we approach children with a respect for their eagerness to learn and if we honor the integrity of their taste. Then, instead of teaching young people as if we were feeding them packaged prescriptions, we inspire them and challenge them to invest their efforts and ideas in learning to read.[1]

ROMA GANS

TO THE READER

Before you read this chapter, think of all the systems, or methods, of teaching reading with which you are familiar and ask yourself, "Through which of these methods could creativity be developed?" Also review any organizational plans for teaching reading with which you are familiar. Do some of these plans make the development of creativity an impossibility? An organizational plan sets conditions for the development of creativity and thus is very important in considering the creative teaching of reading.

1. Roma Gans, *Common Sense in the Teaching of Reading* (New York: The Bobbs-Merrill Co., 1963), p. vi.

WHAT IS CREATIVE READING?

Can a reading program be creative? There are those who feel that all reading is creative because the reader must tap his past experiences and reassemble his ideas and concepts into new meanings. He must give the symbols (words and clusters of words) meaning from his own reservoir of experiences. Therefore, the process is similar to the creative act. But this is a very narrow concept of creativity and of reading. Unless the reading inspires the reader to change his behavior in some manner that will produce a new or different product, we can hardly classify it as creative reading.

Some authors deliberately write to develop creative thinking in the reader. Parts of this book are written with that objective. If, as a result of reading this book, a teacher reexamines her reading program and makes changes in it that include many ideas of her own or ideas adapted from this book, then the reading has been creative.

If the writing of an author has been so beautiful and so inspiring that the reader *thinks* in new ways, he is reacting to creative writing by doing creative reading. However, a reader may enjoy and even cherish the ideas he discovers in beautiful, creative writing without using those ideas to alter his own behavior. Then he is reading creative writing, but he is not necessarily engaging in creative reading.

It is difficult for a teacher to determine whether or not a child is reading creatively by observing him. Observation of his behavior *after* he reads may tell her more, but creative thinking does not always result in a product; it may also result in a process, and a reader may give no outward indication that he has thought creatively.

If a child takes a book on macrame from the library and ties a belt that is exactly like the illustration and directions in the book, she has learned a skill and a technique: she has exhibited her ability to follow directions. If, a few days later, she makes a macrame wall hanging, experimenting with new knots and tying beads and buttons into her design, the reading has led to creative behavior. To some children, this particular book may never be more than an exercise in following directions. But to this child it became the incentive for more creative acts. Her response may have been the result of the classroom teacher's practice of emphasizing creativity in her reading program and testing the children's ability to follow directions by observing each child's behavior rather than by giving pencil-and-paper tests.

This example leads us to the problem at hand: A reading program can be creative only if it conforms to six criteria determined from studies in the area of creativity.

1. A creative reading program has the development of creative thought as one of its objectives.
2. A creative reading program deliberately tries to develop creative behaviors.
3. A creative reading program emphasizes learning by discovery and self-learning.
4. A creative reading program avoids rigid conformity.
5. A creative reading program provides satisfying reading experiences.
6. A creative reading program gives the child opportunities to practice his creative powers.

The following sections discuss the relevance of each of these criteria.

Development of Creative Thought

The objective of developing creativity is important throughout the school day, and reading fits naturally into the fulfillment of this objective in a variety of ways. For example, the teacher makes certain that children have daily contact with beautiful and creative writing by others so that they can see how their thoughts may be communicated *effectively and creatively* as well as *correctly*. The teacher also uses reading as a technique to inspire creative thinking and creative products (like the thinking of the child mentioned above, who developed her creative ideas in working on a macrame wall hanging).

The teacher uses reading as a practice area to develop those components of creativity that fit naturally into the curriculum. The divergent thinking processes that underlie the creative development of children consist of many specific skills, each of which must be developed, either separately or together. Those generally taught as part of the reading program are:

1. Visual acuity
2. Ability to organize
3. Independence
4. Ability to redefine

FIGURE 3–1. *Measures of creative reading.*

 5. Associational fluency
 6. Expressional fluency
 7. Word fluency
 8. Ideational fluency
 9. Ability to elaborate
10. Ability to evaluate
11. Sensitivity to problems
12. Ability to analyze and abstract
13. Ability to synthesize
14. Ability to think abstractly
15. Ability to retain
16. Ability to identify
17. Ability to concentrate
18. Possession of a wide range of information
19. Openness to experience
20. Ability to perceive
21. Ability to draw analogies

Research has shown that creative children have developed these skills to a more refined degree than have noncreative children.   Teachers will recognize many of the above characteristics as objectives already stated in many teaching manuals.   While they are developing these particular skills they are contributing to the development of many component parts of the creative act. Add these objectives to others that develop creativity and we can see how the teaching of reading contributes strongly to creative development.

Other creative techniques for the teaching of reading include the following: The teacher encourages children to read to seek new information to help them *pass judgments* and *make decisions,* two of the necessary skills of a creative thinker.   The teacher uses reading as a way to introduce children to flights of the imagination in stories, poems, science reports, and news and allows time for discussion so children may see that one symbol can provoke a variety of interpretations.   The teacher encourages children to write and print their own messages to be read by others so that they come to understand the techniques of printed form and the need for clear communication.   The teacher keeps the organization of the reading program individualized.   (While it is recognized that some reading skills must be developed in groups, the bulk of the reading program should be geared to each individual child's interests and abilities.)   The teacher carefully scrutinizes the current reading program and removes the blocks it sets in the way of creative teaching and creative development.

Many barriers to the creative teaching of reading have risen in the past twenty years.   Among them are the following:

1. Patterns of grouping for reading that do not meet individual needs in children and that often destroy the ego-concept of a child so that he loses his desire to read because he associates reading with unpleasantness
2. The pseudoscientific concept that all children can be taught to read in the same manner
3. The slavish dedication to commercial textbooks and workbooks that contain a reading program supposedly arranged in scientific sequence
4. The lack of consideration of the socioeconomic level or racial background of the children in the school when selecting reading materials
5. The extreme pressure placed on children to read because of the recent criticism of the public schools
6. Many teachers' lack of understanding of the exact place of reading in the school program, as well as their lack of understanding of the total reading act
7. The excessive emphasis placed on reading periods rather than an emphasis on reading as a skill to be used all day
8. The inability of many schools to keep reading on a personalized, or individual, level
9. The lack of recognition of the change in emphasis and need for reading in the space age
10. The inability of textbooks and reading programs to produce material within the child's range of experience and interest
11. Some teachers' lack of understanding of the structure of the English language
12. Some teachers' lack of understanding of the sub-skills necessary for reading development
13. The overuse of the Round Robin technique of reading practice

Comments on each of these barriers will be further developed throughout the following pages.

Uncreative teaching procedures cannot be justified in terms of sound education. If the learning process is creativity itself, then the teaching of reading must be an individual process taught by teachers who care enough about each child to make sure that he assembles his known experiences into new concepts each day and discovers or creates new skills that open new vistas to him.

Development of Creative Behaviors

Developing techniques and skills in children through their actual reading (as described in the macrame illustration above) is one way a reading program can develop creativity.   But, it can also be developed in less obvious ways.   When teaching phonics, for instance, Mrs. Ellis was trying to communicate the idea that when one prefix is used at the beginning of many different words, it sounds and looks the same on each word, and it tends to change the meaning of the root word.   The children were exploring the prefix *re*.   They were listing all the words they could think of that began with that prefix.   The list included *repay, replay, reverse, rebuild, reply, recess,* and *recycle*.   As Mrs. Ellis printed the words on the chalkboard, she wrote the prefix with fluorescent chalk (which looks like ordinary white chalk in the daylight) and wrote the rest of the word with regular white chalk.   She cleverly manipulated the two pieces of chalk so that children could not detect that she was shifting them.   After the children had given her all the words they could think of, Mrs. Ellis asked them to watch carefully to see if they could notice something important. She then asked Charles to switch off the classroom lights while she turned on the black light located under the chalkboard.   Immediately, the *re* on each word glowed a bright pink.

The children quickly noticed that each *re* came at the beginning of the word, that each *looked* and *sounded* the same, and that *re* placed before the root word seemed to change its meaning.   From examining the list, they thought *re* must mean "opposite" or "back" or "again," as it does in *repay, replay, recycle,* and *rebuild*.   The dictionary helped them to see that adding *re* to a word changed the meaning of that word.   For example, the root of *reverse* came from the Latin *vertere* ("to turn") and *re* made the word mean "to turn back"; in *reply*, the root came from the Latin *plicare* ("to fold"); and in *recess*, the root came from the Latin *cedere* ("to go"), and *re* made it mean "to go back" or "set back" as a niche in a wall or a return to rest from work.   Actually, in all but one word the prefix *re* means "back."   The children decided that although they would not always know the root word or its meaning, they could be pretty sure that the prefix *re* meant its opposite or to do it over again—to go back.

During this lesson the children were given practice in drawing analogies, in gaining perspectives, in thinking divergently, and in making discoveries.   (We will pursue the discovery technique further in the next section.)   All of these skills are creative behaviors.   The checksheet on pages 80–81 lists those behaviors, commonly exhibited by creative children and adults, that teachers will encourage if they desire a creative reading program. The teacher may write the names of the children with whom she is working in the spaces at the top of the checklist and check the

FIGURE 3–2.   *The creative teaching of reading means individualized teaching* and *group teaching.*

children's characteristics in the corresponding boxes.   Children with the greatest number of checks will be the most creative children in the group.   The list serves as a diagnostic instrument and as a cluster of characteristics that become goals for developing creativity in all aspects of the school program.

Emphasis on Learning by Discovery and Self-learning

In considering the normal developmental characteristics of children, we must not forget the importance of the element of discovery to the child.   One of the greatest fallacies of educational technique is the constant practice of the over-ambitious teacher to cover her material so quickly that the children have little time to discover things for themselves.   At a very early age the child secures great delight in discovering.   As soon as he is able to crawl and walk, he opens doors and closets and explores and investigates to his heart's content.   He observes very quickly how his parents and siblings do things, and he attempts to imitate. The joy in his voice shows his delight in self-accomplishment when he says, "Look, I did it all by myself!"   This desire for independence goes on within him continually.   At first he masters simple accomplishments—pouring a glass of milk, filling a sand bucket, or buttoning his clothes.   In any event, it is a creative achievement and another step in his growth, and the child recognizes it as such.   He loves to learn, he wants to create—he wants

Characteristics of Creative Children

(Most commonly listed in research)

Characteristic	Child																		
1. Sensitive to life experiences																			
2. Reacts more fully to emotions																			
3. Superior verbal facility																			
4. Superior verbal fluency																			
5. Superior verbal flexibility																			
6. General flexibility																			
7. Originality																			
8. Prefers perceiving to judging																			
9. Self-sufficient																			
10. Independent in judgement																			
11. More stable																			

12.	Sense of humor— playfulness																			
13.	More interested in unconventional roles																			
14.	More feminine (masc.) in interests																			
15.	More dominant and self-assertive																			
16.	Often estranged from peers																			
17.	More adventurous and resourceful																			
18.	Great energy—zest— effectiveness																			
19.	Challenged by disorder																			
20.	Less susceptible to group pressures																			
21.	Always baffled by something																			
22.	Constructive in criticism																			
23.	Defies conventions of courtesy																			
24.	Industrious																			
25.	Introversive																			
26.	Receptive to ideas of others																			
27.	Attracted to the mysterious and unknown																			
28.	Attempts difficult jobs (sometimes too difficult)																			
29.	Persistent																			
30.	Self-starter																			

to know!   And he is delighted to discover that he has learned! Thus his inherent drive to create and learn is the greatest motivational device a teacher or parent has in working with children; yet, in our rush to "get them told" we so often kill this joy of discovery—the fun the child has in learning by himself.   The job of the teacher is to facilitate the learning process by setting conditions that lead the child to new discoveries rather than to tell him about everything he meets without giving him a chance to find out for himself.   *Teaching* is not *telling.*   In reading, as in everything else, children must have frequent opportunities to discover their own abilities.   Discovery is part of the process of creativity.

I was visiting a small rural school not long ago.   It was a bright fall day and the children were having a play period out-of-doors. The school itself was a beehive of activity, and the classroom environment was rich with the results of many experiences the group had had together.   In one corner there was a live rabbit, and there were charts on "How to Care for Our Rabbit," "Stories on Our Rabbit," and "Fluffy, Our Rabbit," as well as poems about rabbits.   On an attractive reading table the teacher had arranged a great many preprimers.   She had also torn up old readers and primers and had stapled between covers of brightly colored construction paper stories that pertained to the many activities going on in the room.   On many there were pictures of rabbits, and lettered below them were the same words that appeared on the reading charts.

While the adults were talking, a first-grader left the rabbit cage, went over to the reading table, and selected a picture book. The teacher's watchful eye observed him carefully.   Finally, he put down the picture book and noticed the books the teacher had made.   Picking one up, he came to her and asked, "Miss Ellis, is this a book about rabbits?"   "Yes, it is, Peter," she replied.   "Wish I could read it," Peter said as he flipped the pages.   "I bet you can," said Miss Ellis.   "Aw, Miss Ellis," he grinned, "I can't read a *book!*"   "Why don't you try?" she encouraged.

Peter opened the book to the first page.   He looked at the picture and the line printed below it and he read, "I am a rabbit."

His eyes widened and he turned the page.   Again he read, "I am white."   The next pages went faster and faster, and his face and body became more and more animated as he read page after page.   With eyes wide and starry he clutched the finished book to his breast, looked up at the teacher, and said, "Why, I can read!"

She answered calmly, "Why, of course you can!" but he

did not hear. He walked slowly to the doll bed in the housekeeping corner, sat on the bed, opened the book, and again reread the pages. After he had completed the booklet, he held it close to him and laughingly said to himself over and over as he rocked back and forth, "I can read! I can read! I can read!"

Teacher said, "Peter has begun to read."

When the children came in at her call, she assembled all the grades together and said, "We have a surprise today. Something exciting has happened. Peter, do you want to tell them what you discovered you could do?"

So Peter shared his new ability with the group. Immediately four other first-graders wanted to know if they could read the books. Soon all the books were shared, and four more children "discovered" they could read. The older children were loud in their praise, and the first graders spent the whole afternoon listening to each other read. The books went home with the children, who departed eagerly, exclaiming, "I'm going to show my mother how I can read," or "Wait till Daddy hears I can read."

The masterful handling of this situation is impressive. How skillfully the teacher had paved the way for discovery, how well she had utilized the discovery to further motivate the children! All her hours of preparation, vocabulary-building, and chart-making had been repaid in this moment, and the wise and skillful manner in which she waited for the children to discover books is an example of the type of teaching we should be doing to build positive attitudes and a love of reading.

Children are often plunged into reading texts without having had wise and careful preparation. So many school systems have become "manual-bound" that results in reading are often measured by achievement tests, with little attention to enthusiasm and general attitude and the degree to which these are used. Positive attitudes towards reading cannot be measured by an achievement test. Actually, one of the best evaluations of a good reading program might justifiably be empty library shelves.

Because they are prepared by experts, manuals can be of invaluable help in planning creative reading lessons, but they should not be followed automatically. Page-by-page dependence on a manual can often make even an interesting story dull.

One reading series includes a story about a surprise. In the story, Uncle Tim comes to visit. He has a surprise, but it must wait until after dinner. But amazing things happen during the dinner. The dog asks for food, the roast turkey on the table shouts when it is about to be cut, and events in general become

most confusing.   In the end, of course, it turns out that Uncle
Tim is a ventriloquist, and the surprise in his bag is a puppet.

According to the procedure detailed in the manual, this
story, like scores of others, is supposed to be introduced by having
the teacher put the new words on the board.   The teacher and children discuss the words.   Then the teacher reads verbatim the manual's printed introduction to the story.   Next, the children discuss
the pictures.   Teacher asks questions printed in the manual.
Then the children read laboriously, page by page, to find the answers to the questions.   In one school, this delightful story was
taught to one second grade by a veteran teacher using this routine.   A few children were interested; the rest gazed around the
room, fidgeted, yawned, and were scolded because they did not
pay attention.   Their entire approach to the reading group was
one of apathy.   Another teacher used the material in the reading
manual but adapted it to her own particular group.   She operated
on the premise that there are at least three basic ways to motivate
children: (1) through meeting their immediate needs and interests, (2) through content that is appealing, and (3) through
technique.   This teacher made reading exciting by an excellent
"technique" motivation.   She taught the story in the following
manner:

During the planning period she placed before the class a
suitcase with a paper saying "SURPRISE" on it.   "What is this
word?" she asked.   When the children told her, she said, "Yes,
and in the suitcase is a surprise.   But we won't be able to find out
what it is until Timmy's reading group meets—but let's put it in
our plans."   So she scheduled a surprise on the board for eleven
o'clock.

At the appointed time, the children gathered eagerly to
find out the surprise.   Each guessed what it might be, and each
word was printed on the board.   After each child had offered a
suggestion, teacher said, "No one has guessed it yet.   I'm going
to give you some clues.   Let's see if you're good detectives."   Little
by little, she gave an introduction to the story similar to the one
in the manual.   As she talked, the new words were brought into
the conversation and lettered on the board.   Finally she said,
"Our last clue is in the reading book.   Johnny and Mary get the
same surprise as we are to have.   Let's read their story.   Let's
look at these words on the board, too, because Johnny and Mary
used many of these words in trying to find out their surprise."

So the story was read, and the suitcase was opened.
When the puppet was taken out, each child had the opportunity to
speak through it, telling how he liked the story.   The group then

dramatized the story simply, using the books for their speaking lines and inviting other children to observe.

The development of commercial materials that encourage self-learning has reached unprecedented proportions. Available materials provide skill exercises and reading matter for all ability levels of children and for most of their differing interests.

The teacher who does not have access to as many of these materials as she needs, however, can develop her own strategies and materials to develop self-instruction. First of all, children can learn a great deal from each other, and large groups can be broken down into couples or smaller groups so that a child who has mastered a skill may give individual attention to a child who has not.

Cards can be developed to provide work contracts for the children. Often, tapes can be made to go with the cards so that a small group working together may be looking and listening to sounds or practicing exercises in word construction. Much of the material that the teacher distributes to children to work on as part of her regular lessons can also be put on cards to be used independently by children working alone. Many of her practice assignments can be put on tapes. Children can help to make both cards and tapes.

A classroom library (which will be discussed on page 128) is also a good device for self-instruction. It should include books that match the ability of all age levels, and that cover as many of the wide variety of interests that children have as possible. Children learn to read best by reading. When books are within the children's range of ability and interest, they are more likely to use them. Generally they will select material within their range of reading ability.

Avoidance of Rigid Conformity

Flexibility is a characteristic of the creative teacher. Her program must be so flexible that each child is working at his own reading level; each child is stimulated to read, for his own personal interests and reasons, from a variety of sources; each child is evaluated in his reading according to his own growth and abilities, and each child has his own personally prescribed reading program. This program will use many books of all kinds, including those that encourage creative thinking and develop techniques and skills for creative work. The child's experiences in the acquisition of reading skills will be rich and varied and will not (in fact cannot) be confined to pre-planned manuals and workbooks.   The teacher will not feel she must cover *every page* in a text or *every page* in a workbook.   She will use such materials with caution and discretion, giving each child only those materials that are beneficial and that have meaning to him.   She will give individual, small group, and large group instruction, determining which type of instruction will be best for each child, and she will be as inventive and creative as she can be in her presentations.

Seeking novel and highly motivating strategies to use in her reading program, Miss Farnsworth noted that an excellent collection of Weston Woods (and other) filmstrips was available in the school library.   Rather than showing these filmstrips to the entire class as she had done up to that point, she set up a school library corner containing the books about which she was able to borrow filmstrips, along with a number of individual viewfinders.   Children were encouraged to look at the filmstrips as a technique for making a decision about which book to read next. This was Miss Farnsworth's own idea and paid big dividends in her independent reading program.

Fostering creativity, we have mentioned above, means fostering individuality, and vice versa.   This means that each child progresses at his own rate and takes some responsibility for learning on his own shoulders.   Fostering creativity also helps each child to respect his own interests and to gain new experiences.

Provision for Satisfying Reading Experiences

To be satisfying to the child, his daily reading must cover a variety of needs.   During one day a ten-year-old can read a note left by his mother in his lunch box, signs on the billboards on the way to school, road signs, notices on his class bulletin boards, notes from his buddies, a poem aloud over the loudspeaker system, some material about salamanders in a book from the library, material from another book on the life of an astronaut, a story to develop his oral reading ability in his reading group, a test in arithmetic and one in root words, the titles on television programs, a page or two from his Cub Scout Manual, and a story from *Boy's Life* before going to bed.

All of this reading is meaningful and therefore satisfying to the child (with the exception perhaps, of the story read to develop his oral reading skills and his tests, although they *could* be satisfying and meaningful). To be satisfying, reading takes place for a purpose. Consequently, a satisfying reading program is one in which children learn the skills of reading in meaningful ways, *not simply to learn words and skills;* what they *learn* must be applied practically to make the child a better equipped and happier individual.

The child will gain satisfaction from his reading when he does it for any of these reasons: (1) for pleasure, (2) to find out facts and to learn about interesting subjects, (3) for the beauty of the words, (4) to learn how to do or make things, (5) to communicate with others, (6) to use records, (7) to be challenged, (8) to discover new things, (9) to empathize, and (10) to stimulate his imagination.

The basis of creativity, we have said, is divergent thinking. This type of thinking is characterized by the ability to come up with new solutions to problems. Most current reading textbooks concentrate on the development of convergent thinking, which emphasizes memory or recall of answers already known by someone, generally the teacher. In divergent thinking, the child invents the answers. More of our reading should stress this highly satisfying activity of children. But few current readers do stress open-ended problems that call upon children to create new answers by synthesizing, making inferences, passing judgments, and making decisions.

Part of the plan for developing satisfying reading experiences will be to place the child in many open-ended situations that exercise his divergent thinking abilities. The child will be given the opportunity to select his reading material from many options. The material will help him to become sensitive to his own values and to the life styles of others. Much material should be provided that will help him to understand and recognize his contributions to his world.

Provision of Opportunities to Practice Creative Powers

A creative reading program will provide activities that allow each child to put his new knowledge to work, helping him further to develop originality, fluency, and a sense of humor. Reading is always done for a purpose, and the teacher must always keep in mind the objectives for developing creativity.

Mr. March's daily reading program included a variety of purposes for reading in each of the subject matter areas. When the children entered the classroom, they read from the chalkboard the options for the day. From that list they selected the activities they preferred and plotted a daily schedule. In arithmetic they read problems from a chart that they had helped to construct. The chart gave the cost of various staples as they currently appeared at six supermarkets in town. The children had worked on neighborhood committees and had collected the prices after school. In Social Studies the children read for a variety of reasons: John was collecting data on the Eskimos so that he could make a report to an interested group, Helen and Dorothy were making their own filmstrip on the Alaskan Highway and were collecting information for it, Roger was reading about the Alaskan Indians in order to create an Indian diorama with a group of boys. One child had discovered Ramona Mager's book *The Blind Boy and the Loon,* and the children were taking turns reading it to each other, chapter by chapter.

In Science the children were working by contracts. Each child had chosen one major project and two minor ones to complete by himself in a three-week period. Some children were reading and taking notes, some were reading in order to set up a science experiment, and some were reading to construct charts or structures for a variety of purposes (for example, one group was building a gerbil house).

In a creative reading program, all stimulation for creative behavior does not necessarily originate with the teacher. It may come from the ideas the children have once they become interested in a topic. The teacher's role is to provide a wealth of material on topics in which the children are interested and to help the children channel their new information and skills into creative outlets.

In terms of the objectives of modern education, instructional materials cannot be effective if they emphasize any one area of the child's growth over another. They must not, for instance, do the child's thinking for him if he is to be taught to think for himself; they must in no sense be used to "fill in" time if he is to develop a worthwhile use of leisure time; they must have purpose if he is to gain knowledge and skills; they must not create mental blocks within him but must encourage learning if he is to have sound mental and physical health. If individual differences are to be met, the same books, workbooks, and materials cannot be used for everyone in the same class. If we are to develop responsibility, independence, and cooperation, instructional materials must be designed for individual problems, as well as for mass education.

A teacher must realize that she herself knows best the

problems and abilities of her group. She must come to know that it is the children she is teaching—not the book. She must realize that her years of training give her the privilege of knowing how to teach better than the average layman, and that even an intelligent layman could teach reading if the only process involved was reading a book (the manual) and doing what it said. As a professional person, it becomes her duty to invent and create new ways of teaching reading so that each child learns to read and *a remedial program is unnecessary*—corrective programs perhaps, but not remedial. She must learn to teach as individually as possible, and if this is prohibited by the large number of children, she must teach well by groups or by some personalized program.

Teachers who understand the development of children will use each child's language experiences at any given point to develop new uses for language. These experiences will be reassembled into new learnings integrated with the life activity and the creative drive of each child. His reading development can be the most creative of his experiences if he approaches the threshold of children's literature with a drive to read and a body of skills he knows how to use.

AN HISTORICAL PERSPECTIVE OF THE TEACHING OF READING

Great controversies have been waged over the methods of introducing formal reading to children. Until forty years ago reading was taught almost entirely by a very complicated, and often unrealistic, phonics system. This system did not produce many efficient, enthusiastic readers among average and below-average children, so a break was made, and the *sight method* of teaching became popular. Under the old phonics method, reading was introduced through a memorization of the alphabet and its basic sounds, a study of phonics, and word analysis. Advocates of the sight method of teaching beginning reading made these points:

Reading is a skill and a tool. Children do not read for reading's sake. They want their reading to tell them something. They should begin to read at once, and the sight method permits this.

Motivation is very important to reading. The best motivation for a child in reading is to discover that he *can* read. A child can begin to read very simple stories immediately through the sight method. It is true that he probably cannot figure out

new words at the very beginning of his reading experience, but
the job of the teacher is to see to it that the words he knows are
used over and over in new context and that his sight vocabulary
grows a little every day.

With the sight method, children learn more quickly be-
cause they have only two things to remember: the shape of the
word and the sound for it.   In a phonics approach to reading, the
child is burdened by many things to remember: the names of
consonants and their sounds, the names of vowels and their many
varied sounds, the sounds for speech consonants and consonant
blends, the sounds for unusual letter combinations, and the fusion
of this variety of sounds into a sensible word symbol.

The phonics approach to beginning reading must resort
eventually to the memorization of many "sight" words because of
the many exceptions to all rules of phonics.   Also, some authori-
ties say that from 15 to 25 percent of the language is irregular.
This often creates great confusion in a child.   Take the letters
ough, for instance.   A child reading along comes to the sentence,
"The bird sat on the bough."   He looks at the picture for a clue to
the new word and reads, "The bird sat on the branch."   The
teacher immediately corrects him and tells him the sound for
ough is like "ow."   A while later the young reader comes to the
sentence, "The meat was tough," and reads it, "The meat was
t-ow."   The teacher explains that *ough* also says "uff" and that
he must remember both sounds.   Later he reads, "Billy looked as
though he could sing," and he reads it, "Billy looks as th-uff he
could sing."   Again he must learn a new sound for *ough.*   And
then he encounters the word *thought.*   He must choose from all
these sounds the one that gives the sentence proper meaning.   It
would be just as easy for him and would facilitate his reading if
he memorized each of these words rather than taking the time to
interrupt his reading to sound them all out.

The phonic approach to beginning reading requires a care-
fully controlled vocabulary development program.   Often this
forces a teacher to slavish dedication to a commercial reading
series.   Much of the creative work of the children is not used because it does not fit into the highly developed sequential acquisition of skills.   But if the context of the commercial text being
used is not about the life experiences of the child, he soon loses
his motivation for reading.

Spoken language is learned through imitation.   The child
uses language as communication years before he is able to identify nouns and verbs and long before he is able to analyze the
structure of language.   These skills come after oral facility with

language has been established. A child learns to read many words naturally from television, from his book, from billboards, and so forth, without ever having to know the alphabet or the phonic sounds of the alphabet. Whole words have meaning; to distort them means to remove much of this meaning. Just as the kindergartner on page 37 did not recognize the crumpled chair and the nursery-school child on page 37 did not recognize the dismantled tables, so do many children not recognize common words when they are syllabicated or broken up phonically. The study of the structure of words is more sophisticated than the memorizing of shapes and not totally necessary for the recognition of words.

Skills in reading do not consist entirely of being able to call out words. Habits of good reading must be established from the onset of the formal reading program, or the child may be hampered a great deal in his reading development. Good eye movement is essential from the start. Good readers read for ideas. This often means they read groups of words as one idea. Children can be taught to read that way. "In the box," "to school," "around the corner," "said Billy" are good examples of phrases that can be read as one word because they contain one idea. Reading by ideas helps children to obtain speed and better comprehension in reading. A good reader has about three fixation points across a line of the printed page. An overdose of phonics may cause children to stop unnecessarily to look at parts of words rather than to read for ideas.

This simple device, which has appeared in many magazines, illustrates the above concept. Read the idea in each box quickly.

Each phrase is so familiar that it is read as one word. Only by careful examination can the reader notice that there are double articles used in each phrase. Good readers would not notice them at a glance. Only plodding, slow "word" readers would be aware of the double articles at a first reading. Even beginning reading can be taught by thought units.

There are so many exceptions to word-attack rules (such as those centered around the use of a double vowel) that children learn them best after *they have learned to pronounce a word from memory.* The sight reader is handicapped temporarily by not being able to recognize new words, especially if they are out of the realm of his experience. Consequently, as soon as the habit of reading has been established and the child is reading smoothly and with good comprehension, this handicap is overcome by using the reading vocabulary he has acquired to teach word recognition skills and to develop reading skills.

Since the early controversies over sight versus phonics teaching, much research in the total area of language and linguistics has added to our understanding of the teaching of reading. Some important new concepts have been added.

Part of the communicative power of language lies in its rhythm, pitch, tonal quality, and intonation. A baby has no understanding of words as such, yet he very often cries if he hears a loud noise or if someone shouts angrily at him. Conversely, he smiles, coos, and gurgles at the soft, comforting words of his mother. His reaction here is to the *music* of language, not the language itself. Linguists tell us that this musical quality is a major part of communication and should never be omitted in instruction in any of the language skills, reading included. The child who reads, "Paul—went—down—the—street," with every word sounding exactly the same, has been handicapped in reading development because too much concentration has been placed on words rather than meaning and intonation. The child might as well be reading words in a list rather than words arranged in a sentence for the purpose of communicating an idea. This implies that the rhythm of language is important to the understanding of language. Although this is especially true in oral reading, it is also true in silent reading. While reading silently, a child does not *hear* intonation but he thinks it.[2]

Linguists are telling us also that

> no one can get meaning from the printed page without taking in whole language patterns at the sentence level, because these are the minimal meaning-bearing structures of most written communications.[3]

This minimum requirement from the linguist's point of view tends to reinforce one of the viewpoints of the advocates of

2. Carl A. LeFevre, *Linguistics and the Teaching of Reading* (New York: McGraw-Hill, 1964).
3. Ibid., p. vii.

the sight method—that children should be taught to read by thought units.

Reading should be taught in connection with the other skills of language. This was illustrated by the lessons described in Chapters 1 and 2.

Our concept of the reading process has been expanded. Horn points out that the author of a book

> . . . does not really convey ideas to the reader: he merely stimulates him to construct them out of his own experiences. If the concept is . . . new to the reader, its construction more nearly approaches problem solving than simple association.[4]

Reading, then, encompasses mechanical processes and mental processes, and teaching must be directed to the development of both of these processes.

To comprehend printed material, the reader must perceive entire language structures as a whole—as unitary meaning-bearing patterns. Meaning-bearing language structures can be taught to children as a base to the reading process.

Although the basic philosophy of the linguistic approach to reading focuses on letters and words as the most significant units in methodology, LeFevre says

> . . . in my approach to reading instruction the word is treated as a minor language unit for many reasons. Some of these reasons are linguistic, others are pedagogical. In English the word is an unstable element, whether it is taken as a semantic or as a structural unit. The most significant structures in English are intonation patterns, grammatical and syntactical word groups, clauses, and sentences.
> Single words, analyzed and spoken in isolation, assume the intonation contours of whole utterances. Single words thus lose the characteristic pitch and stress they normally carry in the *larger constructions that comprise the flow of speech and bear meaning.* This automatic upgrading of words may lead many learners to "read" word by word, or by pattern fragments, without regard for whole structural patterns that carry meaning. This upgrading may thus contribute to the frequency and extent of serious reading disability among pupils of all ages. So far, little has been done to develop reading of American English by its known structures instead of by its vocabulary.[5]

4. Ernest Horn, *Methods of Instruction in the Social Studies* (New York: Charles Scribner's Sons, 1937).
5. LeFevre, *Linguistics and the Teaching of Reading,* pp. xvii–xviii.

LeFevre, a linguist, proposes a sentence method of teaching reading that applies a linguistic description of American English utterances at the sentence level to their graphic counterparts, written and printed sentences. He bases his method on fourteen assumptions gleaned from the knowledge of linguistics. His assumptions include some of those mentioned above: that children should learn to read and write the language they speak and understand, that they develop a consciousness of pertinent language processes and their interrelationships with graphics, that analytical slicing of larger language segments into smaller segments should be done only to the extent that the reading process requires it, that the child learning to read should practice reading entire meaning-bearing language patterns at the sentence level, and that all aspects of the language arts program should be coordinated.

We tend to be extremists in educational practice. We tend to throw out one system of reading and adopt another one because all children are not reading as well as we wish. We do not seem to learn by experience. Many schools threw out the sight method of teaching and went back to the phonics method, forgetting that the reason the phonics method was discarded in the first place was because *it* was not producing the kind of readers we hoped for. It is like throwing out the baby with the bath water. Many schools today, because of this policy, are actually *creating reading disability* among many children. The current situation regarding remedial reading bears out the truth of this statement.

Each system of reading has contributed to our understanding of the total reading process, and each has inherent in it many ideas that have helped in teaching the majority of children to read. But no *one* system has yet solved the multitude of reading problems in any *one* school. Modern trends tend to be more sensible in that they realize the value of each of the many systems and adapt their strong points to some new reading plan. But no *one* system is ever going to work with *every* child, and the only sound philosophy a school can possibly have is this: Any system of reading is justifiable if it teaches all children to read up to their ability, but no *one* system ever does!

Dechant has made an excellent summary of numerous fallacies concerning reading methods and gives the following pertinent examples:

1. Learning the letters of the alphabet is a handicap to successful learning of reading.

2. Learning to read and reading by a mature individual are the same process and involve the same factors. Because the letter is not the meaningful unit of perception in reading, it therefore cannot be the initial step in learning to read.

3. With the right method *every* child can learn to read. And there is but *one* right method of teaching reading.

4. Every phonically-trained child is necessarily a word-caller. Indeed the child of very low IQ may become a word-caller because it is easier for him to learn to pronounce words than to learn and remember word meanings.

5. The reading readiness program exists *only* because present methods of teaching reading are so slow and so unsuccessful that we must justify our delaying of formal reading instruction until the child can be more successful with it. And it protects the teacher when certain children make no progress through the first grade.

6. Whenever our "favorite" method doesn't work, it must have been taught improperly.

7. The phonics approach interferes with the child's ability to take meaning to and from the printed page and keeps him from thinking with the material.

8. Phonics is best taught incidentally. It should be introduced only after the child has learned a certain number of words by sight to help him to read words with which he has difficulty.

9. The phonics approach is wrong because phonically-trained children do not read as rapidly nor as fluently as analytically-trained children. This may be true of beginning readers, but does drilling children to handle very rapidly a small, controlled vocabulary in grade one necessarily guarantee that they will be able to handle longer and less-controlled vocabularies in sixth grade?

10. The whole word method is completely visual, and the phonic method is completely auditory.

11. Drill in phonics will cause children to dislike reading.

12. Children learning to read by the sight method will develop a permanent interest in reading.

13. The developmental reading method prohibits children exploring and broadening their interests. (The individualized reading program is thought to allow children this opportunity.)

14. The so-called "contextual reader" is the best reader . . .

15. Practice alone will help the pupil to improve. Some proponents of the individualized approach seem to be falling into this error . . .

16. The controlled vocabulary in the basal series is more insipid than the vocabulary used in phonic materials.[6]

Many of these fallacies exist because of lack of understanding of the reading process, but most of them stem from the fact that educators have tried to defend systems of teaching that they were using. Each can be true or not true, depending on the teacher. The creative teacher will recognize all of these fallacies of thinking as possible outcomes of poor teaching. She will not close her eyes to the fact that each of these statements may be a truth (especially one such as No. 11) when the teaching of reading is a mechanical process that is imposed on a child rather than an organic process that grows from within him.

CURRENT METHODS AND PLANS OF TEACHING READING

Confusion often exists between *reading methods* and *plans for organization*. The Initial Teaching Alphabet concept is a new *method* for teaching reading, but Individualized Reading is an *organizational plan* for teaching reading. New methods result from deeper understandings gleaned from research in the areas of methodology, linguistics, communications, language, and so forth. New plans of organization are simply ways to arrange a teaching day so the methods can be most effectively employed. The Individualized Reading concept offers no new method of teaching; it simply offers a plan for organizing a school day so that we may best put to use those methods with which we are already familiar. Every new method and organizational plan is a creative idea that has contributed to our understanding of the reading process and how reading might be taught. But none is the answer to all problems everywhere. A summary of methods and plans may help in the understanding of how creative teaching can be developed.

Methods of Teaching Reading

The following review of the most common current practices in the teaching of reading evaluates each as it relates to the creative development of children.

6. Emerald V. Dechant, *Improving the Teaching of Reading* (Englewood Cliffs, N.J.: Prentice-Hall, Inc., 1964), pp. 77–78.

Phonic Approach. This is a system that develops efficiency in word recognition by employing the speech sounds of the English language in a sequential pattern. It utilizes the forty-four most frequently used speech sounds in English. It begins with the teaching of short sounds of five vowels and progresses to the study of the ten most frequently used consonants. Consonants are soon blended with vowels in pronouncing units or syllables. The system develops from the known to the unknown, from simple to complex, and left-to-right eye progression is assured because children always attack new words at their beginnings.

The phonics approach supplies the child with a reading vocabulary approximately equal to his speaking vocabulary. It is designed for use in *all* basal reading series and integrates the total language arts program.

Basal Reading Texts. This approach to reading provides a series of basal materials that is supposed to provide for a systematic and sequential development of all the skills, understandings, and abilities necessary in interpreting written symbols (the total reading act). The materials are designed as a base of operations, however, not as a scientific exposition of the reading process. They can only be considered as part of the total reading program.

Language Experience Approach. This method recognizes that an oral-language background and an experience background are basic to vocabulary development and word recognition throughout the elementary grades. It pays homage to the logical sequence of development of language mentioned previously in this book. The language experience approach has three aspects: (1) it continues to give children experiences that can be expressed orally with words they will soon read, (2) it studies the English language and develops a form of personal expression, and (3) it relates ideas of authors to personal experiences, using a wealth of materials, to build reading skills. The lesson taught in Chapter 2 is basically a sample of this approach to reading, which has much in common with the linguistic approach advocated by LeFevre.[7]

Initial Teaching Alphabet. This medium, commonly known as the ITA, has broken down the English language into forty-four new characters that provide each major phoneme of English with its own symbol. This eliminates the complicated process, often so confusing to children, of associating inconsistent character-to-

7. Carl A. LeFevre, *Linguistics and the Teaching of Reading.*

symbol relationships as they appear in current spelling forms. The spellings of this new alphabet provide the learner with a consistent alphabet code. The alphabet is designed to facilitate transition to the traditional alphabet once reading fluency is reached with the ITA alphabet. This method claims to make the reading process simpler, quicker, and more successful. Sir James Pitman, of London, England, has promoted this system and claims it is a medium, not a method. But, because of the definition of method suggested above, it is classified as a method here.

Words in Color. The most important contribution of this approach is its full and rapid extension of the linguistic capacities of the learners. It develops the children's ability to read, write, and spell with meaning all language they can already use as meaningful speech. Color is used to help solve quickly and easily the problems created by the ambiguous grapheme-phoneme relationship of English without affecting the usual spelling. The many spellings of each sound are printed in the same color, and each of the many sounds of one spelling is printed in a different color.

Linguistic Approaches. Many linguists would object to the implication that there is such a thing as a *linguistic approach* to the teaching of reading. They feel that the linguist is a scientist, whose mission in life is to search for truths (in this case, truths about the structure of language), and he should not concern himself with method. Nonetheless, the work of the linguist *has* affected method ever since Leonard Bloomfield, one of the first linguists interested in reading, published definite suggestions for the teaching of reading. Although modern linguists have deviated a long way from Bloomfield's teaching suggestions, many textbook companies are advertising their reading systems as *the linguistic approach* because they are built on a study of the structure of language.

The *linguistic approach* has come to mean this among teachers and educators: a system of reading based on the research findings of the linguists that deal with the structure of language. Confusion has resulted from the use of the label because as research has unveiled new truths, the linguistic approaches have changed, but the label has remained the same. Currently, therefore, one cannot tell by the label what is in the package. This confusion is compounded by linguists who write articles in which they start by taking the position that linguists are not concerned with method but then go on to define their own methods of teaching reading. Although some of these methods may be proper in terms of the structure of language, they have been exceedingly dull and unmotivating to children. Consequently, they have helped little to diminish the children's reading problems.

Some current confusion also results from the fact that there are several types of linguists, each representing a different aspect of language research. This fact is not always made clear in their writings.

One type of linguist is concerned with an analysis of the sounds of spoken and written language. This person is called a *phonologist*—one who identifies the phonemes (basic sounds) of the language. He recommends that reading be taught as a process of translating phonemes into words. In a phonological approach to reading, a child first learns the sounds of groups of letters, then learns words, and then proceeds to larger units of sentence structure. It is not important to the phonologist whether or not the translation of letters or letter clusters is accompanied by meaning of what is read. The use of pictures is avoided so the child can concentrate on the sequence of letters as his only clue to unlocking the sound of the word. Children read by relating large units and patterns of their speech to symbolic representatives, the printed words.

A second type of linguist is the *structuralist,* so named because he has researched and studied the structure of language to a refined degree. The structuralists, unlike the phonologists, are greatly concerned with meaning, and some structuralists believe that the sentence is the basic unit of meaning.

Structuralists study the elements of language that result in the communication of ideas. These elements include word order, word function, and word position. The structuralist studies word groups that modify, expand, or change basic expressions. He studies the signals of intonation, such as pitch, stress, pause, and rhythm. He also researches such subjects as the identification and frequency of types of sentences and grammatical inflections or word changes to indicate tense.

The structuralist believes that the reading process is a recognition of the structural principles of word order. A few hundred structure words link other words into groups, and each group must be read as a unit.

One structuralist mentioned frequently in this book is LeFevre. He stresses recognition of large speech patterns such as simple sentences and questions; structural elements such as

noun groups, verb groups, phrases, and clauses; and function
words such as auxiliary verbs, articles, prepositions, and grammatical inflections.

Some structuralists insist that, in the primary grades at
least, good reading means reading aloud.   Children should be
taught to consider other clues in arriving at meaning: clues like
capitals and periods, the order and grouping of words, the importance of modifiers, and the grammatical inflections of number,
tense, and possession.   Children should understand normal sentence order and should also be aware of the great possibilities of
variations when function words such as *the, into,* and *when* are
applied.

The third type of linguist studies the psychology of language and is known as a *psycholinguist*.   The psycholinguist con-
cerns himself with such problems as the relationship between
decoding and encoding, the relationship of context to comprehension, the facets of language that relate to reading instruction,
and the appropriate settings for reading growth.

Some characteristics of the linguistic approach to reading
may be summarized as follows: (1) Beginning reading material
contains words that the child knows and that he recognizes as
words he already speaks.   (2) As a basic requirement for beginning reading, the child must know the alphabet and be able to
identify the individual letters by name.   He must be able to determine immediately whether two sequences of two or three letters are alike or different in respect to both the individual letters
and their order.   (3) Early in the reading process, independent
"extensions" of the root words are created to build the pupil's
ability to read hundreds of words he has never seen written before.   (4) Reading for meaning requires the building of situation meanings out of words and sentences.   Therefore, books
without pictures force pupils to read for meaning rather than
guessing by using picture clues.

More recent advocates of the linguistic method (LeFevre,
for example) stress the importance of teaching reading in a
thought structure (such as the sentence) and have also emphasized the importance of intonation in the understanding of implied meanings.

One strategy to emerge somewhat successfully from the
teaching of the linguists is the *graphoneme concept,* which deals
with the structure of root words.   Within English words there is
generally a stability in the relationship between graphic representation and oral pronunciation: the closed syllable (a syllable
that begins with a vowel and ends with a consonant, semi-vowel

or "silent" *e*). Such a structural unit is called a graphoneme. The teacher uses this stable element in words to promote independent decoding of any vocabulary unknown to the child.

The word *graphoneme* is a combination of the words *grapheme* and *phoneme.* A *grapheme* is the smallest distinctive unit of an alphabet: any letter or combination of letters representing a speech sound. A *phoneme* is one of a group of distinctive sounds that make up a language. The words *cat* and *bat,* for instance, are distinguished by their initial phonemes /k/ and /b/. A phoneme is the smallest unit of language that can differentiate one utterance from another. One phoneme can change the entire meaning of a sentence; for example, *A bird in the hand is worth two in the bush* is changed completely when read "a bard in the hand is worth two in the bush." Phonemes are not so much a set of sounds as a system of differences between sounds. A good reader must know these differences. A character, or symbol, that represents a single speech sound is called a phonogram.

In the graphoneme concept a control of phoneme-phonogram relationships is exercised rather than a control of the *number* of words introduced to each child in basic readers. When emphasis is placed on the internal *structure* of words, the pupil learns that parts of words are useful in attacking new words.

Research shows that the graphoneme concept can be implemented in programs of beginning reading instruction without specially prepared reading materials. Since a high degree of stability was found to be present within the structures of the 149 words common to the basal reading series most often used in today's primary classrooms, those words can form a core of structural elements that can be significant in teaching pupils the skills of decoding.[8] In the graphoneme method, teachers first teach those words in which stability exists, postponing the teaching of irregularities until pupils have acquired enough reading skill to adjust to the differences that exist in word structures.

Jones[9] designed a program and accompanying materials for the teaching of reading through the grapheme method in Alaska and has experienced outstanding success with native children.

8. Virginia W. Jones, "Utilizing the Graphoneme Concept in Teaching the Independent Decoding of Reading Vocabulary," in *Decoding and Learning to Read* (Portland, Ore.: Northwest Regional Educational Laboratory, 1967), pp. 17–25.
9. Virginia Jones, *Decoding and Learning to Read* (Portland, Ore.: Northwest Regional Educational Laboratory, 1967), p. 8.

Patterns of Organization for the Teaching of Reading

Personalized or Individualized Reading. Because reading ability
is closely related to intelligence and other factors, such as emotional and social adjustment, reading level and ability will vary
greatly from child to child. Any personalized approach to reading
is beneficial to children. A total personalized, or individualized,
reading program, where each child develops at his own rate of
speed and in accord with his own interests, *is* possible.[10] In such
a program none of the stages in reading development are skipped,
nor is the methodology for teaching reading greatly altered. The
difference is largely in the organization of the classroom program.

In organizing a class for individualized reading instruction, the commonly accepted pattern of grouping children according to reading ability or in relation to reading problems is
unnecessary. Each child selects his own reading materials, and
the teacher so organizes the day that she may spend time hearing
each child read.

Because the program is one of self-selection, the individual
interests and purposes of the children can be realized and abilities
can be developed as rapidly or slowly as a child's inherent growth
pattern permits.

Individualized instruction in reading does not mean that
children never meet in groups. They often do, because some
reading is taught best in groups. Also, in developing an individualized reading program, teachers discover that small groups
of children have similar problems or need help in similar skills,
so they group these children together.

The individualized reading program recognizes the simple
fact that no grouping eliminates individual differences. Almost
no two children read at the same level or want to read the same
material at the same time. The teaching of reading as individually as possible gives each child the opportunity for reading
without interference, competition, or distraction from other members of a group who may be reading faster or slower than he. In
addition to his right to proceed at his own rate, he learns many
skills in the self-selection of materials.

Creative teachers have had the success that might well be
expected from such a reading program. The number of books
children read under the guidance of these teachers has sky-

10. Jeanette Veatch, *Individualizing Your Reading Program* (New
York: G. P. Putnam's Sons, 1959).

rocketed. Interest in reading and associated skills has developed to unexpected proportions, and the skills of reading seem to have developed as much.

Multilevel Reading Instruction. This approach to reading is designed to meet the individual differences that occur in each child's reading process, developmental growth, and ability to learn. The SRA laboratories worked out materials to aid the teachers in developing each of these strands of development.

The teacher introduces the learning laboratory process to the class as a whole, and then supervises its use by individual children. The materials can be used in a variety of combinations, so that a great deal of self-learning is fostered, and the teacher is free to help those who need it. The pupil learns the names and sounds of the ordinary English alphabet, its phonic and structural sight-sound combinations, and linguistic word patterning as units of thought. He then proceeds to decoding meanings from more complex units. This type of organizational plan generally leads into an individualized reading program. Actually it contributes no new way of teaching; it is simply a plan whereby known methods may be employed more individually.

The Ungraded Reading Program. This organizational plan grew out of the concept of the ungraded school and is often used by schools as a step toward complete ungradedness. As such, it is actually a misconception of ungradedness and is practically the same plan of organization employed by what was once labeled the Joplin Plan. In essence, the purpose of ungraded reading programs is to regroup children in schools where there are several groups of children at each grade level so that each teacher does not have many reading groups in her classroom. Teachers share the children during reading times—one teacher may work with a slow ability group, one with an average ability group, and so forth. The theory is that each teacher, having a narrower range of reading ability with which to deal, can devote more time and help to the individual student. Many variations of this plan are now in use in many of our schools.

Departmentalized Reading. The concept of departmentalization as practiced in the high schools and junior high schools has been projected into the elementary schools. Children go from teacher to teacher for each subject. During reading period the children are grouped by ability levels, and the wide range of reading within any one group is reduced, thus making more individual help possible for each child.

Ability Grouping.   Children are homogenized according to ability in order to diminish range in reading ability and to provide more individual attention for each child.   In the ungraded and departmentalized reading programs, this plan is prevalent in one form or another.

Grouping within the Classroom.   This plan has been popular for many years and still is considered the most sensible by many educators.   The children are grouped by the teachers for reading instruction during various times of the day.   Groups are flexible, and children may be shifted from group to group as their reading problems change.   Children are basically under the guidance of one teacher, and she is responsible for helping each child.   The groups are built around common problems of the group members. Many schools use a variety of basal texts under this plan so that the various groups work with different materials, all the materials being geared to the ability level of the group.

Team-teaching Plans.   In some schools the above plans are often called team-teaching plans because teachers share students and do some planning together.   However, they are responsible largely to one or two reading groups, the core of which may or may not be the students in their own home rooms.   Such reading plans are unjustifiably called team-teaching, for true team-teaching means that teachers are willing to subject their methodology to the scrutiny and evaluation of their peers.   Under a *real* team-teaching plan this element is essential.   One teacher may teach a reading skill while others watch and then, in conference, all evaluate the lesson so that lessons continually improve.   Planning sessions are an integral part of team-teaching. Some days one teacher takes a large group; on other days that group is broken down into smaller groups.   Thus, all teachers are teaching at a given time.   The basic philosophy behind this plan is to make instruction ever more effective and to meet the individual needs of students as much as possible.

The Open Classroom.   In the last few years many schools have begun to establish some form of open classroom, adapted from the British Infant School plan.   The open-classroom concept is a throwback to the philosophy of John Dewey with a few alterations, the main one being that the new schools are constructed to fulfill learning interests by using space in ways quite different from the ways in which it was used in the graded classroom of the past.

In Dewey's philosophy, children centered their activities around the solution of a problem or series of problems, and interests were often created artificially by the teacher. The open classroom, on the other hand, sincerely builds its curriculum on the problems and interests of the individual children.

The open school has eliminated grade rooms and has substituted cubicles and partially walled-in areas that are set up as centers of interest. Children are free to move about from area to area. Gone from the open school are the grade lines; children of several ages work together or help each other. Each teacher is responsible for one group of children, but she is also responsible for any other children who may become interested in the projects or skills being developed in the area in which she is working.

In the British Open School, planned subject matter, or content, is secondary. Teachers stimulate interest in subject matter by setting up the centers, and children study what they are interested in. The school's main goal is to develop the skills needed to live effectively in a democratic society. One of these skills is reading. The story of Charlie at the very beginning of this book tells how a British child is introduced to reading on his first day of school. The teacher follows a British system of teaching reading that combines many of the properties of reading systems described above. The reading program is highly individualized. Teachers help children individually, and older children help younger children. The system is based on the building of a sight vocabulary and the repeated use of the words in the sight vocabulary in new contexts. Then the words of the sight vocabulary are printed on cards so that the children can discover likenesses and differences (analogy) in words.

Eric, one of Charlie's friends, wanted to show me how he could read. He read two or three books he had written. The teacher, who stood by watching and listening, said, "Show Mr. Smith how you can make a story with the cards, Eric." Eric led me to the reading center and took an individual reading pocket chart from many on a shelf. He also took out a box of words. He set the pocket chart before him and spilled the words on the table. Just as he had hunted for shapes for making a puzzle but a month earlier, he now hunted for the shapes of words to recreate his story in the pocket chart.

Later, his teacher wandered by and said, "Can't you make a story about Mr. Smith?" Eric brought her a pack of blank cards, all the same size as the ones he was using to reconstruct his story. "What do you want me to print?" asked the teacher, taking out her flo-pen.

"Mr. Smith," Eric answered.   So his teacher printed my name on a card and stood by while Eric made his story.   When he couldn't find some words in his box of words, his teacher printed them on a card.   Soon he had composed this story:

> *Mr. Smith came to visit.*
> *He is from the United States.*
> *He liked my story.*
> *He will stay to lunch.*

Such activities lead quickly into a study of phonics, structural analysis, and word attack skills.   Much emphasis is placed on the use of trade books that tell stories and give information. Little emphasis is placed on workbooks or ditto sheets: the child is encouraged to apply his reading skill to creative ventures. Basals are used with children who need them.   The activities of

FIGURE 3–3.   *A letter from a child in an English open school.*

the children center around the library and several quiet library centers are set up where children are encouraged to read alone a great deal of the time.

METHOD, ORGANIZATION, AND CREATIVITY

In Chapter 1, the principles of creative teaching and the basic principles of creativity were stated.   Which of the above teaching systems and plans for organization contribute to the development of creativity, and which do not?   Both systems *and* plans must be considered, for creativity is a *process* and a *product* and the process of creativity is made possible by the conditions set for it in the schoolroom.   The organizational plan of the classroom constitutes one of the major conditions for developing or hindering creativity.

Reading can be creative in both process and product.   It may seem at first that, since reading is the recognition of words whose patterns are already formed, it is largely a convergent thinking exercise and allows for little creative development.   But, as stated above, reading is more than a set of skills; it is a *problem-solving* situation.   The reader must choose from all his experiences those meanings that the author intends to convey by the particular choice of a word.   He must evaluate, make decisions, pass judgment, think critically—sometimes creatively.   He must at times be spontaneous in his reactions, flexible in his interpretations, original in his thinking.   All of these skills are concerned with the development of divergent thinking processes. When reading lessons are designed to develop these skills, creativity is being developed in children.

Creativity may also be developed through the process of learning to read.   At times the total creative process may be noted, as in the reading lesson described in Chapter 2 of this book (see page 22).   At other times, only certain *skills* of creative growth are developed in the reading process.   When reading is creatively taught, problems are posed to children, who become involved with them and struggle through each problem until insight (or discovery) comes.   The teaching of each reading skill —even those that often appear to be uncreative—can be used to develop the children's creative thinking processes.

Note how Miss Rogers taught the application of beginning consonants through the use of discovery.

The first-grade class had been collecting pictures that illustrated all the sounds of the beginning consonants and pasting them on large charts around the room. They had played many games with beginning consonants and knew them well. Miss Rogers next wanted these children to see how the application of these consonants could create new words.

One day David spilled some ink. He cleaned it up and later, when the class made their customary reading chart of a summary of the day's work, the children put this sentence on the chart: *David spilled the ink.*

After the chart had been read, Miss Rogers said, "I'd like to come back to one word in our story and have some fun with it." She wrote "ink" on the chalkboard. "What is this word?" she asked.

The children told her. "Now look at our charts around the room," said Miss Rogers. "We know most of the sounds of those letters. Can any of you put some of those sounds with this word and discover a whole new word?"

In a second, Jerry had caught on. "Pink," he said.

"Very good," encouraged Miss Rogers, "any others?"

Soon the words were flowing from the group. Miss Rogers printed each word on the chalkboard.

Jennifer raised her hand, "Miss Rogers, could we do that with other words, too?"

"Well," asked Miss Rogers, "could we?"

"Yes," said Jennifer, "we have the word 'art' on the chart and I could make 'cart' from it."

In a few minutes the children were trying to make new words from all of those on their charts. Josie made another discovery. "When you say the words together it makes poetry." So they discussed how rhyming words sounded alike at the end.

"They look alike, too," said Alice.

"What part looks alike?" asked Miss Rogers, pointing out that rhyming words sounded and looked alike at the *end.*

"I have an idea," said Miss Rogers, remembering a Dr. Seuss book she had recently read. "I will give each of you a large piece of white construction paper. You will put any small word you can think of at the top of the paper and put below it all the words you can make from it. Then we'll put all our charts on the bulletin board so we can share what we have learned. Maybe some of you can take them home and have your brothers and sisters think of words that can be made like this. And there's something else. I'll bet after you make them some of you can use them at the end of sentences to make a poem!"

The next morning the bulletin board was covered with the charts as children shared their words. About half of them had tried them out in poems. This was David's:

David's Yink

I have a Yink
My Yink is pink
He likes to drink
He likes to drink pink ink.

The *process* of teaching reading skills can be creative. When it is kept in its logical sequential developmental place in the child's learning experience, it can produce some creative products as well.

Method and Creativity

Creative teaching *could* be applied to each of the above systems of teaching reading. In all truth, however, it must be observed that only one of these systems is designed to develop creativity, *and if most of them are followed in the form advocated by their creators, they tend to limit creativity rather than develop it.*

The phonics approach is very limiting. I believe that primary reading, especially, must follow the language sequence development. It is true that some children learn to read words without saying them first, but they are an exception, and all children *think* the words if they do not say them. If a teacher is to build a thorough understanding of phonetic analysis, she can do it only on the material with which she is provided: the speaking vocabularies of her pupils. The alphabet of sound is learned before the alphabet of letters. And some sounds are more prevalent than others in different cultures and in different towns and in different schools within each town. These are the sounds that should be taught first.

Bobbie, who lives in a railroad town, comes in to the classroom saying, "Choo-choo-chug-chug," as he imitates a train; the teacher shows the children how Bobbie's sound would look in print—and they *discover* the *ch* speech consonant at the beginning of the words. On the other hand, Mike, who lives near the airport, brings in an airplane and says, "Whirr, whirr—swish, swish, swish," as he flies his toy plane through the air. His teacher has material for working on other sounds. A rigid, preconceived program in developing sounds is even more difficult for children to comprehend than a rigid, preconceived development of words.   Neither contributes much to the development of creativity.

Advocates of the phonics approach to *beginning* reading feel that there are too many words to memorize by sight, so teaching the components of words is a more logical approach.   This logic can be challenged when we consider that every word consists of many components and that these components are less meaningful to the child than the whole word.   It is no more difficult to memorize a host of words than it is to memorize a host of meaningless sounds for each letter in the word or for groups of letters in the words.

The sound elements in the phonics approach are reduced to forty-four, but in application there are many more combinations a child must learn.   Phonics strives to bring out the consistencies in the language, yet many of the rules it advocates are not consistent.   One of the most common rules given to children at an early age is the one defining the use of a double vowel in a word—that when two vowels appear together the first one usually says its name and the second one is silent.   A study by Theodore Clymer reported in *The Reading Teacher* shows that this rule is applicable in only 45 percent of the English language.[11] Is it, then, a rule?   Clymer found that, of all the so-called rules of language that we give children to figure out new words, only 20 percent were applicable 100 percent of the time.   Some are applicable only 10 percent of the time.   Unless a rule is applicable *almost all* the time, it is not a rule—it is an exception, and learning it as a rule is an example of how we limit a child's creativity. The rule keeps him from experimenting and discovering his own answers when he encounters exceptions to the rule.

Clymer's work supports the fact that the English language (at least that portion of it used for the teaching of reading in the primary grades) is only about 80 percent phonetic.

When adapted to the children's use, *the basal reading text* program can provide a medium for developing creativity and for promoting creative teaching.   But when it is followed rigidly, page by page, it can contribute little or nothing to creative development.

The teacher's manuals of many current basal readers propose that teachers follow specific steps when teaching lessons. One such basal proposes the following steps:

11. Theodore Clymer, "The Utility of Phonic Generalizations in the Primary Grades," *The Reading Teacher* 16 (January 1963): 252–258.

1. *Preparing to Read* (the teacher suggests a motivation, establishes a background for the reading, introduces new vocabulary, and reviews the purposes for the reading)
2. *Interpreting the Story* (includes silent reading of the story sometimes after the pictures have been studied, discussion of the story to check the comprehension of the readers, and oral rereading of the story or parts of it for clarification of discussion or to focus on some excerpt of literary merit)
3. *Skill Lesson* (includes the application of skills and abilities and the subsequent checking of comprehension with work sheets and workbooks)
4. *Enrichment Activities* (includes dramatizations, scroll movies, etc.)

The question that comes to mind in reading the basal readers and the manuals that accompany them is, How scientific is this sequence of steps in the teaching of reading? The answer is that it is pseudoscientific at best. In the individualized reading program, the first steps are already taken care of. A child reads what he had been motivated to read both inside and outside of school. He masters new vocabulary words as he confronts them in his reading, for his purpose is always for enjoyment. When preparation is needed for material, it is always material that is being imposed on the child for reasons other than his own. Such motivation is logical in upper primary and middle grades, when a teacher must prepare children to read about strange places and peoples in a social studies lesson, but that is not generally the type of material that appears in beginning reading books. In many schools children read every chance they get, motivated always by their own interests and activities. Consequently, the first step suggested by the manual can be challenged by new modes and approaches to reading. It can also be challenged in terms of the concept of motivation. Using the same approach every day soon kills that particular approach as a form of motivation, for the children become bored. A different approach every day is a creative approach to reading, and the illustrations found on pages 3, 22, and 108 are examples of how creative teachers can motivate children to exciting reading experiences through new approaches to reading.

Interpreting the Story in most manuals means asking the children a series of low-level questions that check comprehension largely through predetermined acceptable answers. These questions make little allowance for divergent thinking or for the child's own interpretation of the story. Questions could be more creative and could place more emphasis on the creative if they dealt more with the literary value of the story. For example:

"How did the author make you feel by using certain words on page 29?"

"I felt like singing some of the words in this story. Did any of you feel the same way?   What words did you feel like singing?"

"On page 82 the author told me something about Aunt Cordelia that made me like her a lot better.   Did any of you have this experience?   What words did the author use to do this?"

"What did the author mean, do you think, by the words 'a ribbon of light' in describing the road?"

These questions allow a child to give his interpretation of passages through his own feelings and tastes rather than those imposed on him by the values of his teacher.

Comprehension of any story can be easily checked in a multitude of ways: through dramatizing it, by making a scroll movie (which checks comprehension of sequence of events better, perhaps, than any other device), by having a TV retelling of the story, by asking questions not directly answered in the story but inferred by the circumstances (such as "What season of the year was it?"   "Why is *yellow* an important word in this story?"), by having some role-playing, by shadow-plays, and by a variety of other ways.

Skill lessons, those that grow out of an experience with a story, can be motivating and creative.   Reread the lessons on pages 3, 78, and 108, all of which contained some fascinating skill application due to the alertness and ingenuity of the teacher.

Enrichment activities, the last step in most manuals, should come first.   If the logical sequence of language development proceeds from experience to listening to oral expression to reading to written expression, then the kind of experiences often suggested in the manuals under enrichment should logically come at the beginning of the lesson.   Stories about farms, cows, sheep, horses, equipment, and the country, as well as movies about them, slides about them, and pictures of them, provide a logical vicarious experience for children who cannot have a direct experience visiting a farm.   The words (the vocabulary) of the farm get into the children's speech in meaningful context so that the children understand the words when they read them in print. Experiences are basic to the development of reading vocabulary and should precede the teaching experience rather than follow it. Dramatizations, filmstrips, role-playing, dioramas, etc., all contribute more to a reading program than just enrichment.   They can provide the core to meaning in reading and will develop creativity in children as well.

Consequently, the rigid adherence to steps in a manual can be greatly challenged. No research proves that this approach to reading can produce better readers than other methods. In light of newer strategies, some of these steps seem antiquated and irrelevant. Certainly, when they are rigidly followed, they destroy the ingenuity of the teacher as well as that of the child.

The language experience approach is the one from which illustrations in this book have been most commonly selected. It offers unlimited opportunity for creative development in teachers and children.

The initial teaching alphabet is sound in many respects and allows a flexibility in using the consistent alphabet code. But it is also very limiting in that it restricts written communication to the group exposed to ITA. One of the strongest criticisms against ITA is that it distorts the visual image of the true shape and spelling of English words. Because so much emphasis is being currently placed on the *image* of the word for correct spelling purposes, critics of the plan agree that while children may read sooner and better, they will have problems in transferring to the regular traditional spelling of words. Supporters of the plan claim this is not the case, and one piece of research has supported their claim.

The words in color approach to reading does not distort the traditional spellings—in fact, it emphasizes the problem areas of words so that children may fix them better in their minds. This method of teaching, when used judiciously, could lead to extensive creative development.

The linguistic approaches, in early stages of development, were limiting in some ways yet creative in others. They were limiting in that Bloomfield's[12] first program for the teaching of reading through the linguistic approach was very detailed and demanded excessive conformity. It was creative in that children could explore and invent new words. Sounds were used in new word forms in Bloomfield's materials whether they made a *real* word or not. (Criticism was leveled against this technique because some educators felt that young children, with limited experience and limited vocabularies, were confused because they

---

12. Leonard Bloomfield, *Language* (New York: Holt, Rinehart and Winston, 1933); Leonard Bloomfield and Clarence L. Barnhart, *Let's Read: A Linguistic Approach* (Detroit: Wayne State University Press, 1961).

could not tell the nonsense words from the words they did not yet know. Their desire to make sense out of their reading was challenged.) Recent approaches (such as that advocated by LeFevre) can contribute a great deal to creative development in teachers and children.

The graphoneme concept, which is a linguistic approach, accents the structure of words and the importance of meanings, so it is extremely flexible in developing creative traits. Skills taught in this program enable the child to learn by discovery.

Organization and Creativity

Some *plans of organization* set conditions for enhancing the creative process. Among these is the *individualized reading plan.* If properly carried out, it can provide a highly creative, efficient, and individual reading program. The SRA (Science Research Associates) materials are designed for individual use and can do a great deal to help children develop their own reading skills. As a self-learning device, they can be a springboard for much creative development providing they are used discreetly and with other reading activities.

The ungraded reading program, if isolated from a total ungraded school situation, is not conducive to the development of the creative process. Reading is isolated from the other language skills; the experiences of the children do not provide a base for the development of language, and often children do not know the teacher well—nor she them. It has been stated that a prerequisite to teaching reading is that teachers must know their children and their experiential background. This organizational plan seems to violate most of the necessary conditions for creative development. Some teachers manage to teach creatively and develop creativity with this plan, but it is very constricting at best.

Departmentalized reading and *ability grouping* plans have the same drawbacks as the ungraded primary reading plans. Obviously, a truly creative teacher may make her lessons with these groups very creative, and some aspects of creative development may be realized, but the consistent, planned program in creative development cannot be carried out when so much preplanned material is shoved at the children, especially if there is little carry-over into the other areas of the curriculum.

Grouping within the self-contained classroom has tremendous potential for creative teaching and creative development. In this situation, the teacher and children know each other well, reading can be an integral part of the total curriculum, the teacher can contrive experiences throughout the day to be used in the reading time, flexibility of scheduling is possible, progress in creative development can be more carefully evaluated, language arts can be taught as coordinated units, interests of the children can be utilized in developing vocabulary and reading skills, flexibility of grouping is possible, and the teacher can help children throughout the day.

In the true concept of the nongraded school as advocated by Goodlad and Anderson,[13] the aspects of the total school program would also apply to fostering creative development through the teaching of reading.

Team-teaching plans obviously can contribute to developing the creative process when they are *real* team-teaching plans. When they are team-teaching in name only, the limitations in developing creativity are the same as those mentioned above under *departmentalized reading.*

The Open Classroom plan of organization is highly flexible and makes possible the application of all the creative approaches to reading. Emphasis is placed on the individual and self-learning. The element of discovery plays an important part in the program, and each individual is responsible for his own learning. Reading often results in creative behavior. It is so integrated with all learning during the school day that it is almost impossible for a child *not* to read. Skills built in one area are often done so with the thought in mind that they can also be applied in the development of reading (such as developing motor coordination, perception, analogy, and visual acuity). Teachers may work with groups or individuals according to their needs, and any type of grouping is possible.

Schools tend today to label themselves as structured or unstructured. For some children, a very loose type of organizational plan seems to provide the best impetus for learning. For others, some structure (and even tight structure) seems to encourage learning.

Grimes and Allinsmith showed the high achievement of highly anxious (and compulsive) children in a structured setting, their significantly lower relative achievement in an unstructured setting, and the resulting underachievement when their high anxiety was combined with low compulsivity.[14]

13. John J. Goodlad and Robert H. Anderson, *The Nongraded Elementary School* (New York: Harcourt, Brace and World, 1963).
14. J. W. Grimes and H. Allinsmith, "Compulsivity, Anxiety and School Achievement," *Merrill Palmer Quarterly* 7 (1961): 248–271.

FIGURE 3–4. *Designing the setting for the spring Art and Music Festival provides experience in manipulating shapes, colors, and sounds and reading for pleasure, factual knowledge, and interpretation.*

The type of classroom organization necessary to achieve maximum results in reading may well be a combination of structures throughout the day, rather than a superstructure or a laissez-faire structure. In planning a flexible system of structures, the teacher will need to know the needs and learning patterns of each child.

WRITING BEHAVIORAL OBJECTIVES FOR THE CREATIVE TEACHING OF READING

It is currently fashionable to write objectives in behavioral terms. This practice is based on the concept that education is the process that changes human behavior. In order to teach effectively, the teacher must measure the results of her teaching in terms of the changes in behavior that result from her lessons. For example, she says to herself, "As a result of this lesson, the children will know the beginning sound of the consonant *p*." Now she must also think of a way she can prove to herself that each child has learned the sound of /p/ and thus changed his word attack ability—modified his behavior, so to speak. She adds this to her objective so it reads, "As a result of this lesson, each child will know the beginning sound made by the consonant *p* as shown by his ability to find and underline said sound on a worksheet (p. 28 in workbook) when it is read aloud by the teacher."

She may also want to state the lowest degree of acceptable performance she can allow for each child.

Thus, the teacher sets out to state what she is to do and how she can determine whether she has done it.

The process is logical for the teaching of simple cognitive learnings. Like all new ideas, however, the writing of behavioral objectives has become almost a fetish in some places, and teachers often spend more time writing objectives than they do teaching to accomplish them. There are many arguments presented in the literature both for and against the writing of behavioral objectives. Common sense should dictate to each teacher whether or not they are suitable for any particular lesson or group. In creative teaching they have value only for those lessons designed to develop specific cognitive learnings. Inasmuch as the writing of behavioral objectives deals only with objectives and evaluation and ignores strategy, method, and technique, they are of limited use in developing creativity, for we know that creativity is a process as well as a product and any behavior change that results from creative teaching is an outcome of *what happened* to the child *during* a lesson. Method determines the attitudes, knowledges, and skills a child will learn. One teacher may drill the children in beginning consonant sounds all the time, day after day. Each day she may give the children a worksheet from the workbook. Each child may attain the minimal score acceptable by the teacher, but that does not indicate that the child is able to really apply his learnings, nor does it measure more important things: the attitude of the child towards learning in general and reading in particular, his feeling for books, his appreciation and understanding of processes, and his feeling about himself.

On the other hand, a teacher like Miss Rogers (see page 108) has inspired the children to discover their own learnings, with the result that she is able to develop their skills in a fraction of the time that it takes the teacher mentioned above. How necessary is it to *measure* the change in attitude of children who squeal with delight over the fact that they are able to figure out a word because of some new skill they have learned? Are not the sparkle of the eyes, the proud stiffening of the backbone, the pleased lift of the chin, and the skipping of many feet logical and worthwhile evaluations of children's progress, of the way they feel about themselves, and of the way they feel about learning?   One teacher teaches what children need to know as revealed by their experiences; another teaches what *she* thinks children need to know.

One of the greatest criticisms about the writing of behavioral objectives is that they void the essential criteria for creative teaching and for the teaching of reading by almost any technique.   Creative teaching and teaching of reading must, to a large degree, be an individual process.   One of our greatest national assets is the individual differences in children.   Each child has his own learning pattern and his own pattern of growth. It is incredible to think that behavioral objectives can be written for each child for every cognitive learning he is to experience each day.   The teacher's time may be better spent in keeping a record of what the child can do and planning next steps for teaching him what he does not yet know.   Not long ago, experts were spoofing the concept that each child could be taught reading individually in the classroom, but it is being done very effectively through various individualized reading approaches using machines, in programmed learning systems with individualized reading programs, and in the open classroom concept (see page 115).

Consequently, any advocate of creative teaching finds only a limited use for behavioral objectives.   They make teaching so simple and learnings so minute that they often lead the teacher down a primrose path of false complacency.   Education is more than the ability to learn facts and parrot them back.   Real change in people comes as a result of experiences that create changes in attitude, values, knowledge, morals, and concepts.

The writing of behavioral objectives *can* result in creative lessons—that fact needs to be made clear.   But there are other aspects about the use of this strategy that need to be discussed, not for the purpose of discouraging the young teacher from using them but to help her understand their logical and proper use. Many graduate students in my classes have abandoned the use of this very worthwhile skill because of the following reasons: (1) writing objectives is too time consuming, (2) lessons planned tend to be uncreative, (3) the teacher becomes insensitive to children's needs in attempting to meet the objectives, and (4) the objectives tend to result in dull lessons.

In the following discussion, I have attempted to point up

the specific cautions that must be exercised in using behavioral objectives.

Mager, a pioneer in the use of behavioral objectives, lists the following criteria for a behavioral objective:[15]

1. It names a specific overt behavior.
2. It tells exactly what the behavior consists of.
3. It may need to exclude related but unwanted behaviors.
4. It describes the conditions under which the behavior must occur.
5. It specifies the criteria of acceptable performance.

The term *behavior* refers to any visible activity displayed by a learner (student). Mager defines this as *overt action*. *Terminal behavior* refers to the behavior you would like your learner to be able to demonstrate at the time your influence over him ends.

Some criticisms of the system of writing behavioral objectives have already been pointed out. Others include the following:

1. In writing behavioral objectives, according to Mager, the teacher must specify what the learner must be able to *do* or *perform* when he is demonstrating his mastery of the objective. The behavior observed may be verbal or nonverbal, but the teacher can only infer the condition of his intellect by observing his performance.

This concept appears to be in conflict with the concept of creative teaching. The written statement implies that the teacher must be able to predict the acceptable response that any given stimuli will evoke in a learner. While this may be possible in some cognitive learning, even there it cannot always be accomplished. Take the first-year teacher, for instance. She has not yet taken her children through enough experiences to be able to predict the terminal behavior of the individual children, however much she knows about children in general at the age level of her students.

In creative teaching, direct, positive outcomes are unpredictable. If a certain amount of predictability is necessary to determine acceptable terminal behavior, then it is impossible to write objectives for the development of creativity in behavioral terms.

2. Most texts define behavior as *overt action*, assuming

15. R. F. Mager, *Preparing Objectives for Programmed Instruction* (Palo Alto, Calif.: Fearon Publishers, 1962).

that overt action can be interpreted by the teacher as a sign that the objective has been met.   Overt action may be that a child is able to name the parts of an airplane.   In her plan, one teacher wrote: "As a result of this lesson, each child will be able to name at least 90 percent of the parts of an airplane from a diagram." So the objective is met—the lesson is a success.   Overt action may be a child underlining a page of nouns in a workbook.   That is the terminal part of an objective on recognizing nouns.   But has the child's *psychological* behavior really changed?   The teacher cannot tell at this point; she can only wait and see if this bit of knowledge changes the child's actions within the next days. Often the checking, or testing, of a bit of knowledge or a skill does not insure a change in behavior.

In creative teaching a knowledge is learned and *provision is made to put it to new use.*   The degree to which a child is able to use a new knowledge or skill is every bit as valid an evaluation of teaching as his ability to respond properly in a pen-and-paper exercise.

I have a friend who makes pots.   He is fascinating to listen to, and my appreciation of all pottery has greatly increased from hearing him talk and seeing him at work.   I am sure my behavior towards pots has changed greatly since I knew John.

But my overt behavior has not changed in any noticeable way.   I go to John's house for the evening and we always wind up in his studio.   Sometimes I even try to throw a pot for fun. I leave his house and go home, and the next day I go about my business.   I do not run downtown and buy a potter's wheel.   I do not seek out a teacher.   I do not buy any books on pottery.   I do not rush to the stores and museums to see displays of it.   My overt behavior has not changed.   Now, had John said to me after my attempt to throw a pot, "Let's see how many of the steps in throwing a pot you can remember," or "Let's see how well you remember the nomenclature of the process and tools," the chances are I could have passed the test.   But I did not take such a test. *My overt actions did not change.*

Something else did change, however.   I never see a pot but that I analyze the process by which it was made, I evaluate it as good or bad or mediocre or fair, and I react to it aesthetically. But the very factors that *did* create change in my behavior are often disregarded when behavior is predicted, and the behavior that really changed is often disregarded even though it may be the most valuable outcome of the entire lesson.

Might not the same situation apply to almost any school experience?   Writing the objective in behavioral terms does not insure that the teacher will make teaching and learning any more relevant or creative; it will not insure accomplishment of the desired terminal behavior; it will not insure a correct interpretation of the child's behavior at the terminal point; and it does not measure creative production, though it does not interfere completely with creative teaching.

3. A teacher's interpretation of children's overt action can be a risky business when dealing with creative children. All our research to date draws attention to the fact that teachers do not understand creative children and misinterpret their behavior down the line. It seems that predetermined terminal behavior patterns allow for no originality or uniqueness of response in children—and the creative child who is already discriminated against becomes the victim of another "system."

4. It must be remembered that one of the goals of creative teaching is to develop divergent thinking. One of the characteristics of divergent thinking is that it does not have closure —or terminal behavior. Since behavioral objectives imply a terminal behavior, creative teaching cannot be stated in behavioral objectives.

5. In creative teaching, almost *any* response is acceptable, at least at the time it is offered. Judgment on ideas, poems, stories, and other creative products is deferred until the child feels himself finished—*then* the ideas are acted upon, the poem is evaluated, etc. This cannot generally happen during a single lesson. An incubation period must be allowed.

6. McAshan says the primary reasons for the current emphasis upon writing behavioral objectives are to aid in curriculum planning, to promote increased pupil achievement, and to improve the techniques and skills of program evaluation.[16]   In theory this concept seems valid. In practice it is difficult to achieve.

In the taxonomies designed for stratifying thought processes and related questions, creativity has been placed in the category of synthesis.[17]   No one studying creativity today will accept this categorization. Creativity is more than synthesis. As Carl Rogers has said, "Creativity is problem solving plus."[18]   Syn-

16. H. H. McAshen, *Writing Behavioral Objectives: A New Approach* (New York: Harper and Row, 1970).
17. B. S. Bloom et al., *Taxonomy of Educational Objectives, Handbook No. 1: The Cognitive Domain* (New York: David McKay, 1956).
18. Carl R. Rogers, "Toward a Theory of Creativity," in *Creativity and Its Cultivation,* ed. Harold H. Anderson (New York: Harper and Row, 1959), p. 72.

thesis is a high level of *convergent* thinking, but creative thought is *divergent*. To think and produce creatively one must synthesize knowledge relating to a specific subject and then project or hypothesize something new that can be done with this synthesized knowledge. Our definition of creativity says it is taking our past experiences and putting them into something new or different. This is going beyond synthesis. And because each individual has different experiences and different knowledge, how can we say what he will create? We cannot. If we could, it would not be creative.

Perhaps one of the difficulties of stating all objectives for creative teaching in behavioral terms comes from a confusion about whether creativity is a logical thought process or not. Research has shown that although there seem to be certain steps in creative processes, there are many kinds of creative thought patterns and many kinds of creativity.[19] Perhaps creative thinking belongs to the affective domain: to be creative means to become involved, to respond emotionally, to give of the heart as well as the head. Affective learnings are not easy to describe in behavioral terms.

7. In using behavioral objectives to guide learning and teaching one must remember that an objective only sets the purpose of the lesson and the manner in which the learning is to be evaluated. The procedure of the lesson—that is, the teacher's methods—can be as creative and unique as desired. In this sense, behavioral objectives may be used just as they are used in any other lesson, as was shown above. Unfortunately, so much emphasis is put on the *writing* of objectives that the procedures of the plan are not as carefully worked out.

8. Divergency in thinking is developed over a long period of time and cannot be identified in one lesson or stated in one objective. It is difficult to see how the objective to develop divergency in teaching can be stated in behavioral terms.

The true test of the effectiveness of the teacher's teaching and the student's learning *comes in the days following the lesson* when each teacher must observe any changes of the behavior of the children!

9. When cognitive learnings are involved in a creative lesson, they may be identified and written up in the original lesson plan. Creativity is often relegated to the background, and

19. Mary Lee Marksberry, *Foundation of Creativity* (New York: Harper and Row, 1963).

the cognitive learnings become the most important part of the lesson.

I question the validity of this action, for I feel that the creative part of the lesson is more important, and many knowledges, though important, are incidental. The teacher's diagnosis of the children's work after each lesson and then remediation to individual's problems call for a *set* of objectives rather than a few or, if needed, different objectives for each member of the class. Then the teacher teaches, by group or to individuals, those skills or knowledges that each child has not yet mastered. This cancels the need for the latter part of the usual behavioral statement such as "The student is to be able to complete a twenty-five-question multiple choice examination on parts of speech. *The lower limit of acceptable performance will be twenty items answered correctly within a period of twenty minutes.*"

The italicized part states acceptable performance. Actually, no performance less than perfect is acceptable in mastering reading skills. To deny a child the right of additional instruction in reading because he met the minimal requirements stated in an objective is to handicap him for life. Behavioral objectives, if not carefully controlled, may create sloppy and incomplete teaching.

In teaching reading skills, the teacher should use a system that allows students to receive individual help and guidance—the goal being perfect performance (provided, of course, the child is not somehow handicapped).

10. Too often we speak in terms of what a student—any student on any level—does instead of *how* or *why* he does it. In creative learning, the *how* can be as important as the result because creativity is a process and a product. Consequently, if behavioral objectives are to set means for measuring creative development, they must be more concerned with process than with a terminal behavior at the end of a period of time.

To state objectives in any form is not to achieve them. The methodology is still the important thing. Evaluation simply tells whether the method worked and what the teacher must teach again.

Curriculum development involves a precarious combination of artistry, dedication, and experience and a difficult mix of scholars, teachers, school administrators, and children. Realistically, emphasis in any program should be on the *method* best suited for *each* child to do what he is able, not on a statement of a final product expected from a total group, within which there are some children who cannot ever reach the goal and many who have already mastered the goal before the lesson begins.

Evaluating in terms of behavioral objectives means evaluating that which outwardly *appears* to be so in a specific situation at one specific time. The long-range view is neglected: those changes in behavior that take place over a longer period of time (in essence, the *real* objectives behind each teaching act). The application of learnings in this instance is largely the outcome of a stimulus-response situation and is not concerned with the true changes in behavior that come after the lesson is over, such as the later application of learnings in direct use in everyday living.

There is a certain amount of dishonesty in writing behavioral objectives if the constituency of the group is not known. This is true, of course, of the writing of any kind of objective. To be absolutely honest, a teacher must evaluate her own skill in teaching by evaluating the skills or knowledges the children already possess at the *beginning* of the lesson. It is always possible that the terminal behavior is the beginning behavior, and the child does not need the instruction. Discovering this at the beginning of the lesson keeps the teacher from kidding herself into believing she has taught something that she has not.

We must modify our concepts of behavioral objectives when we write for creative teaching. We can write only to a predictable point, and we cannot always describe the product as a behavioral change.

In Mr. Cline's lesson at the opening of Chapter 5, his objectives are listed in an acceptable form. Mr. Cline did not spell out exactly how he was to determine whether or not he had met his objectives, for he could not. He understood his children and knew that each child would reveal in his own way whether or not the lesson had been successful. His objectives are open-ended, so he can keep in mind his goals (for example, to build a sight vocabulary) yet, at the same time, use the children's former learnings to develop new material. It was unnecessary for me, an observer, to check out Mr. Cline's objectives with a batch of dull workbook exercises or tests. Anyone who had spent a delightful afternoon in that classroom with those children knew that they were happy, they were learning, and, what is more, they *loved* to learn. Mr. Cline knew every child, and each one left the classroom that day smiling and with a feeling of success.

So it was in Mrs. Douglas's open classroom in England (see pages 3–6). The concern for each child was beautiful, and each was learning in his own way. Each teacher in the school had objectives for every child, but they were not written in terms of a predictable behavior. The philosophy there was that each child, although similar to other children in many ways, has his own growth pattern and his own manner of learning and should be encouraged to follow them. Five of the children I met in the upper primary school (ages eleven to twelve) still correspond with me. All I can say is that they write beautifully and know every bit as much about punctuation and capitalization as their American cousins. As for reading, they all read. I found no child who wasn't reading something. The concern, again, was to help each child learn according to his own individual way and to keep the love for reading alive. No one was interested in grade-level achievement because there were no grades. Each teacher knew everything a child had read or was reading and could work individually or in groups with those who were having trouble in any way.

They all knew about behavioral objectives but felt they were highly impractical and of dubious worth in a system where children learned according to their own abilities and drives. They felt that knowing each child individually was a more humane way of approaching education than setting goals for whole classes of children.

READING MATERIALS

Very few current reading materials are constructed to develop creative processes in children. In fact, one of the most devastating blows to the creative process is the teacher's slavish adherence to exercises in the workbooks. Workbooks can make a contribution to creative teaching, but few of them do at present.

In developing creativity, we strive for a new product, for uniqueness and difference. Yet countless exercises in workbooks have children drawing an object to resemble a pattern already placed on the page. "Color it like this." "Make it red." "Draw three balloons like this one." These directions may be a check on reading comprehension but, because of their excessive repetitiveness, they are fatal to creative development. If creative development is to be one of the major objectives of the elementary school, we cannot negate what we do at one time of the school day by the materials we use at another time. And we do not have to. Look at these exercises:

On this page there are four boxes.   In each box draw
something that you saw on the way to school this morning.
The word "red" is printed at the top of this page.   In
the first box draw three red things you have at home; in the
second box draw two red things you have in your room; in
the third box. . . .

Make a picture of your favorite friends and then put
the number of friends you have drawn in this box.

Such exercises check reading comprehension and the
same concepts as the ones stated in the workbook above.   But
such a difference.   One removes patterns, challenges the child's
imagination, stimulates his flow of ideas, encourages originality;
the other flattens creativity into a prescribed answer.   In assigned seat work and in exercises designed to build reading
skills, creative products can be encouraged, divergent as well as
convergent thinking processes can be put to work, open-ended
situations can be utilized, individuality can be stressed, new
knowledges and skills can be applied, problem-solving processes
rather than busy work can be employed, the individual component skills of creativity can be practiced, all areas of the curriculum can be correlated, and *every* activity can be meaningful
and productive.   These are the essentials of creative development
listed in Chapter 1.

Many reading materials are adaptable to the development
of creativity in children.   Others, such as the teaching machines,
concentrate on convergent thought processes in the teaching of
skills and are not.   One of the most needed commodities in the
elementary school today is a rich variety of independent reading
activities geared to developing the creative process.   It is hoped
a start has been made by the suggestions in this and the other
volumes of this series.

SETTING CONDITIONS FOR THE CREATIVE
TEACHING OF READING

It is difficult, because of the many systems and organizational
plans currently in vogue, to prescribe the most fruitful conditions
that should be set in the classroom in order to develop reading
that results in creative behavior.   Such conditions have been implied in the above material.   Each system or organizational plan
requires unique material.   One open classroom situation may use
a highly developed series of skill cards, graded in order of diffi-

culty, which may be used individually by children; another open classroom may use tape recorders with earphones by which children who are working alone can receive individual instructions from a teacher or have exciting stories read to them.

But regardless of the uniqueness of the programs and the materials used, there are some common considerations for setting up a reading environment. Attention should be directed toward setting these conditions within the framework of *any* system or plan.

Physical Conditions

1. To be successful, any program now needs a wealth of materials in order to operate. These materials include:

films
filmstrips
viewfinders
viewfinder strips
tapes
tape recorders
records
record players
storybooks
children's magazines
books of subject matter references
craft books
books on skills building in many areas
dictionaries
encyclopedias
glossaries
pictures
posters
artifacts
books on poetry
catalogues
supplementary readers (all levels)
art and music books
trade books (all levels)
picture books
skill cards (individualized reading materials)
books that provide open-ended problems

All of these materials are not necessary for a creative reading program, but they are highly desirable. If they are not all available, teachers may find their own creativity greatly challenged in devising substitutes or alternates for some of them.

2. Each classroom should have a reading center, even if a school library or a resource center exists. A classroom library center serves purposes that a school library cannot. In the open school situation, however, the library is often the hub of the school, and it provides an ideal core for developing a creative reading program.

3. The children should set up the plans for keeping the reading center functional and attractive. They should share materials through the use of attractive bulletin boards, displays, and book programs (see page 308). If possible, the reading center should be isolated from the general flow of room traffic so that children who wish to concentrate can do so with a minimal amount of distraction. If possible, a rug and some easy chairs should be placed in the center so children may be comfortable when they read. At home, few of us read for pleasure while sitting rigidly at a table. Soft furniture will also greatly help the acoustics of the reading center.

4. Near the reading center, or as a part of it, there should be a research center. It should contain the materials that need special kinds of reading skills (such as encyclopedias, dictionaries, glossaries, reference books, maps, charts, globes, atlases, and almanacs) and, perhaps, a radio or television set.

5. It is important that the reading center be informal. It should have seats that move, desks and tables that can serve many uses, plenty of shelf area, and cubicles nearby where individuals and small groups may work and not disturb others. The reading center must be well lighted and well ventilated.

6. Materials must be easily available to the children. Books should not be placed on shelves so high as to be out of reach. Files must be on the level where children's eyes can readily read the tabs. Tapes must be stored so that the titles can be easily read. Listening machines must be on low tables where the children can easily plug into them.

7. The objectives of a creative program should be the basis for planning the reading program (see page 74). Natural links between reading and creative development should be exploited.

Intellectual Conditions

1. A creative reading program is one that challenges every child. It calls for a wealth of materials, much of which will be

of the trade book nature. It will include many books of creative writing, such as Maurice Sendak's *Where the Wild Things Are.* It will avoid the class or group meetings where any child must sit and be bored while other children wade through material he has already read.

2. Such a program should emphasize reading material that can be used meaningfully at once: convergent learnings should be put to divergent uses. Open-ended stories should be included in the reading center.

3. Drawing from all the contributions of research, this program should devise a plan of word recognition and skills building for each child, built around his needs and interests rather than imposing any one system on him.

4. Such a program requires a school library with many resources, such as the one mentioned above. This is actually a reading resource center rather than a traditional library. In the open classroom situation, this resource center is often the hub of the school. In schools not structured by the open classroom concept, the main library should be supplemented by a library center in each classroom, stocked from the main library. Materials in these centers should be changed frequently to meet children's growing and changing interests. Children should always have access to both centers and should receive instruction at an early age in the use of library materials (see page 285).

5. Regardless of the teaching strategies or the organizational plans, the teacher should share creatively written reading materials with the children continually. A story or poem should be shared every day in addition to passages to confirm facts or to provoke thought. Reading must be valued. Children should be encouraged to read to each other.

6. Children should be taught library and book skills (see page 285). Part of the love of books comes from handling them, from learning to check them out for other children, and from learning to classify, categorize and assemble materials for reading. The more the children handle books, the more pictures they see, the greater the impetus for reading and the appreciation of literature.

7. The reading program should include a planned program in children's literature (see next chapter) and a series of worthy, childlike activities that deal with affective as well as cognitive learnings.

8. All areas of the curriculum should be used to further the reading abilities of the children. New vocabulary should be

introduced in meaningful ways throughout the day, and much reading should evolve from teacher- and child-made materials, such as Charlie's book, Eric's charts, and Peter's story.

9. Children should be encouraged to share reading materials through exciting ways such as those mentioned above and through creative book reports and presentations, such as those shown on pages 307–320.

10. The teacher should keep a careful, individualized system of records from which she can see at a glance the progress a child is making and a history of the reading materials he has used. Diagnosis of the child's reading difficulties should be placed in a prominent place on each of these records, and a planned program for subsequent teaching steps should be outlined. The records should be so planned that notations made in them daily can be simple and direct but can tell any teacher immediately what she needs to know at any time.

Harootunian found that reading ability was associated with such intellectual variables as word fluency, ideational fluency, speed of closure, and flexibility of closure in seventh- and eighth-grade students.[20] Each of these variables is a component of creativity. Harootunian's study suggests that similar relationships may exist in elementary school students. His study also makes us wonder if a positive correlation exists between creativity and high reading ability. Research remains to be done in this area.

Social-Emotional Conditions

1. To develop a creative reading program a pleasant environment is necessary. Children should feel that they are members of a congenial, cooperating group. This does not mean that all children conform to all activities. It does mean that they learn when it is necessary to conform in order to maintain group cooperation and when they may remain individual. Studies show that highly creative children are neither compulsively conforming nor nonconforming. They tend to conform when it is for the good of the group.

2. The child must experience success in what he is trying to do. No child should leave the school in the afternoon feeling that he has failed. Every child can be made to feel successful

20. Berj Harootunian, "Intellectual Abilities and Reading Achievement," *Elementary School Journal* 67 (1966): 386–392.

with some phase of reading during the day.   A creative product often makes a child feel worthy.

3. Creativity and achievement must be valued by the teacher. Children value that which their teachers value. The value of creative thinking and creative productivity is reflected in things the teacher says.

4. Teachers must be sensitive to the needs of children, stressing and praising differences, uniqueness, and originality rather than likeness and commonness.

5. Teachers should accept silly ideas as a sign of creative thinking and help all children to accept the creative child.

6. The atmosphere in the classroom must be permissive to the extent that children are free to experiment, explore, take risks, make mistakes, and be adventurous.

7. The organizational plan must allow children to feel comfortable working by themselves, to know where materials are located, and to feel free to move about and work with other children.   The classroom teacher need not be the only teacher in the classroom: children can help.

8. Records (other than those of achievement and diagnosis) should be accumulated on the factors that influence reading growth in each child.   Conditions in the child's home life can affect his ability to read even before he enters school.   Parental attitudes and the nature of the home environment are important ingredients of motivation.   In her research of children who learned to read before entering school, Durkin concluded that whether or not parents read to their children and felt a responsibility for helping them to learn to read made the biggest difference in whether or not the children read before school entrance or soon after.[21]   Studies by Kramer and Fleming show that parental-child rearing conflicts (conflicts between parents over how the child is to be disciplined) impede reading progress,[22] and studies by Mutimer et al. show that failure of children to establish sibling identification as well as identification with the same-sex parent also impedes reading progress.[23]

21. Dolores Durkin, *Children Who Read Early* (New York: Teachers College, Columbia University Press, 1966).
22. David P. Kramer and Elyse S. Fleming, "Interparental Differences of Opinion and Children's Academic Achievement," *Journal of Educational Research* 60 (1966):136–138.
23. Dorothy Mutimer et al., "Some Differences in the Family Relationships of Achieving and Underachieving Readers," *Journal Genetic Psychology* 109 (1966): 67–74.

Psychological Conditions

For children to read comfortably, certain psychological factors must be taken into consideration, whether or not the reading is to develop creative behavior:

1. The child must not feel threatened. An atmosphere of controlled permissiveness must prevail so that the child is willing to take risks.

2. Children must be aware of self. They must understand that, although they are alike in many ways, they are each uniquely different from anyone else. They should be able to accept differences and realize that it is common and valuable to be different.

3. Children should be open-minded—open to the ideas and feelings of others and able to empathize. They should be able to accept ideas that are different from their own. The teacher must work toward developing these traits.

4. Children must experience success and feel secure in their learnings.

5. The teacher should provide motivation and tensions to agitate creative thinking and creative production. Sometimes this can be done with individual children (as Miss Douglas motivated Charlie), and sometimes the entire group should enjoy a lesson (such as the one Eric and his classmates shared in this chapter). Frequent adventures into creative reading for the purpose of inducing creative activity should be experienced.

6. The attitudes of the teacher are of utmost importance. Creative teachers develop creative children. Even if a teacher is not artistic, she can help children develop their creativity if she values it and understands how it comes to be. A teacher should be relaxed and happy with the children. She should plan well enough to feel confident in her work with them. She must respect each child and be willing to listen to his ideas and plans. She must be courteous and patient with pupils. She must see discipline as self-discipline: the ability of individuals to become independent enough to take the responsibility for their own behavior, including their own learnings.

The *anxiety level* of a classroom appears to have some effect on reading development. Nevelle et al. found, for instance, that reading-comprehension gains among boys enrolled in a six-week summer program were greatest among the middle-anxiety-level group; high test anxiety appeared to have an inverse relationship to comprehension gains, though not to *vocabulary* gains.[24]

Expectations of status-seeking parents who exploit their children may cause high anxiety levels in children. Illnesses at home, the absence of a parent, inability to play a sex role, and a multitude of other causes for anxiety should be considered by the teacher as she attempts to reduce high tension stimulants in the classroom.

SUMMARY

All reading is not creative. To teach reading creatively a program must deliberately attempt to develop creative behavior. It must be flexible in its plan, its adjustment to individuals, and its expected outcomes. It must provide satisfying reading experiences and encourage each child to practice his creative powers.

Creativity *can* be developed in the teacher and the student through the teaching of reading. Some of the systems for teaching reading currently used in our schools provide little chance for creative development, while others appear to provide countless opportunities for it. Some plans of classroom organization deny the full development of teacher and student to their creative potentials; others seem to promote it. Almost no independent reading materials currently used in our schools consistently provide for creative development. A careful scrutiny of teaching plans, organizational plans, and teaching materials must be made if the teaching of reading in any school is to promote creative teaching among its teachers and creative thinking among its pupils.

Inasmuch as creativity cannot be taught but can be fostered, certain conditions must be set in the classroom to develop a good creative reading program.

When a creative instructional program is added to the inherent ability and personality of each child, reading can become a day-by-day experience in creative development.

TO THE COLLEGE STUDENT

1. At the beginning of this chapter you were asked to review methods and organizational plans for the teaching of reading

24. Donald Nevelle et al., "The Relationship Between Test Anxiety and Silent Reading Gain," *American Educational Research Journal* 4 (1967):45–50.

and check them in terms of developing creativity. Did your analysis agree with the author's viewpoint?

2. Check your own reading ability. If a reading clinic is available on your campus, ask the director to speak to your class about reading disability in college students and give a demonstration reading diagnostic test. How do you account for your own reading disabilities?

3. College students often complain that the large numbers of readings required from them for each course make it almost impossible for them to read what they want to read. Do you feel you would read more or less under a freer reading plan than now exists in your college? Think of all the plans you could use, if you were a college instructor, to motivate your students to free reading, and then suggest ways such plans could be initiated. Perhaps your college instructor may permit you to work one or more of these plans on a trial basis.

4. Examine the material you have read this week in terms of *how* you read it. Which assignments did you read quickly? Which did you read slowly? Which did you read over? Which did you enjoy? Was your rate of reading faster for some than others? Do you read material you like quickly or slowly? What generalizations can you make from this examination?

5. Many college students identify closely with *The Prophet,* by Kahlil Gibran. If you haven't read it, do so, and then determine whether it was a creative reading experience for you.

6. Observe the list of components of reading on page 74. Assign one topic to a group and break your class into groups. Brainstorm the ways you could develop your component creatively *or* design one lesson showing how that particular component could be taught creatively. Share your ideas with the class.

TO THE CLASSROOM TEACHER

1. What method of teaching reading are you currently using? What organizational plan are you currently using? Make a conscientious list of the ways your method and your organizational plan hinder or encourage the development of creativity.

2. Examine Dechant's list of fallacies regarding reading (see pages 94 to 96). Have you believed any of these fallacies? Submit yourself to some critical and creative thinking and determine why they are fallacies.

3. How can you turn the heterogeneous grouping of children in a classroom into an asset to teach reading creatively?

4. Think of all the ways by which you can teach phonics creatively.

5. Using Clymer's report as a basis (see page 110), determine which vowel rules should be taught as rules rising from generalizations and which are really exceptions to a generalization. Then determine more creative ways to teach the exceptions than those advocated by your basal series.

6. My first teaching was in a one-room rural school containing all eight grades. On my arrival at the schoolhouse, I discovered I had *no* beginning reading books. There were five children in the first grade. How would *you* go about teaching reading in this situation?

TO THE COLLEGE STUDENT
AND THE CLASSROOM TEACHER

1. Make a list of the conditions you must set in order to teach reading creatively. A review of Chapters 7 and 8 of *Setting Conditions for Creative Teaching in the Elementary School* may serve as a guide.

2. Following is a list of statements collected from faculty meetings and discussion meetings. Analyze each comment and discuss the fallacies of the thinking behind each:

> Our principal insists each child read two preprimers, two primers and two first-grade readers before we are allowed to promote the child to the second grade.
> We must work harder at teaching reading because half of our children were below grade level on the achievement test.
> We don't begin social studies until the third grade because reading is so important we spend most of our time on it.
> We are going to ungrade our reading program and I'm glad. It will make it so much easier for the teachers.

3. Using material from the preceding chapters, plan a program for teaching adult illiterates (of average or above-average intelligence) how to read.

4. Make a list of as many situations as possible where reading skills may be developed without small group meetings.

5. Refer to the lesson at the beginning of Chapter 1. Plan a good reading lesson for culturally-deprived, average-intelligence children that will attain the same objectives as the lesson

described in Chapter 1 without grouping the children (that is, individual differences will be met within the total class group).

6. Design some independent reading activities that will develop creativity in children. Take stock of some of the independent activities you are already using and evaluate them according to their value in creative development.

7. Using the chart of characteristics of creative children on pages 80–81, visit a classroom and observe the children to see if you can identify creative behaviors. After you have decided which students are the most creative according to your analysis, compare your findings with the teacher's feelings.

8. Observe some reading lessons in a nearby school or a campus school and categorize them along a continuum from creative to noncreative. Establish criteria for making your choices at several points along the continuum.

9. Consider this situation: Miss Barnes brings to class a copy of *The Wizard of Oz*. She reads part of it to the children to prepare them for the national broadcast over television during the coming evening. The children all watch the TV show and have a wonderful discussion of it. As a result of this experience, they take turns reading the rest of the story to each other. Then they rewrite the story into scenes and present it as a play for the entire school. Is this a creative experience? Why or why not?

SELECTED BIBLIOGRAPHY

Abercrombie, D. O. *Studies in Phonetics and Linguistics.* Oxford: Oxford University Press, 1965.

Allen, R. Van. "Write Way to Reading: Language-Experience Approach." *Elementary English* 44 (May 1967):480–485.

Baker, S. S. *Your Key to Creative Teaching.* New York: Harper and Row, 1962.

Barbe, Walter B. *Educators' Guide to Personalized Reading Instruction.* Englewood Cliffs, N.J.: Prentice-Hall, 1961.

Bloomfield, Leonard, and Clarence L. Barnhart. *Let's Read.* Detroit: Wayne State University Press, 1961.

Bond, Guy, and Eva Bond Wagner. *Teaching the Child to Read.* 4th ed. New York: Macmillan, 1966.

Carrol, John B. "The Analysis of Reading Instruction: Perspectives from Psychology and Linguistics." In *Theories of Learning and Instruction*, pp. 336–353. (Sixty-third Yearbook, pt. 1, National Society for the Study of Education). Chicago: University of Chicago Press, 1964.

Chall, Jeanne S. *Learning to Read: The Great Debate.* New York: McGraw-Hill, 1967.

Clymer, Theodore. "The Utility of Phonic Generalizations in the Primary Grades." *Reading Teacher* 16 (1963):252–260.

Cooper, Bernice. "Contributions of Linguistics in Teaching Reading." *Education* 85 (May 1965):529–532.

Covington, Martin V. "Some Experimental Evidence on Teaching for Creative Understanding." *Reading Teacher* 20 (1967): 390–396.

Curry, Robert L., and Toby W. Rigby. *Reading Independence through Word Analysis.* Columbus, O.: Charles E. Merrill Publishing Co., 1969.

Dale, Edgar. "Education for Creativity." *The News Letter* 30, no. 3 (December 1964).

Darrow, Helen Fisher, and R. Van Allen. *Independent Activities for Creative Learning.* New York: Teachers College, Columbia University, 1961.

Darrow, Helen Fisher, and Virgil M. Howes. *Approaches to Individualized Reading.* New York: Appleton-Century-Crofts, 1960.

Dickinson, Marie. "Through Self-Selection to Individualizing Reading Procedures." In *Readings in the Language Arts in the Elementary School,* edited by James C. MacCampbell, pp. 366–374. Boston: D. C. Heath, 1964.

Downing, John. "The Augmented Roman Alphabet for Learning to Read." *Reading Teacher* 16 (1963):325–336.

Durkin, Dolores. *Phonics and the Teaching of Reading.* Rev. ed. New York: Bureau of Publications, Teachers College, Columbia University, 1969.

Durr, William, ed. *Reading Instruction: Dimensions and Issues.* Boston: Houghton Mifflin, 1967.

Fitzgerald, James A., and Patricia G. Fitzgerald. *Fundamentals of Reading Instruction.* New York: Macmillan, 1967.

Fries, Charles C. *Linguistics and Reading.* New York: Holt, Rinehart and Winston, 1963.

Goodlad, John, and Robert H. Anderson. *The Nongraded Elementary School.* New York: Harcourt, Brace and World, 1963.

Goodman, Kenneth S. "The Linguistics of Reading." *Elementary School Journal* 64 (April 1964):355–361.

Gray, William. "Reading as Experiencing, Thinking and Learning." In *Readings in the Language Arts in the Elementary School,* edited by James C. MacCampbell, pp. 411–425. Boston: D. C. Heath, 1964.

Green, E. *The Learning Process and Programmed Instruction.* New York: Holt, Rinehart and Winston, 1963.

Harris, Albert J., and Edward R. Sipay, eds. *Readings on Reading Instruction.* New York: David McKay Co., 1972.

Harrison, Maurice. *The Story of the Initial Teaching Alphabet.* New York: Pitman Publishing Corp., 1964.

Heilman, Arthur W. *Phonics in Proper Perspective.* 2nd ed. Columbus, O.: Charles E. Merrill Publishing Co., 1968.

Hernandez, David E. *Writing Behavioral Objectives.* New York: Harper and Row, 1972.

Hersch, Richard, and Stuart Cohen. "A Case Against a Case Against Behavioral Objectives." *Elementary School Journal* 71 (May 1971):204.

Jackson, P., and E. Betford. "Educational Objectives and the Joys of Teaching." *School Review* 75 (Autumn 1967):250–266.

Jacobs, P. M., and L. S. Maier. *A Guide to Evaluating Self-Instructional Programs.* New York: Holt, Rinehart and Winston, 1965.

Jones, J. Kenneth. "Colour as an Aid to Visual Perception in Early Reading." *British Journal of Educational Psychology* 35 (1965):21–27.

Jones, Virginia W. *Decoding and Learning to Read.* Portland, Ore.: Northwest Regional Laboratory, 1967.

Kohl, Herbert. *The Open Classroom.* New York: Vintage Books, 1969.

Krathwohl, David R., Benjamin S. Bloom, and Bertram B. Masia. *Taxonomy of Educational Objectives: Handbook II: The Affective Domain.* New York: David McKay Co., 1964.

Lee, Doris M., and R. Van Allen. *Learning to Read through Experience.* New York: Appleton-Century-Crofts, 1963.

McAshen, H. H. *Writing Behavioral Objectives: A New Approach.* New York: Harper and Row, 1970.

MacDonald, James B., and Bernice J. Wolfson. "A Case Against Behavioral Objectives." *Elementary School Journal* 71 (Dec. 1970):205.

Mager, R. F. *Preparing Objectives for Programmed Instruction.* Palo Alto, Calif.: Fearson Publishers, 1962.

Oettinger, Anthony G. "The Myths of Educational Technology." *Saturday Review,* May 18, 1968, pp. 76–77.

Popham, W. James, and Eva L. Baker. *Establishing Instructional Goals.* Englewood Cliffs, N.J.: Prentice-Hall, 1970.

Robinson, H. Alan, ed. *Meeting Individual Differences in Reading.* Chicago: University of Chicago Press, 1964.

Robinson, Helen M., ed. *Innovation and Change in Reading Instruction.* Chicago: University of Chicago Press, 1968.

Rogers, Vincent R., ed. *Teaching in the British Primary School.* New York: Macmillan, 1970.

Spitzer, Lillian, comp. *Selected Materials on the Language-Experience Approach to Reading Instruction.* Newark, Del.: International Reading Association, 1967.

Stauffer, Russel G. *The Language Experience Approach to the Teaching of Reading.* New York: Harper and Row, 1972.

————. "Linguistics and Reading (ed)." *Reading Teacher* 18 (December 1964): 172–231.

Vilscek, Elaine C. "What Research Has Shown about the Language Experience Program." In *A Decade of Innovations: Approaches to Beginning Reading*, pp. 9–23. Newark, Del.: International Reading Association, 1968.

Weber, Lillian. *The English Infant School and Informal Education.* Englewood Cliffs, N.J.: Prentice-Hall, 1971.

CHAPTER IV

Literature and the Reading Program

Childhood will have no difficulty with literature if it has a chance to develop its own native gifts in language. This, of course, is not the whole story, but it is one of its most important chapters.[1]

HUGHES MEARNS

TO THE READER

Before you read this chapter, look at the bibliography on page 152. Find one of the anthologies of children's literature in the library and enjoy some children's stories and poems. You will enjoy this chapter more if you spend some time browsing through a children's library first.

INTRODUCTION

The skill-building program described in the first three chapters of this book constitutes one half of a good reading program; the other half is a rich program in children's literature. Reading skills are learned so that children may be able to read the litera-

1. Hughes Mearns, *Creative Power: The Education of Youth in the Creative Arts* (New York: Dover Publications, 1958), p. 75.

ture written for them.   A good school library is essential, therefore, in developing a well-rounded reading program.

Children's literature makes definite contributions toward
creative development in boys and girls and offers many opportunities for creative teaching.   Literature is the creative product
of the minds of creative people.   As a painting serves to fire the
imagination, so does a fine story, a well-composed poem, or a
good book.   Children who write their own literature are always
eager to see what others write.   True literature stimulates the
imagination and contributes to the children's concept of the use
of imagination in creating.   The creative teaching of literature
can contribute to creative development in many ways:

1. It can stimulate children to write for themselves.
2. It can provide a means of therapy for troubled children.
3. It can help children build skills in expression, in defining, and
   in elaboration.
4. It can help build a colorful vocabulary that will assist each
   child to express himself better.
5. It can serve as the basis for constructive daydreaming and
   complete identification with a problem (so necessary for creative problem-solving).
6. It can make children more discreet in passing judgment and
   making choices, especially in the use of words.
7. It can be the perpetual source of creative stimulation for every
   child.
8. It can develop a sensitivity to places, sights, sounds, words, life
   problems, and people.
9. It can help children build a set of standards and values regarding creative writing.

Literature should not be *taught;* it should be *read* and
enjoyed.   The teacher's job in sharing a story or a poem with children is a simple one: she is an intermediary between the author
and his audience, and her major duty is to try to put across the
author's ideas as though she were a substitute for him.

Through literature the child develops his tastes in reading
for pleasure.   If he experiences satisfaction in the stories the
teacher reads, he will seek out this satisfaction in other stories.
Satisfaction, happiness, contentment, fun, joy, positive release,
pleasure—all of these feelings should accompany the literature
period in the classroom.

Literature fulfills a need in the modern school that does
not confine it to the language arts alone.   It touches on every
aspect of living and therefore should become an integral part of

FIGURE 4–1.   *Reading* Mr. Popper's Penguins *stimulates interest in a whole unit on penguins.*

the entire school program.   At least once every day, and in some instances many more times than this, a teacher should read a poem or story to the children regardless of age range or grade placement.   The wealth of available material gives her resources for every occasion.

Although literature is often classified among the fine arts, in the elementary school it can be combined with any area of the school curriculum.   Social studies books can only be, at best, a summary of facts about a country or a period in history.   They do not have the space to give children the feeling of the way of life in any given country or any period of time.   Without the "feeling" element, facts cannot help children understand life in a time or place different from their own.   Reading about Switzerland in a social studies book is one thing, and reading *Heidi* is another.   Facts about the Revolutionary War cannot impart to children the terror, the suspense, the fear, the bravery, the courage, the compassion, or the hatred that war arouses in the hearts of men, but reading *The Matchlock Gun* or *Drums Along the Mohawk* can.   Social studies books reach the minds of children, but literature reaches their hearts.

Good literature recaptures the *mood* rather than the *facts* of life.   The life of a bygone period of time is reconstructed, a strange place comes alive, or a feeling or mood saturates the listener to the extent that the author is able to communicate in an imaginative manner.   It is not the *story* of Tom Sawyer and

Huckleberry Finn that makes *The Adventures of Tom Sawyer* a delightful book—it is the author's unique ability to make every boy today feel a kinship with Tom because he understands Tom through the genius of the author's communicative power. Tom makes fires glow in the hearts of fathers, bringing back the carefree adventurous feeling of their own boyhoods; the author evokes nostalgic memories through the magic grouping of words. So literature can transplant us to another world and another period of time; it can create an emotional situation, a mood or tone, and a feeling. We experience sadness, love, joy, disgust, hatred, sympathy. This we do through empathy, our ability to project ourselves into the situation and live within the consciousness of the characters created by the author.

The therapeutic value of literature must be recognized. Creative writing provides emotional release, and, in reading the writings of others, many children are able to project themselves so that they receive help with their own problems. They come to understand human nature by learning that their problems are not unique.

The field of literature, then, belongs in the area of the creative arts, for it has aesthetic values; it belongs to the field of language arts, for it is the most perfected use of symbolic communicative tools; and it belongs to the area of the social sciences, for it develops knowledge and understanding. More intimately than any other subject-matter area, literature, as children write it and read it, goes hand-in-hand with goals of the modern school. It *is* communication through creative experiences.

CRITERIA FOR CHOOSING LITERATURE FOR CHILDREN

Literature is concerned more with the telling of the story than the plot. It is the raising of the commonplace to the beautiful by caring enough to choose exactly the right word in the right place. Leland Jacobs[2] gives five criteria for selecting literature to read to children:

1. The story should have a fresh well-paced plot.
2. It must have unique individuality.

2. Leland B. Jacobs, "Children's Experiences in Literature," in *Children and the Language Arts*, ed. Virgil E. Herrick and Leland B. Jacobs (Englewood Cliffs, N.J.: Prentice-Hall, 1955), p. 194.

3. It should contain plausible, direct conversation.
4. It must have well-delineated characters.
5. It must have authentic outcomes.

Jacobs also feels that good children's literature must be free from obvious sentimentality while rich in honest sentiment; it must be free from direct moralizing but rooted in genuine spiritual and moral values; it must be free from cuteness and triteness; it must be vigorously unhackneyed and distinctive; it must be free from talking down or misunderstanding of children's abilities. He feels good literature has "memory" value—there is a residue of meaning after time lapses.

Many surveys have been developed to assist the teacher in the selection of appropriate literature for various age levels.[3] These surveys show that children tend to have specific interests at different ages, but with the changing interests there remain some persistent overall ones. Children tend to maintain an interest in machines, nature, everyday experiences, holidays, love, fun stories and poems, and make-believe.[4]

Young children prefer literature that has one main plot. They want to be able to anticipate the outcome of the story. They like literature that sets a mood, and they like direct conversation. They enjoy colorful, tongue-tickling words and prefer simple, natural climaxes in their stories. They like stories developed around one main character, and generally they prefer one boy or girl hero, although sometimes an animal hero will act as an acceptable substitute. And they like literature with illustrations that also tell the story.[5]

As children grow older, they develop a keener interest in animals, especially specific animals, such as horses or cats. Older children like folk literature and stories of American folk heroes. They like modern magic, stories about contemporary experiences, historical fiction, regional fiction, and intergroup fiction. They enjoy reading about child life in other countries and like biographies and books about science. They also like stories built around such themes as sports, games, religion, arts, crafts, heroes,

3. George Norvell, *What Boys and Girls like to Read* (Morristown, N.J.: Silver Burdett Co., 1959); Mary Eakin, *Good Books for Children* (Chicago: University of Chicago Press, 1962); and Dora V. Smith, *Fifty Years of Children's Books, 1916–1960, Trends, Backgrounds, Influences* (Champaign, Ill.: National Council of Teachers of English, 1963).
4. Jacobs, "Children's Experiences in Literature," pp. 196–198.
5. Ibid., p. 198.

humor, mystery, travel, and nature.   They like to read about children with their own characteristics and problems.[6]

In choosing books for children's reading, or in guiding children in the selection of their own reading, teachers will keep in mind the following sources: contemporary literature, great stories and classics, realistic tales, fanciful tales, stories of fiction, stories of information, current material in periodicals, popular materials and distinctively literary reading matter, anthologies, and inexpensive books on children's literature.

In summarizing research in the area of reading preference, Harris indicates that the following broad generalizations may be made:[7]

1. Interest in book reading tends to increase with schooling, at least through early adolescence, and then to stabilize or to decline.
2. Interest in newspaper and magazine reading follows a similar pattern beyond the primary grades, with greatest interest being shown in the comics and in sports.
3. Fiction is preferred to factual exposition.   Prose is preferred to poetry in both elementary and secondary school.

Children's preferences among the types of illustrations appearing in children's books have been studied only to a limited extent.

CREATIVE TEACHING OF LITERATURE

A good story or a good poem will stand by itself; it needs no embellishment.   Because this statement is obviously true, librarians and teachers sometimes frown on any activity that detracts from the story or poem being read to the children.

While the basic criterion for using any piece of literature *is* that it communicate effectively and beautifully, much can be done to develop children's taste in literature.   Today's children are exposed to much cheap, yet often impressive, writing.   They become confused when no attempt is made to help distinguish the difference between good and poor literature.   Children are not

6. Ibid., pp. 200–204.
7. Theodore Harris, "Reading," in *Encyclopedia of Educational Research*, 4th ed., ed. Robert Elbert (New York: The Macmillan Co., 1969), pp. 1069–1104.

FIGURE 4–2. *Using classroom materials, one child makes a mural of her favorite book,* My Friend Flicka.

born with a set of standards and values. These they develop as a result of the understandings they glean from their experiences. Setting conditions for the creative teaching of literature means that the teacher provides experiences that help each child to become more selective in his reading, more critical of the type of material he reads, and more sensitive to good writing.

Inasmuch as empathy is necessary in order to experience literature, and the ability to project oneself into any situation is dependent on one's own related experiences and feelings, it is not enough that children hear good literature in the classroom—they must *experience* it. This means that while sometimes the reading of a poem or story will suffice in itself, in most instances conditions must be set so that the children can experience or live the material being read. It is this additional attention paid to the "good" stories and poems that makes children realize they are special. By living and feeling the story with the characters, and by learning to express their own feelings in carefully chosen words, they come to see the skill of the author—and to appreciate the quality of the work. Through classroom experiences with literature, they build their own values and standards and learn to evaluate the writing of others.

In setting conditions for developing a love and appreciation for literature there are a few hints a teacher might follow:

1. *Remember that it is not only the plot that makes the story a good one; it is the way it is told.* Encourage the children to use the author's words as much as possible. Be sure that the Elephant's Child does not look only for the crocodile but for "the great grey greasy Limpopo River all set around by fever trees."

2. *Remember that children can interpret the author's words only in light of their own experiences.* Do not try to force your interpretation of a story on them. Let them dramatize or retell it in their own way. Although their interpretation may not be the same as yours, the retelling does give you an opportunity to correct gross misconceptions.

3. *Remember that enjoyment of the piece of work, not perfection of performance, should be the goal.* Should some child's or some group's contribution be exceptionally well-received, the class may work on it to "polish it up" for other classes or for parents. This should only happen occasionally, for polished performances take too long to prepare. Children should receive enjoyment from experiences with literature every day.

4. *Continually draw attention to phrases or words in the writing that make it unique or give special delight.* All over America children love to chant:

I meant what I said
And I said what I meant
An elephant's faithful
One hundred percent.[8]

or

Listen, my children, and you shall hear
Of the midnight ride of Paul Revere —

and

"The time has come," the Walrus said —

and

Speak for yourself, John

and

Fourscore and seven years ago

Phrases lifted from literature are as much a part of life as learning itself.   To know them is part of the children's rightful heritage.

The teaching of reading and the enjoyment of literature go hand in hand.   In skill-building reading periods, children learn the tools needed to unlock the joys concealed in the world of books.   Children come to school with a reservoir of literature of some kind in their background.   Much of this can be used to teach reading.   Miss George, for instance, printed the favorite phrases of her children on a chart before the room, and the children learned to read them the way they learned to read an experience chart.

The first reading chart composed by the class may well be their first experience at composing literature.   A sensitive teacher will make certain that these first charts *are* good literature, simple as they may be.   A good program in the enjoyment of literature and poetry may grow out of the first compositions of the children.   The account of the stories composed by the slow first grade in Chapter 2 shows how a lead is provided for the teacher to read *The Fir Tree* and other related stories.   The chart about

8. From Dr. Seuss, *Horton Hatches the Egg.*   Copyright 1940, 1968 by Dr. Seuss.   Reprinted by permission of Random House, Inc.   Reprinted in British Commonwealth by permission of Wm. Collins Sons & Co.

the bus driver (described in Chapter 3) was the teacher's cue for reading *The Little Red Automobile* and other stories. As soon as children write their own stories, the stories may be placed on charts and read and enjoyed by other children. Every topic suggests a work of literature or a poem that will help children understand the power of effective communication. An understanding and appreciation of good literature develops most readily when children write their own and then discover that others enjoy the power of expression through words.

SUMMARY

No reading program is complete without a planned parallel program for the enjoyment of literature. All the language arts become meshed in a final product when children write their own literature and read the effective writing of others. All the teaching of listening, speech, oral expression, reading, and handwriting skill is directed to this end. None of the teaching of any of these skills of communication is of any substantial value unless it results in the application of the skills in effective writing for oneself and enjoyment of the writings of others.

The teacher may develop an appreciation for literature in her classroom through these techniques: (1) exposing children to good writing; (2) using literature creatively as a tool for teaching other subjects; (3) carrying on discussions that emphasize style above plot; (4) integrating literature with subject matter; (5) making literature relevant to children, and (6) encouraging the children to create their own literature by having a program in creative writing run parallel with a program in developing appreciation in literature.

Special conditions must be set in the classroom for the creative teaching of literature.

TO THE COLLEGE STUDENT

1. Using the criteria stated in this chapter for good children's literature, bring a collection of children's books to class and evaluate them. Which books do you feel are especially creative or contribute to children's creative development?
2. Discuss the following questions in class:

    a. What part do picture books play in a literature program? Are picture books good literature?

    b. How does television contribute to an appreciation of good literature in children?

    c. What makes a classic in children's literature?

    d. What authors do you remember from your childhood? What authors do children currently enjoy?

    e. How can literature develop creative components of the intellect?

3. Plan a social studies unit that you could teach entirely through children's literature.

4. Read *Island of the Blue Dolphins,* a Newbery Award book by Scott O'Dell, and discuss all the ways you can think of in which it could be used in the classroom in connection with various areas of the curriculum.

5. Design and illustrate a children's story or book. Try it out on children and note their reactions.

6. Set aside a short period of time in class, and ask one student each session to read a child's book or story. Rediscover for yourself the delightful world of children's literature.

7. Have each student make a list of the books he remembers from his childhood. Make a composite and note which books were enjoyed most by the members of the class. Check your favorite books against the favorite books of children today. How well has your choice withstood the element of time?

8. Assign some members of the class to select passages from current literature, both good and poor. Have each member read one of his selections without naming the source. Ask the class members to rate the passages on the following basis:

    a. Excellent piece of writing (good literature)

    b. Good piece of writing (fair as literature)

    c. Fair piece of writing

    d. Poor writing (poor literature)

After all passages have been read and rated, expose the sources. Can you identify good literature?

TO THE CLASSROOM TEACHER

1. Examine your daily program for the past week and notice the amount of time you spent on children's literature. Do you have a well-balanced reading program?

2. Examine your classroom and note the stimuli you have provided for interesting children in literature. Are you doing enough? How can you do more? How can you get the chil-

dren to help?   Have you provided materials on many reading ability levels?

3. Observe the books your children cherish.   What clues does this observation give you for creative teaching in your classroom?

4. Outline a plan for teaching the history of the United States through the use of children's literature.

5. Think of all the ways you can teach art through the use of children's literature.

6. Collect specific stories from children's literature that lend themselves to: (a) the building of values, (b) the solution of children's problems, (c) the development of appreciations, and (d) the development of empathy.

TO THE COLLEGE STUDENT AND THE CLASSROOM TEACHER

1. Collect specific stories from children's literature that lend themselves to interpretation through puppetry, dramatization, dance, pantomime, shadow plays, and music.

2. Discuss these questions and statements together:
   a. To what degree should a teacher impose her standards for good literature on children?
   b. By what techniques can a teacher develop good literary taste in children?
   c. The filming of children's classics often destroys children's joy in reading the books.
   d. The violence on television is no greater than that to which children have been exposed in such stories as *The Red Shoes, Hansel and Gretel, Grimm's Fairy Tales,* and *Red Riding Hood.*
   e. Children today do not seem to have much use for poetry. Boys, in particular, regard the reading of poetry as "sissy." How might this specific characteristic be identified with creativity?
   f. The lack of an appreciation of poetry by elementary school children is caused by the fact that it is not a part of the general school curriculum in most schools today.

3. Some literature written for children is appreciated more by adults.   Can you find such books?   How do you explain their popularity among adults?   Read some to children and note their reactions.

4. Make a list of all the children's books or stories you remember that you did *not* like as a child.   Why did you *not* like them?

Check them against the criteria for good literature stated in this chapter and decide whether or not they could be classified as good literature. Reread some of these stories now and see if you still feel the same.

SELECTED BIBLIOGRAPHY

Adams, Bess Porter. *About Books and Children.* New York: Henry Holt and Co., 1953.

Allen, Patricia, comp. *A Catalog of 3300 of the Best Books for Children.* New York: R. R. Bowker Co., 1963.

Anderson, William, and Patrick Groff. *A New Look at Children's Literature.* Belmont, Calif.: Wadsworth Publishing Co., 1972.

Arbuthnot, May Hill. *The Arbuthnot Anthology.* Palo Alto, Calif.: Scott, Foresman, 1961.

Arbuthnot, May Hill, Margaret Mary Clark, and Harriet Geneva Long. *Children's Books Too Good to Miss.* 4th ed. Cleveland: Western Reserve University Press, 1963.

Arbuthnot, May Hill, and Zena Sutherland. *Children and Books.* 4th ed. Glencoe, Ill.: Scott, Foresman, 1972.

Carlson, Ruth Kearney. *Literature for Children: Enrichment Ideas.* Dubuque, Ia.: William C. Brown Co., 1970.

Chambers, Dewey W. *Children's Literature in the Curriculum.* Chicago: Rand McNally, 1971.

Clark, Margaret M. *Keeping Up with Children and Books, 1963–1965.* Palo Alto, Calif.: Scott, Foresman, 1966.

Dalgliesh, Alice, and Annis Duff, comps. *Aids to Choosing Books for Your Children.* New York: Children's Book Council, 175 Fifth Ave., 1962.

Doyle, Brian. *The Who's Who of Children's Literature.* New York: Schocken Books, 1968.

Duff, Annis. *Bequest of Wings.* New York: Viking Press, 1961.

————. *Longer Flight.* New York: The Viking Press, 1965.

Eaton, Anne Thaxter. *Treasure for the Taking.* New York: Viking Press, 1957.

Fenner, Phyllis. *The Proof of the Pudding: What Children Read.* New York: John Day Co., 1957.

Fisher, Margery. *Intent upon Reading.* New York: Watts Publishing Co., 1962.

Georgiou, Constantine. *Children and Their Literature.* Englewood Cliffs, N.J.: Prentice-Hall, 1969.

Gillespie, Margaret. *Literature for Children: History and Trends.* Dubuque, Ia.: William C. Brown Co., 1970.

Huck, Charlotte S., and Doris Young Kuhn. *Children's Literature in the Elementary School.* New York: Holt, Rinehart and Winston, 1968.

Jacobs, Leland B., ed. *Using Literature with Young Children.* New York: Teachers College Press, Columbia University, 1965.

Johnson, Edna, Evelyn R. Sickels, and Frances Clarke Sayers. *Anthology of Children's Literature.* 4th ed. Boston: Houghton Mifflin, 1970.

Ladley, Winifred C. *Sources of Good Books and Magazines for Children.* Newark, Del.: International Reading Association, 1970.

Lanes, Selma. *Down the Rabbit Hole: Adventures and Misadventures in the Realm of Children's Literature.* New York: Atheneum Press, 1972.

Larrick, Nancy. *A Parent's Guide to Children's Reading.* Columbus, O.: Charles E. Merrill Publishing Co., 1960.

———. *A Teacher's Guide to Children's Books.* Columbus, O.: Charles E. Merrill Publishing Co., 1963.

Nelson, Mary Ann. *Comparative Anthology of Children's Literature.* New York: Holt, Rinehart and Winston, 1972.

Reasoner, Charles F. *Releasing Children to Literature.* New York: Dell Publishing Co., 1968.

Robinson, Evelyn R. *Readings about Children's Literature.* New York: David McKay Co., 1966.

Sayers, Frances Clarke. *Summoned by Books.* New York: Viking Press, 1965.

Smith, Lillian E. *The Unreluctant Years.* Chicago: American Library Association, 1963.

Strang, Ruth, Ethlyne Phelps, and Dorothy Withrow. *Gateways to Readable Books.* New York: H. W. Wilson Co., 1958.

Walsh, Frances. *That Eager Zest.* New York: J. B. Lippincott, 1961.

Ward, Martha E., and Dorothy A. Marquardt. *Authors of Books for Young People.* New York: Scarecrow Press, 1964.

Whitehead, Robert J. *Children's Literature: Strategies of Teaching.* Englewood Cliffs, N.J.: Prentice-Hall, 1968.

PART 2

The Nurture of Creativity Through Reading and Literature

My six-year-old came bouncing down the stairs, all scrubbed and starched. Her eyes gleamed with anticipation, her face glowed in animation. She looked good enough to eat, and it was with considerable restraint that I suppressed a wild desire to crush her to me in a joyous shower of affection.

She was going into the first grade, and this was the first day of school.

"Would you like some cereal this morning?" Mother asked.

"Yes," she answered.

Mother put the cereal box on the table with the bowls. At the very top of the box in small print were the directions for opening it. Patty pointed to it and looked at me. "See that?" she said.

"Yes."

"Well, when I come home today I'm going to be able to read it!"

Such are children's aspirations and expectations on their first day of school. What miracles they expect from teachers! Charlie's teacher knew how to meet this challenge to a degree. Unfortunately, many teachers do not. They squelch the child's aspirations for himself and substitute their mediocre aspirations, which are contrived for the average children in a group. Isn't there a way to keep this joy for learning alive? I believe so.

Excessive conformity serves as an anticatalyst to the development of creativity. I recognize that many of the skills necessary for effective reading mentioned in Part One of this volume must be taught through conforming, convergent thinking processes. But I also feel that the conformity suggested by our current reading programs has been exploited to excess with the damaging result that children have suffered in their attitudes toward reading and in their acquisition of the necessary skills for reading. I am convinced that intelligent teachers could find more creative methods of teaching these skills to children and have more rewarding results if they were not inclined to follow preconceived methods so religiously.

It is with this conviction in mind that I have chosen the material for Part Two. This material does not suggest a step-by-step development of a reading program. Because of space limitations I have attempted to show, instead, how several of the creative teachers I have observed have effectively taught the necessary skills by encouraging the children to use their own creative abilities.

I have chosen to include, as much as possible, illustrations that demonstrate one or more of the principles of creative teaching outlined in Chapter 1. These illustrations are concerned not only with the development of necessary reading skills, but also with the development of divergent thinking processes—and, consequently, the development of creative powers in our boys and girls.

CHAPTER V

The Creative Teaching
of Beginning Reading
in the Primary Grades

. . . A molehill can be a mountain to a sparrow. . . .[1]

RUMER GODDEN

TO THE READER

The concept of *reading readiness* grew out of the studies of the
child development psychologists who came to realize that the
acquisition of certain skills and abilities resulted from maturation
and that practice, as such, before the appropriate developmental
age was reached was apt to be of little value and might even
damage the child.   Examine some current readiness programs.
Do they promote this concept or have they wandered from it?
Make a list of the skills children need in order to be able to read.

INTRODUCTION

Mr. Cline's purposes became clear as he developed his lesson in
the first-grade class I was observing.   I listed them in my notebook as follows:

As a result of this lesson the children will:

1. understand the concepts of the words *wonderful* and *beautiful*
    as evidenced by the many ways they use these words in their

1. Rumer Godden, *An Episode of Sparrows* (New York: The Viking
Press, 1935), p. 204.

speech, in forming new vocabulary phrases, and in using them in a book of their own creation.

2. add new words to their sight vocabulary as evidenced by the charts they form using words that describe certain sensory experiences and by their ability to later read these words on individualized sight cards.

3. extend their skills in phonics by dealing with rhyming words as evidenced in a poem they create for their new book.

4. develop creative writing skills as evidenced by the stories and poems they write together to make a class book and the stories and poems each writes individually on his pages for the class's "big" book.

5. have a meaningful, integrated language arts experience (having new sensory experiences, expressing them in oral vocabulary, expressing them in printed symbols, reading the printed symbols, and then using the experiences in personal creative writing) as evidenced by each child's behavior during and following the afternoon's language experience.

6. have practice in reading to an audience as witnessed by their reading of material containing the new words on individualized reading cards.

7. review the phonics already known as evidenced by their oral contributions to the phonics charts and their written contributions to the books (compound words, rhyming words, initial sounds, and common suffixes.)

Mr. Cline had set conditions for his reading class by setting up a tape recorder. He had also placed on the chalkboard tray two cardboard book covers, one bright green and one bright red. Each was hinged along the left border with masking tape so that it opened easily like a big book and was clamped to a cardboard of the same size, which served as a back cover. Neither book contained any pages. On the cover of the red book he had printed the words "BEAUTIFUL, BEAUTIFUL," and on the cover of the green book he had printed "WONDERFUL, WONDERFUL." Several large sheets of chart paper were taped to the chalkboard above the books. The children, returning from lunch, were eager to know what they were going to do with the materials at the front of the room.

Mr. Cline held up the book covers. "Today we are going to work with two words, and I have printed them on the covers of these two books. Can anyone read them?"

Some children could. So the words were read, and a discussion was held about their meaning. Many children told of beautiful things and wonderful things they had experienced. At the close of the discussion Mr. Cline said, "Let's make a list of all the beautiful things we have discussed and put the words on this chart paper."

The list read like this: *mother's roses, a sunset, my puppy, my mother, our school, my doll, a kaleidoscope, trees, flowers, paint, colors, baby sister, baby brother, my church, stained glass windows, music, bubbles, a rainbow.*

A similar list was made of the wonderful things children had experienced. Mr. Cline then continued, "I thought it would be a good idea if we had some beautiful and wonderful experiences together this afternoon, and I have brought in some things I want to share with you. First of all let's look at this picture."

Mr. Cline set a beautiful painting of a rural scene on the chalkboard, and the children talked about it. When Mr. Cline asked for words to describe the painting, the children offered many ideas, which he printed on the vocabulary chart.

"Now let's think about the word *wonderful,*" he said. "I have here three bags. Each has in it something wonderful to feel. I will pass the bags around and each of you may feel what's in them. Tell me how it feels and what you think it is, but do not peek at it."

The bags were passed around, and each child responded to Mr. Cline's directions. Words such as *fuzzy, warm, soft, cuddly,* and *tickly* appeared on the chart, along with such words as *kitty, toy dog, mouse, fur, hair,* and *rabbit,* as the children guessed the objects in the bag.

Next Mr. Cline asked the children to put their heads down on their desks and close their eyes. "There are wonderful things to smell," he said. "Breathe deeply and tell me what you think you smell or what the smell reminds you of." At this point he sprayed pine-scented air spray around the room.

Perfume, mother's roses, deodorant, flowers, shaving lotion, the woods, Christmas trees, cologne, and other words appeared on the chart. There were also phrases such as, "It smells like my Daddy when he is all dressed up to go out with my Mother."

Finally Mr. Cline said, "Keep your heads on your desks and open one hand. I will put something in your hand. Eat it, but do not look at it." He dropped a jelly bean in each upturned palm, and again a flood of words issued describing what it was and how it tasted: *candy, jelly beans, sweet, like perfume, good, sugar, sticky, crunchy, smooth, delicious.*

The children watched Mr. Cline print these words on the vocabulary chart.

FIGURE 5–1. *Mr. Cline's props for a meaningful, relevant reading*
experience.
A beautiful oil painting to see
A wonderful bag of jelly beans to taste
A beautiful scent to smell
A wonderful ball of yarn to feel.

FIGURE 5–1A. *Some of Mr. Cline's highly relevant homemade*
reading materials.
The wonderful *book*

FIGURE 5–1B. *The* beautiful *book.*

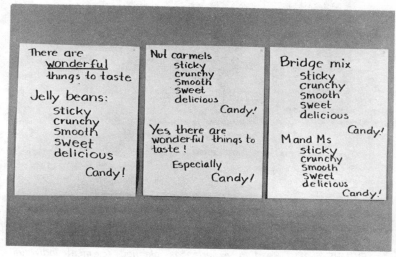

FIGURE 5–1C. *Pages from the* wonderful *book.*

FIGURE 5–1D. *Reading experiences planned to meet individual differences yet to teach the words* wonderful *and* beautiful.

Beautiful light!
Wonderful sight!
Goodbye night!

Soft, soft kitten
Furry and white
Soft, soft kitten.
A beautiful sight!

Mother bird.
Sings away
Beautiful babies!
Wonderful day!

Look, it is morning
And all I can see
Is a beautiful house
And a beautiful tree.

163

"I am going to print a sentence at the top of each of these four pieces of chart paper here on the chalkboard," he said. "See if you can read them."

On each of the four pieces of paper he printed the following sentences:

There are beautiful things to see!
There are wonderful things to feel!
There are beautiful things to smell!
There are wonderful things to taste!

"Now, let's look at all these words we have used today and see if we can write a story or poem under each of these titles. We may want to use other words besides the ones we have put on our vocabulary chart, and we may want to rhyme some of our stories. Think for a while, and then share your ideas with all of us."

Soon the four stories were composed; two of them appear below:

There Are Beautiful
Things to See

Mother's roses yellow and red,
Baby sister in her bed.
A rainbow in the sky,
A puppy running by.
Bubbles in the air,
The ribbon in Mary's hair.

There Are
Wonderful Things
to Smell

Shaving lotion.
Mother's flowers.
Perfume.
Fires burning.
Cakes baking.
The woods.

Mr. Cline then read the stories to the children, using a liner. They then read the stories together and put them on the tape recorder. During the playback, the children read silently from the originals.

A discussion of new words followed. Compound words like *sunset* were utilized to develop the concept of compound words. The rhyming words *red* and *bed, shy* and *by, air* and *hair* were analyzed for phonics development and the application of initial consonant sounds to common endings.

"I wonder how many of you have learned to read some of these words—especially the new ones," Mr. Cline continued. "I have used many of these words and some others to make up new stories you have not read before. I shall pass them out, and you will read them silently. There is a beautiful or wonderful picture to go with each story. If you have trouble reading any of the words, raise your hand and I will come to help you. As soon as each one of you can read your story, you will show the picture and read the story to the rest of us."

Mr. Cline had pasted attractive pictures from magazines and books to large cardboards. He had printed a story to go with each picture. Some had very simple words and sentences, while others had complex ones so that every child, from the lowest ability reader to the highest, would have a story to read. Each story contained either the word *beautiful* or the word *wonderful*.

The simplest stories were one-line ideas that accompanied a lovely picture and said simply "Beautiful baby!" or "Beautiful tree!" The next most difficult was a beautiful picture of a piece of colored burlap. The story read, "Cloth is beautiful." The third was a picture of a United States Marine in full-dress uniform, and the story said, "He feels wonderful!" A colored picture of the Chicago skyline was accompanied by the phrase, "Beautiful, wonderful city!" One picture of a sunrise was accompanied by, "Beautiful light! Beautiful sight! Good-bye night!" A picture of a tree in a farmyard in the early morning had a poem that went:

> *Look, it is morning*
> *And all I can see*
> *Is a beautiful house*
> *And a beautiful tree.*

A more difficult story, which went with another picture of a sunrise, read as follows:

> *This is a beautiful shining day.*
> *It is before breakfast.*
> *The rooster is not up.*
> *The children are not up.*
> *Mother is not up.*
> *Get up, rooster!*
> *Call the children!*
> *Call Mother!*
> *Tell them to see the beautiful, shining day!*

The children enjoyed reading the stories to each other. Then Mr. Cline drew their attention back to the two books with which he had introduced the afternoon's work.

"You will notice," he said, "that these books have no pages in them. I have pages ready that will fit the books, but they're all blank. I am going to give each of you two pages. On one, make something beautiful or wonderful with your crayons. On the other page, write a story about the thing you drew. Then we will read them to each other and put them between the book covers. Use as many words as you want from our list on the vocabulary chart. I will help you with words that are not there. You may want to make poems or stories. Do it any way you like. Go!"

The children who finished first were asked to read a new sentence that Mr. Cline had printed on the board. It said, "There are beautiful and wonderful things to *hear!*" Then they were challenged to draw pictures and write stories for that concept.

This lesson is the essence of creative teaching. It breaks away from stereotyped methods of teaching vocabulary, word recognition, word-attack skills, structural analysis skills, phonetic analysis skills, and the typical sequence of manual-type teaching.

Mr. Cline's plan blasts the theory that children of differing abilities must meet in small groups or other individualized grouping plans every day for reading instruction. Reading in Mr. Cline's room is taught through the natural sequence of language development; children and their spoken vocabularies come first in the process—individual differences are met through the adaptation of the *materials to the children,* not the children to the materials, as so many of our current reading systems demand.

A review of Mr. Cline's objectives as I wrote them in my notebook shows that *each* was met, and met well. An integration of the teaching of language skills makes possible the meeting of multiple objectives so often *not* accomplished when reading experiences are isolated from other language experiences.

A check with Chapter 1 will show how Mr. Cline's afternoon with the children followed the basic principles of creative teaching. His teaching considered individuals, and he accepted all individual contributions. Individual and unique products resulted from his work. Divergent thinking processes were balanced with convergent thinking processes. Open-ended situations were used. At times during the lesson, children faced the unknown, and they created. The process of reading, writing, and teaching elicited the creative products from the group and from individuals within the group. The experiences were success-oriented, problem-solving techniques were employed, skills were developed, words and objects were manipulated and explored, and democratic processes were used.

The lesson was evaluated by the performance of the children, by their obvious enthusiasm for their work, and by the creative products in the group work and in the pages each child made for the two books.

The material that follows contains ideas that may provide some motivation for the teaching of reading in ways as creative as those used by Mr. Cline.

THE READINESS STAGES

In Chapter 2 the various stages in learning to read and the instructional tasks of the teacher were defined. The components of each stage were discussed. These stages are elaborated in the material below.

Children Must Have a Desire to Read

The desire to read can fire a child to explore the reading process and the structure of language so that creative teaching can follow. The first step in the creative teaching process is creating such strong motivation in children that they are almost driven by a passion to learn. Teachers must regard reading as problem-solving and regard the building of a strong desire to read as a motivational-involvement process.

The teacher sets conditions for all reading by making clear to the children the *need* for reading and the joy that comes from being able to read. Some ways teachers can do this follow:

1. Read to the children every day for enjoyment. Let them experience the fun in books.

2. Use books frequently to look up material for them. When children see the teacher use books to identify objects or to find out about them, they will want to learn how to use books too.

3. Keep many picture and simple storybooks around the room where they will be easily available to the children.

4. Keep bulletin board exhibits, displays, book jackets, and peg-board exhibits of good books in your classroom all the time. (See Chapter 8.)

5. Use books and stories as the basis for puppet shows, dramatizations, shadow plays, roll movies, and various other activities, as described in Chapter 8.

6. Make simple books of children's experiences. They can contain paintings, magazine pictures, and simple stories or sentences.

7. Letter notes and messages to the class on the board. List on the board questions children ask. Though the children cannot read them, the teacher can read them to the children, who will come to recognize the value of reading and writing as a method of keeping records.

8. Use the immediate school environment fully. Take children on simple trips to observe the fall foliage, to hear the sounds on the playground, and to observe the play equipment and possible science resources in the school yard. Use these trips as an experiential background for making simple picture books when the class returns to the schoolroom.

Children Must Develop the Ability to Listen

Basic to all teaching in reading is listening ability. Any child who cannot hear the difference in gross sounds is not ready to read, for he cannot hear differences in sounds such as /m/ and /n/.

The Nature of Listening. There are basically four types of listening:

1. Attentive listening
2. Appreciative listening
3. Analytical listening
4. Marginal listening

FIGURE 5–2. *Listening: an important part of reading.*

Attentive listening is the type of listening in which most distractions are eliminated and the attention of the listener is focused on one person or one form of communication, such as a radio broadcast, a play, a television show, a recording, a lecture, and a telephone conversation. Attentive listening is used in many natural ways in the classroom:

1. Preparing to hear the roll, preparing for a lesson, etc.
2. Getting directions for assignments
3. Making daily plans and organizing into groups
4. Listening to someone read in audience-type reading situations
5. Listening to announcements and reports
6. Watching dramatic presentations and puppet shows
7. Listening to lectures or presentations by the teachers
8. Listening to announcements and programs over the school's sound system
9. Listening to directions on the playground and in the gymnasium
10. Taking examinations
11. Taking notes
12. Searching for answers to questions in reading assignments
13. Listening to tape recorders
14. Learning rote poems and songs
15. Learning music and playing instruments
16. Participating in ordinary conversation
17. Participating in the show-and-tell period

Appreciative listening is the type used when one listens for enjoyment. Appreciative listening is not as concentrated as attentive listening. It is more relaxed, and the listener is in a less tense state. Children react to this type of listening in pleasant or emotional ways. Appreciative listening is used for the following activities:

1. Listening to musical or art recordings
2. Listening to radio and television programs for enjoyment
3. Listening to a play, puppet show, or other type of dramatization
4. Listening to a concert
5. Listening to stories or poetry being read
6. Participating in choral speaking

Analytical listening is attentive listening plus, because the listener is expected to respond in one way or another. Therefore, he thinks carefully about what he hears. Activities in which analytical listening is used naturally in the classroom are as follows:

1. Listening to solve arithmetic problems
2. Reading and discussing for the following reasons:
   a. To find specific points, such as "Why was the color blue important to the story?"
   b. To outline (for example, choosing the main scenes for a tape, as suggested on page 296)
   c. To select main ideas (for example, creating a title for a paragraph)
   d. To determine the true meaning of a word as it is used in a new context, such as "The metal on the space ship will *decay*."
3. Discussing social problems (for example, seeking a solution to a playground fight or solving problems through a school senate)
4. Participating in any discussion involving a decision, such as what day to go on a trip or which of two textbooks has the correct facts when the texts do not agree

Marginal listening is the kind of listening in which two or more distractions are present. Children listen to the radio while doing their homework, apparently with no ill effects. Marginal listening would be used naturally in the following instances:

1. Teacher provides music for the children as a background for creative writing.
2. Teacher plays music for rhythms.
3. Children paint to music.
4. Teacher counts while children learn a folk dance or popular dance.
5. Children plan together and then write the plans on a chart or the blackboard.

Setting Conditions for Listening. Listening can be taught creatively and with excitement. So often the teaching of good listening habits is interpreted as meaning a demand for attention or a demand for order. I have seen countless numbers of teachers wasting precious minutes standing before classes of children, waiting until everyone was ready, or waiting because "John isn't quiet." I have also seen teachers who receive immediate response for each listening experience the children are to have, and the children come to the experience eager and excited.

The teaching of listening involves the setting of proper conditions so that listening can take place. These conditions may be *natural* ones. Natural experiences are those in which the conditions present themselves, and the teacher makes almost no preparation because the motivation is so high that the children all listen immediately. On the other hand, conditions may have to be *contrived* by the teacher, who plans, constructs, and uses materials, situations, and gimmicks to motivate children to listen.

One excellent example of such a contrived situation involved the construction by first graders of actual "listening ears" to be worn only when listening was required. This contrived experience was a creative way to help children to approach the beginning steps of attentive listening—simply paying attention!

In the teaching of listening, certain important general conditions are necessary. Before each teaching situation, consider the following suggestions:

1. Be sure the physical conditions are properly set up. Remove all the distractions that you possibly can—both noise and movement. Make sure that chairs face the right direction so that eye strain and uncomfortable sitting positions are avoided. Place materials in a prominent place, and remove materials that are not to be used. Make sure that each child is comfortable and that he can see well.

2. Speak in an animated and interesting manner, as though you yourself can hardly wait to tell the children what you have to say.

3. Make sure that your speaking speed does not exceed the children's listening speed.

4. Help the children make up rules for good listening.

5. Help the children to understand what they have heard, in much the same way as you would check comprehension in a good reading lesson. Ask such questions as, "What did Bill tell us about?" (selecting main idea); "What was the first thing that happened to Bill?" (sequence of ideas).

6. Praise the children often for good listening. When children have followed your directions well, you enhance their motivation by saying, "Good, I am proud that you did such a good job! It shows that we all listened well!"

7. Be a good listener yourself. Teachers often half-listen to a child as their eyes roam around the room taking in all the other children at work. Develop the habit of looking directly at a child when he talks and responding specifically to him.

8. Avoid needless repetition, especially in giving directions. It is better to say, "Do all of you understand that?" than "Listen once more and I'll say it all over again." The child who thinks he has it correct (and most of them will) will not listen the second time. This discourages good listening. Teachers who know their children well will ask other questions such as, "Marcia, can you tell us what we do first?" Such questions will provide a check on the child who is too shy to say he doesn't

understand or the extroverted child who wants to repeat all the directions to his classmates.

9. Avoid needless demands of pupil attention. Instead, try using interesting gimmicks and devices to gain immediate attention.

10. Allow the children to talk.   Remember that most teachers talk too much!

11. Help children eliminate bad listening habits.   Make a list of the poor listening habits you notice in the children and show it to them.   Let the children help eliminate them, perhaps by listing ideas for their correction.

12. Do not place too much emphasis on regurgitative material.   To foster creative listening, seek to develop mental alertness in the children.   Attitude, or *set*, toward listening is important.   Often, children are required to listen for the purpose of reproducing what they hear.   More emphasis should be placed on encouraging them to *think* about what they hear.   Avoid overuse of these reproductive sets, and plan conditions for creative thinking sets.

13. Remember that different kinds of listening require varying degrees of attention.   Children can be helped to listen effectively if they are told at the onset of each lesson just how important the listening for that particular lesson is, *how* they can best listen to get from the lesson what they should, and what kinds of listening are needed for the lesson.

14. Above all, be sure that the child has something worthwhile to listen to—a valid reason for listening.

15. Present listening as a social courtesy, but explain that this is not the only reason or the main reason for good listening.

The preceding generalizations apply to all listening periods during the school day.   For the *creative* teaching of listening, others should be added:

1. In the creative teaching of listening, the teacher or the children use a unique or original idea to obtain from the children a required mental response, which sets the stage so that creative teaching may follow.

2. The creative teaching of listening not only develops the skill of listening among children, but also results in an unusual response or a unique product from the children.

3. The creative teaching of listening accents highly motivational tensions; the listening experience is planned in such a manner that tensions are built immediately in children so that

they want to listen. Little or no time is spent in waiting until John is ready or until all are quiet.

4. In creative teaching of listening, the motivational experiences are planned so that divergent thinking processes begin to take place at once. Emphasis is not placed on the attainment of any *one* answer. Consequently, the creative teaching of listening involves *all* children almost immediately (as shown in the opening situation in this chapter).

5. The creative teaching of listening uses many open-ended techniques.

6. The creative teaching of listening may require that some unique conditions be set.

7. Creative listening experiences are the motivational forces that build proper tensions so that creative teaching may follow. As such, they encompass or lead into the basic principles for creative teaching listed in Chapter 1.

Creative Teaching of Attentive Listening. Attention-getters get children ready for any lesson, but they should not be confused with actual lessons planned to develop attentive listening skills. Suggestions for the creative teaching of attentive listening follow.

1. Read stories that draw attention to the value of listening to sounds, words, letters, and sentences.

Examples: "Stories in *The Listening Book,* by Dan Safier; *Ounce, Dice, Trice,* by Alastair Reid; *The Listening Walk,* by Paul Showers; *Word Bending with Aunt Sarah,* by Al Westcott."

2. Use puppets. In the primary grades, the children may have a friend who comes to talk to them once a day. In one room it was Jo-Jo, the puppet. The teacher had made a laundry bag from colorful material. The laundry bag had a slit in the back through which she put her hand. Inside the bag lived Jo-Jo. Every once in a while Jo-Jo came out. He was shy, so he only whispered to the teacher, and she had to relate to the boys and girls what he said.

Jo-Jo always had a surprise in his bag. Some days it was a letter or an invitation from another class. Some days he had a new book or a new game or a new story. One day he had a packet of seeds to plant. On another day he had a note from the principal telling of the Halloween party plans. All the teacher had to do to get immediate silence was to stand by Jo-Jo's bag.

3. Put ten "sound" makers on a table. Fold a piece of cardboard to make a screen to conceal the items. Suggest to the children that they number a paper from one to ten. Call a num-

ber for each item and make the sound. Let the children write down what they think it is. Younger children may raise their hands when they know instead of writing their answers.

After this game has been played a few times, the teacher may ask the children to work in pairs and think up sounds they can use on the rest of the class. When a group is ready, a few minutes may be used each day to develop listening skills.

There are many illustrations of the creative teaching of listening in other books of this series.[2]

Creative Teaching of Appreciative Listening. The following activities will develop appreciative listening.

1. Play some beautiful records and have the children paint, draw, or fingerpaint while the music is playing. (This is also an example of marginal listening.) Suggestions: "Nutcracker Suite," by Tchaikovsky; "William Tell Overture," by Rossini; "Sleeping Beauty," by Tchaikovsky; "A Summer Place"; "Tara's Theme"; "Rhapsody in Blue," by Gershwin; and "Blue Star." A variation is to play the music, have the children listen carefully, and then have them draw, paint, or write what it means to them.

FIGURE 5–3. *Appreciate listening.*

2. James A. Smith, *Creative Teaching of the Language Arts,* 2nd ed. (Boston: Allyn and Bacon, 1973).

2. Have the children participate in choral speaking. It provides endless opportunities for careful listening so that children may work out patterns of their own.

3. Ask the children to listen to TV so that they can reproduce as closely as possible their favorite commercials or the opening phrases of their favorite shows. Then let the children change their selections to suit themselves.

4. Have the children listen to popular music in order to learn to do folk dances or ballroom dances.

5. Have the children interpret music by using simple rhythm instruments.

6. Courtesy is learned through listening. Have the children dramatize social courtesies such as introducing a man to a woman, introducing a child to an adult, conducting a club meeting, answering the telephone properly, and asking a girl to dance.

Creative Teaching of Analytical Listening. The following suggestions are for the creative teaching of analytical listening.

1. Have the children keep a diary over a given period of time wherein they list or draw all the sounds they can remember experiencing during the day. This helps them become aware of the sounds in the world around them.

2. Have the children listen to oral reading for the following reasons:

   a. To find a sequence of events and then list them for some purpose (for example, to make a scroll movie)
   b. To find details to support a statement (for example, "Read some phrases or sentences that show that Caddie Woodlawn was brave")
   c. To find emotional persuasion (for example, to select from newspaper articles emotion-packed words that influence the reader)
   d. To draw comparisons (for example, to make analogies, develop metaphor, and decide how characters are alike or not alike)
   e. To make judgments (for example, to read several facts and then decide on a solution to a problem)
   f. To find relationships (for example, to discover how places and people are alike or not alike, to draw parallels, to study situations)
   g. To make inferences (for example, to find passages that *suggest* ideas, such as "a world enveloped in white" to imply *snow*)
   h. To follow directions and instructions, as in making puppets or constructing scenery

3. Use motion picture films as the basis for creative listening assignments.   For example:

    a. How does the musical score help to tell the story?

    b. Look and listen for these three important facts. (List them.)

    c. How does the opening line of the film set the theme for the rest of the film?

    d. Toward the end of the film there is a line that tells the main theme of the whole film.   Can you find it?

4. Use records such as *Sounds Around Us,* by Scott, Foresman and Company Records for Developing Listening Skills, and *Listening Activities,* by RCA Victor Record Library for Elementary Schools (Volumes I–II).

5. Read a short paragraph containing several words that have the same or similar meanings.   Ask the children to pick out the words that have the same meaning.   Older children may write them down.

> *Example:* Soon the *little* man came to a *small* dining room.   He peered through the *tiny* door and saw a lovely, *petite* room all set up with *miniature* furniture. There were even *minute* dishes on the dining room table.

6. Ask children to listen to special sounds on their way to school and then list them on charts in the classroom in categories such as *beautiful* sounds (birds singing, music playing) and *loud* sounds (the backfiring of a bus, the blaring of a radio).

Creative Teaching of Marginal Listening.   Marginal listening can be developed through these activities:

1. Use a series of pictures that describe an event or a process, such as frosting a cake, making a valentine, or carving a jack-o'-lantern.   Tell about the picture, but omit one of the steps and have the children find the step omitted.

In the upper grades, the same procedure can be followed using words without the pictures.

2. Riddles are fun.   Children can create their own.

3. Take the children on a field trip around the school to listen to all the sounds around them .

4. Run a short cartoon film, then shut off the sound and have the children tell the story or reproduce the speaking parts while the film is rerun.

5. "Musical Chairs" is a good marginal listening game.

Children Must Develop a Large Oral Vocabulary

Creative children are fluent in verbal expression. One way to develop creativity in children through the teaching of reading is to develop oral fluency in all children. A summary of some of the ways previously suggested to bring this about in the kindergarten and primary grades appears below.

1. Encourage the children to tell stories about pictures, experiences, news items, original drawings, and so forth.
2. Also have them retell stories (vary them by having one child tell part of a story, another child continue it, and still another finish it).
3. Have the children listen to stories and poems on recordings, on television, and on tapes.
4. Plan activities with the children (trips, parties, and so forth).
5. Hold class discussions (science, nature study, and such).
6. Encourage children to report on facts—something new learned.
7. Plan for the children to meet and converse in groups.
8. Provide a time to note and tell "number" stories.
9. Provide first-hand experiences ("scuffle in leaves"). Think of words to describe them.
10. Make lists of various schoolroom activities with the children and use them as reference.
11. In sharing time, make up and answer riddles with the children.
12. Encourage children to use different words that mean the same thing (*nice day, lovely day*).
13. Learn opposites (*night, day; come, go*) and make charts with the children.
14. Sing songs together.
15. Listen to records, songs, stories and poems with the children for a variety of specific objectives such as listening for expressions used.
16. View movies and film strips, and discuss them together.
17. Praise children when they use good descriptive words.

    Example: "Peter said, 'The milkweed seed is fuzzy.' Fuzzy is a good word."

18. Display posters about coming events, and discuss them together.
19. Encourage children to label some pictures and books for exhibit.
20. Change the end of a story they have heard. Attempt to motivate their creativeness in making a new ending.

177

21. Start an original story and have children think of an ending.
22. Confront children with problem situations whose solution involves real life experience or activities.
23. Introduce games with speaking parts.
24. Have children compose "thank you" notes and "invitations" orally and then print them on the chalkboard.
25. Use finger plays, for teaching rhythm, expression, etc.
26. Record experiences of trip taken.
27. Have "Show and Tell" periods.
28. Have children dictate stories about their own pictures, experiences, or interests.
29. Read bulletin board announcements, notices, labels, captions, titles of books, signs, and action words to children.
30. Make charts of all kinds:
    a. Word charts (words from projects, books, TV, films, conversation, etc.).
    b. Phonics charts.
    c. Picture charts.
    d. Color charts.
    e. Experience charts.
    f. Weather charts.
    g. Our helpers.
31. Encourage students to make individual picture and word booklets.
32. Have each child make a picture dictionary and a card catalogue.
33. Help the children learn to recognize known words in different context through diversified activities.
34. Allow each child to tell news of his own, or something he has read and heard.
35. Dramatize and pantomime stories with the children.
36. Suggest that children imagine experiences. (How does a small chicken feel when you touch it? Soft, fluffy, warm, cuddly.)
37. Discuss current events, holidays, and things observed in newspapers, magazines, environment, and such with the children.
38. Help your class exchange gift boxes with children in other parts of the country. (Gifts sent from Florida: coral, conch shell, coconut shell.)
39. Associate words with pictures for children.
40. Have children learn words having more than one meaning.
41. Use many word associations, such as, "If you were near a pond what might you see?" (duck, tall grass, trees) "What might you hear?" (rippling water, frogs croaking).
42. List beginning, middle, and end of words, and find likenesses and differences.

Children Must Develop the Left-to-Right Concept

Children do not easily acquire this skill. For the first six years of their lives, children observe objects by studying them from every angle and learn to recognize and name an object such as a chair from the front, from the side, from the back, from underneath or over the top. Then they are presented with reading material and must always remember to look at it one way: from left to right. Many ways of helping children develop this concept can be employed. Some children will have no difficulty with this skill, while others will need a great deal of practice.

1. Show children picture stories of four or five pictures in a sequence, placed from left to right. Have them tell the story by moving along from picture to picture. Point out to the children that we read words the same way—we go from left to right to get the story.

2. Comic strips use this technique and can be effectively employed in some instances. Comic strips with little or no reading are especially effective for this purpose.

3. Take particular care to write or print on the board, or on cards or charts, from left to right so that children will develop this concept through imitation.

4. After picture stories have been read, you can scramble the pictures and have children rearrange them in the correct order.

5. On dittoed sheets, draw two simple devices that children can relate by beginning at the left of the paper and proceeding to the right. For example, the picture of a mouse appears on the left side, the picture of a piece of cheese on the right. The teacher tells the children to take the mouse to the cheese with their eyes. Similar ideas would be to take the baby to the rattle, the dog to the bone, the kitten to the milk, and the block to the shelf.

6. Many primary reading-readiness texts and manuals provide interesting ways to develop this concept. Refer to the teacher's manual to locate such material. This is one way manuals can be of great value.

Children Must Develop Audio Acuity

In order to be able to read, each child must develop a sensitivity to sounds. An infant recognizes gross sounds such as the clanging of a bell, the honking of a horn, or the barking of a dog.   As his sense of listening develops, he is soon able to hum, showing he can differentiate pitch.   His hearing skill must be developed until he becomes sensitive to sounds in words that are very much alike—*men* and *man, catch* and *ketch.*   Finally he must develop a good ear for phonics training—a sensitivity to sounds themselves, such as /m/, /n/, /pl/, /ch/, /ā/, and /à/.   Many suggestions for developing listening skills are listed below.   Others may be found on pages 168–176.

1. Nursery rhymes may be effectively used to develop good listening, to improve speech, and as a beginning for choral speaking.   To improve audio acuity have children say certain nursery rhymes (especially those that are almost entirely direct conversation) in a variety of ways to indicate a mixture of emotions.   For instance, say "Pussycat, pussycat, where have you been?" angrily and have the children give the next line with the proper emotional tone.   Then try saying the same lines happily, sadly, coyly, fearfully, excitedly, timidly and anxiously.   Try this technique with other nursery rhymes, such as "Simple Simon" and "Where Are You Going, My Pretty Miss?"

2. Miss Frey used recordings a great deal to develop audio discrimination among her children.   She encouraged them to note likenesses and differences in the music by:

a. Pretending they were something tall whenever the music went high, and something short when the music went low.   She would stop the music and say "freeze," and some children then held the high or low pose while the others guessed what they were.

b. Doing rhythm patterns to the music.   On fast music they could run, skip, and fly.   Other music might suggest hopping, marching, and jumping.

c. Singing along with records (the children add motions to fit the voice interpretation).

d. Listening to instrumental records (as soon as a child hears a violin he begins to make the motions of the violin).

e. Reproducing the rhythm of the music by clapping, tapping, or snapping fingers.   These sounds can then be combined into a percussion rhythm without the record so that the children can sense a definite beat.

3. Miss Marcus often asked a question by singing it.   The children answered by singing a response that completed the musical tune that Miss Marcus had begun.   She took roll in this manner: she would sing, "Johnny Jones, Johnny Jones, are you here?

Are you here?" to the tune of *Frère Jacques* and he would answer, "Yes, I am, Miss Marcus. Yes, I am, Miss Marcus, here I am, here I am." After the children had used known tunes this way, they made up original ones.

4. Mr. Graves used singing finger plays with his children. Often the forefinger and the middle finger of each hand became the feet for imaginary dolls, and children made up dance steps on the tops of their desks with these "finger feet" to go with recorded music. The children also did small dramatizations of other songs and stories in this manner.

5. When children compose tunes on glasses, flower pots, or spikes of different lengths suspended from a board, it is easy for them to see that the taller the glass or the longer the spike, the higher the pitch. Experimentation with hitting all sorts of materials to determine the kind of sound it makes can lead to a classification chart and help children in refining their ability to recognize variances in pitch.

6. One of the best ways to help develop audio acuity is to provide a music center in the room where children can experiment with instruments. Drums, bells, xylophones, and rhythm instruments can all be played and classified for high, low, and in-between sounds.

7. Miss Ames used many of the traditional patterns of clapping and tapping, such as having the children repeat a pattern of claps and taps that she produced, to develop audio acuity. But she carried this into more creative activity when she asked the children to listen to music or to some sound outside the window and to repeat that sound by clapping or tapping in as many ways as possible. When the rhythm of claps was established, the children used it as a basis for building a clapping or tapping tune. Often various rhythms were combined to make a "clapping" band. At times, various tempos were combined as well as rhythms. Children reproduced their rhythm by striking wood, glass, or plastic. Later these sounds were combined to make percussion tunes.

8. Mr. Richardson taped sounds at home (the refrigerator, radio, telephone, shower), and the children had to guess what the sounds were. However, when a child recognized the sound he did not tell the others. He gave clues to help the others determine the sound. ("It is in the kitchen." "You make this sound every morning.")

9. Miss Yager took her children on "listening" walks where the children listed all the sounds they could hear. A walk around

the school made them sensitive to bird sounds, peepers, blowing wind, and rustling leaves. A walk along the street made them aware of cars whizzing by, horns honking, brakes screeching, and voices shouting. Even a walk down the school corridor made them alert to clocks ticking, typewriters clacking, dishes rattling, and balls bouncing. The children made up listening games in the classroom by "discovering" all the ways they could make noises and then having guessing games to see how many noises they could recognize while blindfolded. These included the sounds one makes by opening and closing a desk drawer, closing a closet drawer, stamping a foot, tapping a bell, closing a book, winding a clock, and bouncing a ball. Often these sounds were combined into a "sound" story (see *Creative Teaching of the Language Arts in the Elementary School*, 2nd ed.). The words to describe these sounds were always placed on a chart before the room.

10. Many of the hearing skills developed through music can be used to appreciate stories and poems. While reading poems, the teacher can have the children clap in as many ways as possible to fit the rhythm of the poem—the children can also be divided into groups, with each group clapping a different rhythm pattern. Some stories lend themselves to soft noises spoken in rhythm as a background for the reading of the story. Dramatization of the stories helps the teacher to point up likenesses and differences and sequences in the story. Sequence can also be developed by determining who speaks first in the dramatization, who speaks next, and so on.

11. As soon as children are able to rhyme words and note the similarities and differences of initial beginning sounds, the children can use cards in a variety of ways. Have the children go through old magazines and catalogues to find pictures to paste on three-by-five-inch cards or cards cut from chipboard. Beginning sounds can then be matched with the pictures on the cards. Each child takes ten cards. If the letter *d* is placed in the pocket chart, every child hunts through his cards to find words that begin with the /d/ sound and places them in the pocket chart under the *d*.

The game Shopping at the Supermarket adds variety to the above suggestion. Obtain a small shopping bag and have the children make picture cards as suggested above. Each child spreads his pictures out on his desk, which becomes the counter for which he is clerk. One child is chosen to be the shopper, and he takes the shopping bag. He says, "I am going to shop for all things that begin with a /b/ sound." He goes from desk to desk, and as he sees a picture he says, "Mary, I would like the butter and some bread please." If the shopper does not take *all* the cards on Mary's desk that begin with /b/ and Mary can catch him, he must give up the shopping bag and Mary takes over.

12. As soon as children can recognize the beginning sounds of their own names, have each make a chart on construction paper, printing the first letter of his name at the top. Under it he will put his name and then all the words or pictures he can find that begin with the same sound as his name.

13. Chart-making to categorize sounds is a worthwhile activity. Such charts may be on the following topics: Words That End Alike; Words That Start Alike; Words That Have the Same Middle; Names That Sound Alike.

14. Rhyming exercises are excellent for developing audio acuity. The teacher says, "What will I do if I spill the ink?" and a child must answer in a statement that rhymes, such as, "Wash your clothes out in the sink." Making original poems or rhymes, supplying missing rhyming words, making charts of rhyming words—all are good preparation for phonics exercises, and all help children develop audio acuity.

15. Play Barnyard Frolic. Assemble two sets of word cards with the name of one animal commonly found on a farm on each card, such as *dog, duck, goat, cat,* and *chick.* Print the word *barnyard* on one of the cards. The leader keeps a complete set of cards for himself and then distributes one card from the second deck to each player. When the leader holds up a card with the word *dog* on it, the child who holds the matching card must "bow-wow" like a dog, and so on. When the leader holds up the card with *barnyard* on it, each child must respond with the sound made by the animal named on his card.

Children Must Develop a Keen Sense of Visual Discrimination

Research shows that creative children have a particularly keen sense of visual discrimination. Thus, in developing visual discrimination, teachers are also helping a child to develop his creative powers.

First a child recognizes shapes of objects about him: a drum, a ball, a swing, an automobile. Then he notices differences between objects of the same or similar shapes: dull or shiny, sad face or happy face, brother or sister. He also develops the concept of related shapes at a very early age: large and small, big and tiny, long and short. To read, he must be taught to select the one shape that is different from the others, and eventually to see differences in word shapes, such as *mother* and *grandmother* and *on* and *no*. In the end he must discriminate between little shapes that are very much alike, such as an *o* and an *a* or a *b* and a *d*.

In a sense, all kindergarten activities are natural readiness experiences in visual perception. The work and play that children do with blocks give them the necessary experience they need to work later with shapes and objects. From their work with paints, clay, cut paper, finger paint, doll furniture, dolls, miniature furniture, toys, and other materials, they gain the experience and concepts essential to the beginning reading program. In this sense, the kindergarten program becomes a most important part of a child's formal schooling.

Conditions can be set for developing skills in visual discrimination in many creative ways:

1. Miss Martin often used her art period to develop a

FIGURE 5–4. *Elaboration of ideas and measures of visual acuity from Miss Martin's lessons with shapes.*

sensitivity to different shapes and the relationship between shapes. She saved all the odd pieces of colored construction paper from the children's art work. Several times a week she would give each child a piece of plain grey, buff, or white construction paper at the beginning of the day. Then she gave him one of the unusual colored shapes from her scrap box. The child could paste the shape on the plain paper and, using *any* medium, make something of it. Very creative and original ideas emerged from this activity.

2. As a variation of this activity, ask a clothier or clothing merchant to save his books of sample cloths for you. Tear out the swatches of sample cloth and use them the way Miss Martin used the scrap pieces of construction paper. Some of the cloth samples will have the texture of fur or will be beaded or brocaded. The additional quality of texture adds to the motivation for creating new relationships.

3. Some games help develop visual acuity. In the Change-the-Face Game, the teacher draws a large face on the chalkboard and hands an eraser and chalk to a child telling him that he may go to the board and *change* or *add* one new feature to the picture drawn there. The child in turn passes the eraser and chalk along to another child. Each change or addition changes the picture and helps children focus attention on one specific part of the total shape much as they will later need to focus on one line to see the difference between the printed *a* and *d*.

4. A variation in this game is to draw a scene on the board that is simply a background, perhaps a mountain and a tree. Each child must add something to the scene. In one class, so much had been added to the scene that the picture was nearly full, so one first-grader drew a tongue hanging from the dog's mouth—and the last six-year-old to draw in the scene drew a fly on the tongue.

This activity may be changed by having the children add to or change the scene as they did with the face in the preceding game.

5. Place several small, familiar objects on a table and cover them with a cloth or paper. Remove the cover, exposing the objects for a few seconds. Then replace the cover and ask the children to name as many objects as they can recall. Gradually increase the number of objects exposed. This game requires careful visual attention.

6. Describe some object and have the children guess what it is. For example: I am thinking of something little and white

FIGURE 5–5. *One teacher's handmade visual discrimination game. All plain shapes are scrambled. Then, children find the shapes that blot out the pictures.*

with long ears and a short tail and pink eyes. Have the children try to visualize the object while it is being described. Describe the clothes and appearance of some child until the children can guess who is being described.

7. Collages are excellent for helping children develop visual relationships. A box of junk (cloth, buttons, candy box papers, cellophane pieces, feathers, cotton, foil, pipe cleaners, and such) can be placed before primary children. From these they can make three-dimensional designs, thus focusing their attention on shapes and their relationships.

8. Walks to gather shapes may be taken as in the listening walk described above. Children collect leaves of various shapes, rocks, twigs, and so forth, mount them on charts, and study shapes. Pictures of objects in the community can be used to note likenesses and differences in shapes (mail boxes, traffic signals, fire alarm boxes, telephone poles). Duplicating various traffic signs is excellent for this, because children often learn to read the word painted on the sign by simply recognizing the shape of the sign.

9. Mr. Rhodes drew a triangle, a square, a rectangle, a circle, and a trapezoid at the top of a large piece of cardboard. The children then hunted for things in the room to fit these shapes. Under the circle they drew a picture of a clock, a thumb tack, a saucer, an ink bottle, a compass, and a telephone dial. Under the square they drew a window, a box of crayons, and a chalk box. Every day some child discovered a new shape to add to the chart.

10. Mr. Rhodes later handed out dittoed sheets covered with circles and asked the children to draw in each circle something in their classroom that fit that shape. The next day he again gave them a sheet of paper covered with circles and asked them to fill in as many things of that shape in their home as they could think of; the next day he asked for round things out of doors, and so on. Dittoed sheets covered with squares, triangles, rectangles, and other shapes were also given to the children. At the end of each day, the children shared their ideas.

11. Twice a week, Miss Ellis arranged a bulletin board on which she put pictures or a series of pictures that told a story; in each, a detail or one of the series was omitted. The sign at the top of the bulletin board said, "What is missing?" Children enjoyed searching for the missing details.

12. A variation of Miss Ellis's plan is to put a foreign picture into a series of pictures and ask, "Which one does not

belong in this story?" Comic strips are excellent for this purpose.

13. Classification games are excellent to help develop visual discrimination and a relationship between shapes and ideas. Children draw or paste pictures of animals or objects found in the home or other items. The teacher (or a child) makes a series of charts such as "Found at the Zoo," "Found at My House," and "Found at the Grocery Store," and the children match the object with the correct chart. Before children can read, a picture of an animal may be substituted for the word *zoo*, a house for *home*, and a store for *grocery*.

14. Find Me games are realistic. The teacher simply starts the game by bringing a book (or any other object) to the front of the room. She says, "Billy, find me a bigger book," and Billy does, while the whole class checks. Other directions, such as "Find me a brighter colored book," "Find me a prettier book," and "Find me a thicker book," sharpen visual acuity and build concepts for difficult words.

15. Comparisons in visual form may be made by matching mother with baby on a flannel board, a chart, or a pocket chart. Many tiny ducks, chickens, rabbits, and other animals are cut from construction paper and distributed to the children. The mother animals are placed before the class and the children match the babies with the mother. A more creative situation results when children are encouraged to make up stories in which the babies are mixed up to begin with but eventually get home to mother. Such books as *Whose Mother Are You?* are very appropriate for reading at this time.

16. Miss Fred made oak tag vocabulary cards cut to the shape of word configurations:

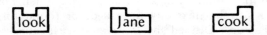

Words were compared for shape in terms of likenesses and differences.

17. Find likenesses or differences. The teacher can make many sets of "twin" cards with dogs, clowns, houses, boys, girls, cats, and so on. The game is to match all the twins to "make them happy." The games of Old Maid and Snap, where this kind of matching is developed, are excellent.

As a more complex step, the teacher can make many abstract designs with lines to help children to increase their ability to determine likenesses or differences. Again working from the simple to the more difficult, the first set of line cards may be made with the different line being a second color (two blue lines and one red). The difference could be in position, for instance, three vertical lines and one slanted line. The difference could be in the number of lines in each group. Each group should be kept together as a set. A more creative element enters the game when children design their own sets, trying to create some that have one card that is almost identical to the others but has one difference, for example.

18. Mr. Good used plain pieces of colored construction paper, which he held before the group. One child would rise when the red sheet was held up and say, "My sweater is red," and another would say, "My bow is red," until all the red objects in the room had been named, and then another color would be used.

19. Miss Farnsworth's group enjoyed a game called, I Went to the Window. A designated child went to the window, looked out, faced his group, and said, "I went to the window and saw a tree." The next child then repeated what the first child had said but added another object. This continued until one row or one group of children all had had an opportunity to go to the window. It is an excellent game for keeping a sequence and developing observation and listening powers.

20. Picture puzzles are always challenging and creative devices for building visual acuity. Enlist the aid of some children in the intermediate grades to make puzzles for the kindergarten. Appropriate magazine covers or pictures from calendars should be pasted on durable cardboard; tablet backs make good mounts. The puzzle should be weighted until the paste is dry. A number of pictures should be cut into two uneven parts. Other pictures should be made into puzzles of three or four parts. Each puzzle should be put in a separate envelope.

21. Set aside a box in which to put things that are used together. Encourage children to bring objects for this box. Pencil and tablet, plastic cup and saucer, doll's shoes and socks, can and can opener, hammer and nail, comb and brush will appear. The activity becomes more creative when unusual things are put together and the child is called upon to relate why. Jonathan put a picture of a cake and a dill pickle together "because," he said, "they are my favorite foods."

FIGURE 5–6. *Readiness materials for developing perceptions and visual acuity: swatches of cloth are pasted at random on paper and children are asked to make something from them.*

FIGURE 5–6A. *Imagination is brought into play when you make something from funny shapes and letters.*

Do You Know ???

Levels 1 and 2 in Room 103
Chestnut Hill Elementary
October 1968

FIGURE 5-6B. *Simple sentences ask riddles in the* Do You Know *book. If you don't know, a picture tells the answer.*

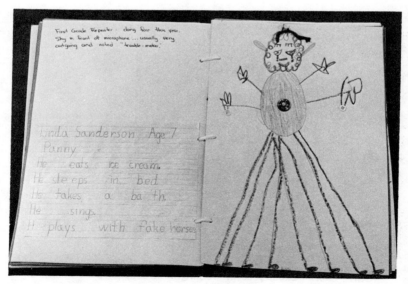

First Grade Repeater - doing fine this year.
Shy in front of microphone... usually very
outgoing and noted "trouble-maker."

Linda Sanderson   Age 7
Panny
He eats ice cream.
He sleeps in bed.
He takes a bath.
He sings.
H plays with fake horses.

FIGURE 5-6C. *The teacher asks, "What is your idea of a Panny? Draw one and we will write a story about it."*

FIGURE 5–6D. *The natural development of visual perception in the very young.*

FIGURE 5–6E. *Experience in working with shapes: perception development.*

22. A variation of the old fishing game may be adapted to many uses. Use a glass mixing bowl or fish bowl. The fish are made of construction paper. On them are mounted pictures that begin with different initial consonants. Place several staples on the heads of the fish. Make a pole with a stick or a pencil with a good magnet suspended from it. The game may be played with two children or a group. They take turns with the magnet to catch a fish. When a child catches the fish, he names the picture that is mounted on it (for example, "ball"). If he can give another word that "begins just like it" (such as "bed"), he can keep the fish. If not, he returns the fish to the bowl. The one with the most fish is the winner.

23. Play Wheel of Fortune Games. Make a large cardboard circle, or wheel, and mount pictures (such as a mitten, baby, cake, and door) on the outside edge. Place a spinner in the center of the wheel. Make a large chart of oak tag (12″ x 18″) showing pictures beginning with the same consonant sounds as the initial words of the pictures on the wheel. Make small circles of colored paper or use kindergarten beads.

Procedure: Child spins the spinner on the wheel. He names the picture where the spinner stops, finds a picture on the chart that "begins just like it," and puts a circle or bead on it.

Suggestion: A more difficult step is to omit the chart and have the child give another word that "begins just like" the one where the spinner stopped. Keep score of how many he got right with a colored circle.

24. No technique helps children hear and see ideas in sequence more readily than a roll movie, where favorite stories are discussed scene by scene. Each child is assigned to draw one scene, and all the pictures are then pasted on a roll of shelf paper and retold as a picture story. The retelling with the pictures helps children organize and remember details that went unnoticed with the first reading of the story.

Game approaches are especially useful with children who are under a great deal of stress, either from their environment or from their own failures in reading. Throughout the program of instruction in reading, games tend to relieve stress in some children and free them to learn. In addition, game approaches such as those mentioned above develop creative growth by increasing awareness, helping children see things in a different way, encouraging exploration and manipulation of objects and words, and demanding flexibility of thinking.

Children Must Develop a Comprehension Ability

Research on the creative personality has shown that creative children are more sensitive to problems than noncreative children are. They like to redefine and rearrange, to bring order out of disorder. They like to produce; they have strong intuition and identification ability. Since all of these skills are also part of the total concept of comprehension skills in reading, a teacher is also developing those aspects of creativity in children when she teaches reading. The mastery of comprehension skill is closely linked to a child's intellectual development and his ability to listen, to conceptualize, and to organize well. Many of the children's general activities can be used to check their comprehension ability in kindergarten and first grade; interpreting the main idea of a story; retelling a story with some specific questions by the teacher to check depth of comprehension; reacting to a story; interpreting a picture story in sequence; finding missing details in pictures and stories; following directions; anticipating endings in stories and poems; putting on finger plays; following sequence in games such as Looby Loo; and discussing material read to them.

Most of these activities are of the type that develop convergent thinking processes. Some that develop comprehension skills *and* creativity are making roll movies, as mentioned above; developing stories or story endings after a fragment of the story has been read; dramatizing stories or poems; pantomiming stories or making puppet plays or shadow plays from them; interpreting the ideas in a story by reading a sequence of pictures; and using the stories as a basis for making pictures, murals, dioramas, and other art work.

It has already been pointed out that much of the material used in commercial workbooks tends to jeopardize the child's creative development by giving him too many patterns to trace or imitate. Excess use of this sort of activity should be avoided. Instead of using exercises that say, "Draw like this," check comprehension in more creative ways. For example, the teacher might give the children these instructions: "Fold your paper into four, and number each box 1, 2, 3, 4. In Box 1 draw something that lives in a tree, in Box 2 draw the part of the story that was funny," etc. This gives the child the opportunity to apply his own creative powers and, at the same time, tells the teacher what she needs to know. (Some other examples were mentioned on p. 126.)

More samples of creative ways of checking comprehension in the primary grades follow:

1. Mrs. Arthur would ask the children questions that were not in the context of the story but could be answered if the children really understood the story.   For example: What season was it?   What time of day was it when Tom lost his cat?   Did Mary and Tom have any relatives living near?   Did they have any friends close by?

2. Many primary teachers have a discussion of important daily news from which a news chart is made on the chalkboard. This is an excellent beginning step in organizing material, choosing main ideas, recognizing proper sequence, and checking overall comprehension.

3. Miss Ellis printed a note for her boys and girls on the chalkboard each day.   At first she used drawings to communicate, but as soon as the children knew some sight words they appeared on the chalkboard.   One such note in the advanced stage said, "Dear Boys and Girls, Good morning.   Today we go to the library.   Please have your books ready."

4. Oral book reports, even from picture books, can help the teacher decide whether or not the child understands what he reads.

5. Miss Jones read stories to her children and then gave them dittoed sheets with three or four sentences about the story. The children put them in proper sequence.

6. Mr. Hayes cut out pictures and made a sentence to put under each one.   Then he mixed up pictures and captions to see if the children could put them together correctly.

Example: Picture of a grocery store.   *Caption:* This is where Mary buys her bread.

7. Make up a story and see if children can read it and then draw a picture to illustrate the story.

Example: Nancy likes the farm.   The sun is shining and the birds are singing.   She is playing ball with Joe.   She has on a green dress and black shoes.   Joe has on brown pants and a yellow shirt.   They also like to swing and go swimming in the pond.   It's such fun on the farm.

8. Mr. Farmer played a short cartoon film and cut off the sound.   The children had to tell the story from the pictures.

9. Film strips with no captions may be used in a similar manner to help build comprehension skills.

10. The construction of many kinds of experience charts helps children develop comprehension skills (see pages 204–215).

Many activities in the upper primary grades develop comprehension and creativity.   A few examples follow:

1. Miss Isaacs, who was using the individualized reading plan, encouraged her children to draw a series of pictures about their book or story and show it to the rest of the class in a miniature roll movie, using facial tissue boxes or shoe boxes as the stage for the movies.

2. The Matching Opposites game is always enjoyed by children. Shoestrings may be attached to a game card. The strings are threaded through holes next to the descriptions. The end of the strings, on the reverse side of the card, should be knotted to keep the strings from pulling out of the hole, and a piece of scotch tape can be used to hold them in place. The strings may then be threaded down to the correct answer.

A little boy   *A hot day*
A cold day   *A rich man*
A poor man   *A big boy*

3. Actual reading comprehension can best be checked when reading communicates—and once again charts of various kinds can be an excellent check on comprehension (see pages 204–215).

Children Must Develop Skill in Oral Communication

Many suggestions for developing oral expression skills in a creative manner were made in Chapter 5 of *Creative Teaching of the Language Arts*, 2nd edition.

A summary of the many suggestions from that book follows:

1. Collect the clever and often beautiful sayings of children, put them on charts, and use them for reading "thoughts." Such sayings as "The seeds are falling with parachutes" are a child's first attempt at literature. Mr. Smith heard one of his second graders make that statement after he blew a milkweed pod.

2. Help children to manipulate and classify spoken words by collecting them on charts with such headings as Soft Words, Heavy Words, Hard Words, and Beautiful Words. Bind the charts into book form as the pages become complete so that children may use them for reference material in their creative writing.

3. Use the Show-and-Tell period in a variety of interesting ways to stimulate oral discussion. Children generally use the

Show-and-Tell period to show interesting items from home or to tell of some exciting experience. But this period may also be used effectively for announcements, for discussions of current events or interesting ideas, for the presentation of a short dramatization for role playing, for short puppet shows, for reports and for demonstrations.

4. Hold discussions each day (perhaps during the Show-and-Tell period) on movies and television shows children have watched. Evaluate assembly programs, present book reports, and make plans during these discussion periods, remembering that words, to become meaningful, must be spoken before they are read.

5. Use audience-type reading situations each day where teachers read to children and children read stories, poems, letters, reports, and announcements to other children.

6. Dramatizations of all kinds encourage oral expression, especially impromptu dramatizations that are not read from a script. Role-playing a scene from literature, a fight on the playground, or an emotional or social problem can release a flood of new words spoken meaningfully in context. Writing and producing scripts, acting out telephone conversations, and reproducing scenes from stories are all aids to the development of oral expression. Inasmuch as the main purpose here is to develop meaningful vocabulary and good speaking quality, a finished product is of little consequence unless the dramatization is to be presented to parents or other children.

7. Television shows and radio shows, both real and pretended, also provide an excellent opportunity for practicing expressive and meaningful dialogue.

8. Loudspeaker systems in some schools serve as a means of helping children to use expression and to receive practice in speaking to groups. Mr. Alexander, the principal of a middle school, scheduled one group to present a short program at the opening of each day. This program included the flag salute, announcements, and something creative by the scheduled group or the individuals in it. Often this was a poem, a song, a choral poem, a short play, a dialogue on a school or current problem, or a short dramatization.

9. Assembly programs of many kinds are always valuable in developing creative oral expression.

10. Having children make tape recordings of stories, poems, songs, choral poems, and dramatizations helps them to improve thir speech habits because they can hear their own voices.

11. Reports by groups of individuals are good oral expression builders, especially when they are followed by discussion.

12. Panel discussions and debates not only provide the opportunity to use words but show the power of words as well.

13. Planning periods at the beginning of each day provide a situation where the teacher may introduce new, yet common, words such as *schedule, conference, assembly*, and *specialist*.

14. Many current games, such as Password, Truth or Consequences, and To Tell the Truth, encourage dialogue and effective oral communication.

15. Playing with words is an effective technique for developing creative oral expression. You can play with words to help children develop the concept of *describing* words.

> Write a story about the children and omit all the *describing* words. Draw a line in the place of each omitted word. Tell the children that you were asked to write a story about them for the newspaper and that you want them to help. Ask each child to think of a describing word. Tell them you are going around the class and will incorporate their word into the story in the order in which it is given (whether or not it fits). After this is done, an hilarious time can be had by the children in reading back the story.
> One such story is reproduced here. The capitalized words designate the adjectives given to the teacher by the group.

A Silly Story

> One FUNNY, SILLY *day in the* NUTTY *month of May, some* BRIGHT, *sixth-grade boys and girls met at the* FABULOUS *Mayville Elementary School to write some* SLOPPY *stories and* CRAZY *poems with their* BEAUTIFUL, ICY *teacher.*
> *The* MISERABLE *class and their* TERRIBLE *teacher had a* SOUR *time. They wrote some* CORNY *stories, some* STUPID *poems and drew some* MARVELOUS *pictures.*
> *When the afternoon was over, the* FAT *teacher got into her* FRUITY *car and drove home. Each of the* GORGEOUS *boys and girls took the* BUMPY *school bus back to their* FANTASTIC *homes and their* SICK *parents. It was a* REPULSIVE *experience to all.*

Once children have had this experience, they will want to write news accounts at home leaving out the describing words so that they may use them in class. This is a great deal of fun with Halloween stories and stories about individuals in the class, providing, of course, the children realize it is done for fun.[3]

16. The creative use of pictures can excite worthy oral discussion and introduce new words on the spoken level in a meaningful way. Teachers can find pictures that will draw from children words describing taste, touch, smell, sound, and feeling. Some pictures that show people with unusual expressions on their faces are useful for developing the imagination through questions such as, "What is this father looking at?" or "What does the baby see?"

Pictures can become good starters for stories or can fire the imagination of the child so that he creates a story of his own. A flood of dialogue can be created by partially covering some and printing below them such questions as "What is it?" and "What is happening?" Some pictures are excellent for encouraging open-ended thinking when the teacher asks such questions as, "What happened *before* this picture was taken?"

Magazines and advertising materials are filled with pictures of beautiful desserts, salads, and other enticing foods. Some of these pictures can bring out some imaginative prose or poetry when the label, "How does it feel to be your favorite dessert?" is attached.

Find pictures of people using one-way communication systems, such as a person telephoning, talking on TV, or using a public address system. Put captions such as these over the pictures:

"What is she saying to you?   Answer her."
"What is he saying?   Tell us."

Encourage children to take turns being the person in the picture and adding the sound to it. The label "Make a sound picture out of me" is a good one to use on a bulletin board with many pictures.

Find unusual pictures, pictures that are misty, or pictures that show a scene taken through a window during a rainstorm. Ask the question, "What words describe this picture?" Unusual words are needed to describe unusual pictures. Find pictures that tend, in themselves, to depict some quality such as strength, beauty, or joy. Use it to develop a specific vocabulary about specific parts of the picture.

17. Choral speaking affords every child the opportunity of

3. Ibid.

saying all the words aloud in a meaningful context.   It provides for creative expression, especially when the children's own poems and stories are used for the spoken material.

18. Chalk Talks are really an old, lost art but can be revived for the purpose of developing vocabulary and effective oral expression.   A few old books include some of the chalk talks popular years ago.   Some teachers have used an adaptation of this idea successfully as in the illustration presented below.

This technique is largely a matter of drawing common shapes on the chalkboard until some child "sees" something in it.   With chalk, Miss Sheckells made large red circles on a paper taped to the chalkboard.   "Boys and girls," she said, "I am going to put some pretty colors on this paper.   When they remind you of something, you raise your hand and tell me."   She applied yellow and red until Anne said, "It makes me think of a clown."

"All right," said Miss Sheckells.   "A clown it shall be.   And while I am making a clown out of my colors, let's think of a poem or story that tells about him.   I'll make him sad.   Maybe we could begin like this: Here we have a sad, sad clown."

She drew the mouth with the corners turned down and then put in a little, perky nose with black chalk.   "What can we say for our next line?" she asked, and Bobby said, "His nose turns up, his mouth turns down!"

"Good," said Miss Sheckells as she continued drawing. She drew the clown a hat and fancy buttons down his front. "Now what else can we say about him?" she asked as she drew large feet on him.

"His feet are big," said Dale.

"That's fine, and we can put another idea with that line," said Miss Sheckells.

"Well, his hands are wide," said Marcia.

"Very good," said Miss Sheckells, and she read the poem again.   "Perhaps we can add one more line that rhymes with "wide"—any ideas?   Why is he sad?"

Judy volunteered the answer, "His nose pulls off.   I know.   I tried."

> *Here we have a sad, sad clown*
> *His nose turns up, his mouth turns down.*
> *His feet are big; his hands are wide*
> *His nose pulls off.   I know.   I tried.*

19. *Sound stories* are very popular.   Sometimes children or the teacher can find stories such as *Gerald McBoing-Boing* or *The Tiger Hunt*.   Many other stories are equally effective when

FIGURE 5–7.   *Here we have a sad, sad clown.*

sound is added to them.   One library assignment for upper-grade children might be to find a story suited to sound accompaniment.

Often the teacher can set up a beginning situation to create a sound story, and the children can take it from there.   Putting such stories on tape contributes to their enjoyment because children hear the total effect better in the playback than they do while making up the story.

A sound story must be one that can have sounds added to it much the same way a round-robin story has words added to it.   Think of noisy situations to get your clue: a visit to a factory, the circus, the carnival, or a state or county fair; a living room with TV set, radio, hi-fi, and people talking; or a busy store.   Start a plot by having a main character enter this situation, and add to the plot by adding sounds as the plot develops.   Then have the children in the room add the noises until the whole story reaches a climax.

20. *Lap stories* are fun for all age levels.   Instead of simply telling a story, the teacher sits down in the middle of a group where all can see and holds a simple piece of wall board in her lap.   With a few props she tells or retells a story by acting it out on her lap board.   The one way a lap story differs from any other storytelling is that the teacher involves the children in the plot.

21. Telling stories by use of a *flannel board* is an excellent way for children to share words they know and to add new ones to their vocabularies.   Commercial cutouts can be used for flannel-board stories.   Old worn-out books provide a wealth of material.   Cut out the pictures and paste a small piece of flannel

on the back of each picture so that it will stick to the board. A new dimension in creativeness is developed, however, when children design and paint their own figures and symbols for use on the flannel board.

Flannel boards serve many purposes besides the telling of stories. Because children must *tell*-about the materials they are putting on the flannel board, vocabulary may be developed in all subject areas.

22. Real creativity is evidenced when children use the flannel board for their own creative work. The ultimate goal is to have children create their own stories and use their own ideas to present them.

23. Puppet shows, especially when written by the children, provide an excellent opportunity for children to speak and see their speech in written symbolic form. There are many kinds of puppets and many ways in which they can be used to develop good speaking habits and effective use of vocabulary.

24. *Shadow plays* provide another excellent way to introduce words into children's oral vocabulary. Here are some ways shadow plays may be used.

Hang a sheet before the room. Place a bright light behind it. Children can make simple shadow scenery by using cardboard or by simply cutting newspaper and pinning it to the sheet. Turn out the light to change the scenery. Be sure the children perform close to the sheet so that they will make clear-cut shadows.

Take a large carton such as a paper towel carton and cut a hole in it to represent a stage. Tape a piece of sheeting or unbleached muslin over the hole. Put a bright light behind the carton. Using the towel carton stage, encourage children to cut out cardboard figures and tape them to long wires. Wire coat hangers, when pulled straight, are excellent for this purpose. These figures can then be pressed against the muslin to create shadows without the operator's shadow showing. The operator must sit or stand behind the light that creates the shadow.

Cardboard figures can also be cut with a tab on the bottom so that they may be operated from beneath the carton simply by putting a slit in the back of the carton and pushing the figures up onto the screen, then moving them about by manipulating the tab.

A simple way to make scenery for this type of shadow box is to paint the scene with thick tempera paint or black flopen onto a heavy-grade Saran wrap. The scene can then be pressed firmly against the muslin, and it will stick. When the light is turned on, the paint or flo-pen ink casts a shadow, making a fixed scene against which the movable figures can act. This technique provides an easy way to change the scenery quickly.

Children Must Develop Skill in Concept Formation

The ability to understand concepts comes largely from experience with the use of words and their application to new situations. Many suggestions for concept development have been given in this book (such as the one at the beginning of this chapter). For other suggestions, see *Creative Teaching of the Language Arts in the Elementary School*, Chapters 5, 6, and 8. In the research on creative personalities, creative children were able to conceptualize better than noncreative children. Helping children to form concepts contributes to their reading skill and creative skill development.

Children Must Develop a Knowledge of the Alphabet

As soon as children begin to hear sounds of letters, the letters should be introduced as symbols to represent the sounds. Letters will be learned individually before they are learned in alphabetical sequence. The latter can be taught as soon as most of the children recognize and associate sounds with their letter symbols. Little use is made of the alphabetical sequence as such much before the upper primary or early intermediate grades, but the letters should be recognized early in the reading program.

Some suggestions for introducing letters may be found in Chapters 7 and 8 of *Creative Teaching of the Language Arts*.

1. Following are some suggestions to help children see the letter sounds in printed symbol form. These may be used as first steps toward building an alphabet consciousness.

   a. Help each child learn the first sound and letter of his own first and last names.

   b. Write on the board *r, h, l, g, f, m, y, w, b,* and so forth, and have a child point to and name the letter that stands for the sound heard at the beginning of a list of dictated words or the letter with which his own name begins.

c. Make large capital letters on oak tag and have various children whose names begin with a capital shown stand and name the letter and sound.

d. Use large pictures that have many objects beginning with the same sound. Identify the letters.

e. Find those words in spelling lists that sound alike at the beginning or end.

f. Make individual sound-picture booklets.

g. Match (oral exercises—each child must say the sound and the word that begins with that sound):

h. Start with a word such as *Dick* (and substitute other letters for the initial consonant to make new words *pick, lick*).

i. List initial sound or sounds on the board and have children find as many words as possible for the sound or sounds listed from their related reading in science or from their spelling lesson.

j. Emphasize both likenesses and differences in words.

2. Many exciting alphabet books are available on the market. These are excellent aids in helping the children *see* the alphabet over and over again.

THE BEGINNING FORMAL PROGRAM

Building a Sight Vocabulary Through Group Approaches

From the examples already given in this chapter and others in this book, the conclusion may be drawn that building a sight vocabulary can be a very creative process. Some further illustrations demonstrate the limitless possibilities for doing this in creative and meaningful ways.

1. Simple charts may be made on the chalkboard each day to plan the day. These charts repeat the words used to date in as many ways as possible. Drawings may be substituted for words unknown to the children. Mrs. Noyes introduced the words *paste, scissors,* and *brushes* on this chart:

Today's Helpers

Bobby will pass the milk.
John will pass the crackers.
Mary will pass the napkins.
Angie will pass the paper.
Peter will pass the paint.

Michael will pass the

Helen will pass the

George will pass the

Of course, the teacher must understand that the child may read the above as "Helen will pass the glue" and "George will pass the shears," but that doesn't matter in this particular situation because the meaning the child is putting to the statement is that which is linked to his former experience with the object in question. He is making the printed symbols communicate. A wise teacher will show him the word *glue* and *shears* at this time and let it go at that. Perhaps the next day she can introduce the synonyms *paste* and *scissors*. There is always a danger that he may not interpret pictures as the artist intended him to. In the beginning stages of reading, the teacher can use the words that the child "reads" into the pictures. Later, she will need to use phonics clues to show him the differences in the words so that he can decode words precisely as they appear on the printed page.

Daily planning can be done on a chalkboard chart each day. Miss Farrell, a kindergarten teacher, saw evidences of reading readiness in a group of her children. She was concerned at the time with helping the children to plan. In brief, she selected magazine pictures of children engaged in schoolroom activities and pasted them on cardboards. As they planned the day together, she placed the pictures in logical sequence on the chalk tray, thus developing the readiness skill of logical sequence. Soon she began to add simple cards printed with these words, "We

play," "We work," "We eat," "We dance."   The children were told
that these labels said what the children in the picture were doing.
After a very short time, she saw children matching pictures and
words.   Finally she was able to use a pocket chart to plan the
daily program.   First she would plan the day with the pictures,
then add the labels, and then allow the children who could do so
to make up a program of duplicate labels on the pocket chart.

2. Charts for unusual days may be printed on the chalkboard:

Happy Birthday!

Today is Helen's birthday!
She is seven.
We will sing to Helen.
We will read to Helen.
We will have a party.
Happy birthday, Helen.

Our Trip

Today is a fun day.
We are going on a trip.
We are going to the War Memorial.
We are going to the circus.
There will be clowns.
There will be elephants.
There will be acrobats.
There will be horses.
We will have popcorn.
We will have coke.
We can hardly wait!!

Saturday and Sunday

Saturday and Sunday!
No school.
We had fun.
Allan went to the museum.
David, Rodriguez and Joel played
*   ball in the park.*
Paula went to her father's office.
Jenny saw a big ship come in.
Ersie went for a ride in the country.
Jonathan and Jed went to the dump.
Sara went to Coney Island.
Saturday and Sunday!
No school!
We had fun!

Look! Look!

Today is a good day.
Someone is coming.
Who is it?
It is Mr. Jones.
He will show us pictures.
They are pictures of our trip
to Mr. Jones's farm.

Christmas!

Today is for Christmas!
We will have our party!
We will have fun!
We will have popcorn!
We will have games.
We will have presents.
We will have a play.
We will sing.
Christmas is fun!

3. Daily news can be printed in chart form on the chalk-board in initial reading experiences to develop a sight vocabulary. Each morning, children who have some important news tell about it. The teacher prints the news on the board in simple sentences. Miss Martin's first news chart looked like this:

Our News

Today is Wednesday.
It is warm.
Bill is sick.
We will take a trip.
We will go to the park.
Today we have gym.

Later, after the children can print, master ditto papers can be lined lightly and one child each day can be assigned to copy the news from the board onto a master ditto paper. On Friday, all the dittoed copies can be run off on a duplicating machine so that each child has a copy of each day's news. These can be stapled between two pieces of colored construction paper and a cover can be drawn so that the child may take home his grade newspaper each week.

After the newspapers are assembled on Friday afternoon, they provide excellent material for reviewing the words learned during the week.

4. Reading directions from a variety of charts helps children to follow directions independently. A sample of one such chart is called "Helping Hands." Each child traces his hand on a piece of oak tag. He cuts out what he has traced and writes his name on the "hand." An 18″ x 24″ sheet of oak tag is divided into as many sections as there are duties in the room. On each section a duty is written. These sections are made into pockets so that the "hand" slides in and out easily and can be readily seen.

The oak tag hands are changed every day or every week, as the children decide.

5. Teaching children to read individually does not imply that each child is always on his own reading program. Common experiences give children common understandings, and these can be employed for group work. Individual teaching does imply that certain individual needs, problems, and interests must be met, for each child may need extra help or attention at some time.

Following are good examples of techniques for teaching beginning reading individually through chalkboard and other charts.

Mrs. Wallace's children come into the first-grade classroom in the morning. There are notes on some of the desks, and on the board are taped a few large sheets of paper with various children's names on them. One says:

> *Billy*
> *Surprise, surprise,*
> *Billy has a surprise!*
> *What is it?*

The teacher tells Billy to read what is under the paper. Billy lifts it up and printed under it on the board is:

> *Go to the kitchen.*

Billy goes to the kitchen and there on the table is a reading chart. It reads:

> *Surprise!*
> *Today is Billy's birthday,*
> *This is a surprise,*
> *Billy will make a birthday cake.*
> *We will have it for lunch.*
> *Surprise us, Billy.*
> *Read the box.*

Pasted on a box of cake mix on the table are directions printed in large letters.

Pour flour in bowl.
Add 1 cup milk.
Stir
Call Miss Wallace.

If Billy cannot read all of this he gets help, but the words are largely those that have come from the vocabulary chart and the reading experiences the group has shared. Billy mixes the cake and calls Miss Wallace. She helps put it in the oven for that is dangerous for Billy to do alone. Miss Wallace and Billy plan to frost the cake and decorate it for the surprise for midmorning lunch. (This experience takes on special significance when we learn that it happened in an educationally deprived school and Billy was a child who had never before had a birthday cake of his very own!)

Similar experiences are had by other children on their birthdays. The same charts can sometimes be used. Later, after the lopsided, irregularly frosted cake is served, the class makes a chart about Billy's surprise, and words are used in new context.

Other children read instructions for simple household duties and for treasure hunts—exciting, important experiences. Mary's note says:

Mary may go to the library.
Find a story.
We will read it.

Sally's note says:

Sally may water the plants.
Sally may set the table.

Other charts on the board say:

Surprise.
Surprise for everyone.
All may peek.
See the surprise.

And under the paper on the board is a picture of some boys and girls giving a play. Under the picture is printed:

Today we will have a play.

Because Miss Wallace knows her children well, she is able
to use their interests to develop personal sight vocabularies.   Each
week each child gets at least one personal note on the board.   An
example of one such chart said this:

Look, Don.
Look and see.
See your surprise!

When Don lifted the flap of paper he found this printed
on the board:

Here is a surprise.
It is for you.
Show it to the boys and girls.
Show it at Show and Tell.

An arrow pointed to an envelope stuck to the board.   The
envelope was labeled "For Don."   Inside the envelope was a stamp
from France.   Miss Wallace remembered that Don is a stamp col-
lector when she received a letter from France.

Individualized reading charts can make reading very
precious and truly communicative to children.   The time a
teacher spends after school each afternoon preparing for such
reading experiences is very small in relation to the results obtained.

6. The teacher can use individual stories the children dictate to her for personalized reading charts for their own books,
as Charlie's teacher did at the beginning of this book.   Occasionally, a story is of general interest and can be shared with the
class.   For example:

The Motorcycle

My uncle Tyrone has a motorcycle.
He brought it to show me on Saturday.
It is all black and red.
It is shiny.
It makes a big noise.
It goes fast.
Uncle Tyrone has a helmet.
He took me for a ride.
I was scared.
But I am going to have a motorcycle some day.

—CHRISTOPHER
Grade 1

7. Objects in the room may be labeled with cards and tags to make simple sentences. Signs such as "This Is the Reading Table" and "Our Library" help children to visualize many words over a period of time.

8. Dramatizations can be used to develop reading skills. After the teacher reads a story, labels can begin to play a part in dramatizing it. The imaginary scenery can be labeled "This is a tree" or "Here is a house." Characters can be labeled "I am Dick" or "I am the mouse." Actions and sounds can sometimes be read from cards instead of being acted.

9. Occasionally a word or phrase that takes on great importance to the children comes up in the classroom, and the teacher may print it on a vocabulary chart for future reference. Words around holiday time may be printed out of context on a vocabulary chart and still have a great deal of meaning to the children. Vocabulary charts are excellent ways to keep the picture and the spelling of current words before the children and are of special value after children begin to write and can use the phrases and words in their stories and poems.

10. Surprise charts are sprung on the children as new arrangements of words already learned. Surprise charts can serve many purposes.

> a. They can repeat words already learned in new and exciting forms.
> b. They can be constructed as riddles.
> c. They can be used as announcements such as the following:

Surprise! Surprise!
Today we have a surprise.
We will go to a play.
It is at 10 o'clock.
It is in Miss Jones's room.
It is about Peter and the Wolf.
That is our surprise!

Look! Look!
We have a surprise!
It is in the room.
It is near the door.
It is something to look at.
Can you find it?

11. Charts can be devised for many other purposes:

> a. To give directions:

Look! Look!

Here is some paper.
Fold it.
Make a book.
Draw pictures.
Tell us about it.

b. To make announcements:

Lunch Today

This is our lunch today—
    Milk
    Hamburger
    Roll
    Potato chips
    Ice cream

c. For daily planning.
d. For long-term planning:

Our Plans for the Circus

1. *We will go to the circus.*
2. *We will draw pictures.*
3. *We will act like animals.*
4. *We will have clowns.*
5. *We will read circus stories.*
6. *We will sing circus songs.*
7. *We will make a book.*
8. *We will have a circus.*
9. *We will make tickets.*
10. *We will invite mothers and fathers.*

e. To use children's individual or group creative writing (see page 213).
f. To list children's questions for science or social studies.   These may later be printed on a card so each child learns to read his one question—and is perhaps responsible for finding the one answer.
g. To evaluate classroom experiences:

What Makes a Good Report?

1. *Speak clearly.*
2. *Think about what you are saying.*
3. *Look at the class.*
4. *Speak loudly.*
5. *Do not speak too long.*

h. To use for reference purposes:

How to Write a Letter

Your letters should look like this:
                              Penfield School
                              Penfield, N.Y.
                              October 26, 1967
Dear Mother,
        We are going to have a play.
Can you come? We will have the
play on _____ at _____
o'clock in Room _____.
                              With love,
                              _____

i. Often the children in the initial reading stages compose letters of thanks on the chalkboard. Then the teacher (or some capable child) copies the letter and sends it to the deserving person. Letters of invitation, announcements, and trip permission slips may also be developed in this manner. At times it is appropriate for the teacher to coach the recipient of the letter to answer the children with a letter printed in simple chart form. All people do not possess the skill of writing proper manuscript, but a letter printed in this style with large lettering, which can be placed on the bulletin board for all to read, is a thrilling experience for the children and a rich experience in communication.

Here is a sample of one such letter written by a father (who was a teacher) to a group of first-grade children who sent him a Christmas gift because he had made them a reading table for their room.

Dear boys and girls,
Christmas was coming!
I had a gift under the tree!
It was from you.
I could hardly wait.
But I did.
I waited and waited.
Finally Christmas came.
I ran downstairs,
I opened my gift,
I saw the tie-holder—
It was wonderful.

It was just what I needed.
I was happy.
Thank you.
This is how I looked when I opened my gift.

your friend,
Mr. Smith

12. The surprise box fulfills the same purpose as a surprise chart except that it makes possible the use of three-dimensional objects in building vocabulary. A large box is cut open at one side so as to produce a "flap" effect. This flap enables the children to raise the front of the box and look inside. On the flap are printed words similar to these:

> *Surprise, surprise!*
> *Look and see.*
> *See the surprise inside!*

On opening the flap the children find an object and a card on which is printed a description of the object. A slit in the top of the box in the back makes it possible for the teacher to print these cards and to drop them in the box easily.

Mrs. Hodges used the box often to introduce new materials to the children. One day, on lifting the box, the children found a lump of clay. On the back wall of the box was printed:

> *Surprise!*
> *Today we have clay.*
> *We will play with it.*
> *Look for it.*
> *Find it.*
> *Play with it.*

On another day she introduced the new reading books through the use of the box. In the box was a book. Behind it was printed this card:

Look!

A new book!
We will read it.
We will each read it.
We will read it at 10 o'clock.

Miss Swengle used a surprise box to stimulate creative writing. She put a music box in the box one day, and behind it she printed:

Look!
Listen!
Hear me!
What do I say?
We will write about me today!

One day she put a beautiful fall picture in the box. Below it she printed:

Tell about me.
Tell about me at Show and Tell time.

Miss Swengle sometimes used the box to introduce letters and invitations.

Surprise boxes can serve a multitude of purposes as well as provide meaningful reading experiences. When placed on a table near the door, they are an excellent motivating device for children as they enter the classroom. Often children can be encouraged to provide a surprise and create a message to go with it after they begin to do manuscript writing.

Setting Conditions for Building a Sight Vocabulary
Through Various Individual Approaches

Reading can be made a personal experience from the start of the formal reading program. Inasmuch as some children are ready to read before others, the individualized reading program has much merit. Where a completely individualized reading program is impossible, attempts should be made to personalize the reading experience in as many ways as possible.

Conditions can be set so that creative teaching of reading on a personalized level can take place. Examples of such conditions set up by creative teachers follow on the next few pages.

1. Miss Wallace (page 208) personalized her reading program for the children by making individual reading charts on the chalkboard.

2. Mrs. Lanning, who knew her first-graders had had an excellent readiness program in kindergarten, brought a camera to school and took a picture of each child on the first day of school. She and her husband were both amateur photographers. They developed many pictures (five of each child) and made thirty prints of the group picture. This was paid for by the parents, who were sent a letter explaining the project along with a routine request for other money the children would need for books, milk money, cafeteria money, and so forth.

Mrs. Lanning arranged her children in groups of five in the classroom. She dittoed these words near the bottom of thirty sheets of paper:

> *I am* _____
> *I am in the first grade.*

Room was left over the printing for each child's picture, which he pasted on the sheet. He then printed his name in the blank space, copying it from a model taped to his desk. During the next two days each child made five copies of this sheet—pasting his own picture and printing his own name on each copy. On the last day of the first week of school, the children swapped copies so that each child had five different pictures with five different names. Mrs. Lanning printed the words "My First Book" on the chalkboard, and the children drew the words on colored construction paper with crayons. They then drew a picture on the construction paper and stapled in the five pages. Each member of this class, at the end of the first week of school, had created his own reading book. Each page of the book repeated the same words except that on each page was a different name to which the picture gave the clue.

The next week a book was made of "My Friends," and this time the children at different tables swapped pictures. A new page was added at the end of this book. It was the picture of the class. Under it was dittoed:

> *This is the first grade.*
> *They go to school.*
> *They are friends.*

With the continued use of drawings and photographs Mrs. Lanning was able to help each child build a sizable library of his own reading books and, of course, a superb reservoir of sight words. The last book of the year was a class yearbook summarizing events of the first grade for the entire year.

3. In Miss Allison's first grade a sight vocabulary was introduced on a personal basis by having the children draw pictures of a trip taken soon after school began. Each child could draw as few or as many pictures as he wished. As soon as he finished his pictures he put them in a logical sequence and brought them to Miss Allison, who sat before a primary typewriter. Each child told about his pictures or told a story about his pictures, which Miss Allison typed on the primary typewriter, helping the child to put it into short phrases with meaningful vocabulary.

Miss Allison skipped several spaces between the stories about the individual pictures. When the dictation was complete, Miss Allison told each child to cut apart the story between the large spaces and paste the story to the proper picture. Each child then stapled his pictures between construction paper covers, and Miss Allison helped him print the name of his book.

Her first reading lessons were built around teaching each child to read the story in his own book. Soon the children were reading their books aloud to the class. Before long they were reading to each other by twos and threes (teaching each other, actually) and finally swapping books.

By the end of her first week of formal reading, Miss Allison had a homemade library of thirty-two books from which to draw. This was increased by thirty-two more the second week and for several weeks thereafter. Before long some children were typing, illustrating, and binding their own books to share with the class.

4. Miss Johns personalized her reading program by having the children use a home experience the first day of school. The children drew two or three pictures of something that happened at home. Then Miss Johns printed the dictated story on the picture. These were bound in construction paper and shared with the rest of the children. Jimmy's is shown in Figure 5–8. Soon Miss Johns's children were also sharing books.

5. Miss Myers ran off dittoed drawings of the new school building on the first day of school. Below the picture she printed "Our School." On the same day she took the children on a tour of the new school. When they returned to the room she had them draw pictures of their trip. She printed stories below the

FIGURE 5–8.   *Pages from a beginning reading book.*

pictures and used these as a personal reading experience for each child.

6. Miss Maggio had each child draw an illustration on one cover of a manila folder.   Then she helped the children print "My Stories" on the cover.   Each day the children had an opportunity to come to Miss Maggio and tell her a story built around an assigned topic.   The first day they told about themselves.   The next day the topic was "My School."   Then they made stories about "My Father," then "My Mother," then "My Pet."   Miss Maggio printed each story on primary paper and put it in the folder.   She used these stories to teach each child his own sight vocabulary. Each child in this room soon had a book of stories different from any other child's.   They were encouraged to illustrate the stories, and soon the books were full enough to be bound.   Children working in small groups read their stories to each other and swapped books, helping each other to learn the new words.

7. Miss Douglas, Charlie's teacher in Chapter 1, started Charlie on his reading program with a book of empty pages.   The open classroom setting encourages individual approaches to reading and gives the teacher enough leeway to draw on the skills of

other children when any particular child needs help or experiences above and beyond those he is able to create for himself.

SUMMARY

A highly creative approach to beginning reading can pay great dividends in terms of the child's attitude toward reading. In this age of technology and canned learning devices, we must not forget that relevancy and involvement are two prerequisites to learning and that to them must be added the supportive words of someone interested and proud of each child's successes, however minor they may be. Individual attention must be afforded each child from the very beginning of his reading program, but there are times when great stimulation and high productivity may result from group work. Both strategies have their place in teaching children to read.

In order for children to read, they must want to do so. They must be able to listen, and the teacher must be able to help them creatively learn to listen. Each child must have a large oral vocabulary, he must have a working knowledge of the left-to-right concept, he must have audio and visual acuity, and he must have a comprehension ability.

It is important that children have a knowledge of the alphabet and a substantial sight vocabulary. In addition to having these, each child must be physically, emotionally, intellectually, and psychologically ready to read. Each of these beginning reading skills may be developed through creative activities.

TO THE COLLEGE STUDENT

1. In the lesson described at the beginning of this chapter, Mr. Cline appealed to the senses of taste, smell, touch, sight, and sound. Little children learn best when what they are learning appeals to all their senses. Compare Mr. Cline's lesson with the one described at the beginning of Chapter 7. Did Mr. Banks follow the same principle in the intermediate grade lesson? How?

2. Reread Mr. Cline's lesson and tell how you would develop some creative experiences in phonics development for the children involved.

3. Are the objectives for Mr. Cline's lesson written in behavioral terms? Is it always possible to write behavioral objectives for

creative outcomes when one of the qualities of creativity is that its outcomes are unpredictable?

4. Why is the quote from Rumer Godden's book *An Episode of Sparrows* particularly appropriate for this chapter?

5. How keen is your visual perception? Do you really notice things—*see* things? Check by trying some of the games suggested on pages 183–196.

6. As a further check of your visual perception, face the rear of the room and then write the answers to these questions:
   a. What is hanging on the wall in the front of your classroom?
   b. How many panels are there in the chalkboard?
   c. Does the doorway to your classroom have a glass panel?
   d. What picture is hanging before the room?
   e. What is currently written on the chalkboard?
   f. Is there a movie screen or a map in the room?
   g. Is there an electric outlet in the front of the room?
   h. What is currently on the teacher's desk?
   i. Who is absent from your class today?

TO THE CLASSROOM TEACHER

1. Did you ever ask yourself *why* a great many traditions exist? For instance:

   Why must children read in periods? *Why not* have language activities all day that include reading such as Mr. Cline did at the beginning of this chapter?

   Why must we give achievement tests in reading? *Why not* find out what maturational skills each child has and take it from there, as Miss Douglas did in Charlie's classroom in Chapter 1 or as Peter's teacher did in the country school in Chapter 2?

   Why must we give achievements tests in reading? *Why not* measure a child's progress in terms of his own records and his own reading. Has anyone ever stopped you on the street and asked you what grade level you were reading at in January of your third year of school? In the long run, does it make any difference?

   Think of other *whys* about reading—and see what you are doing to your children by promoting noncreative practices.

2. How much time do you spend making your children listen to you? How much time do you spend in the teaching of listening? How much time do your children have for reading? How much time do you spend on the teaching of reading? What is the importance of the correlation here?

TO THE COLLEGE STUDENT
AND THE CLASSROOM TEACHER

1. Make lists of all the children's *picture* books you can find that might meet one of the objectives of the reading readiness program described in this chapter.

2. The specific qualities possessed by creative children that may be logically developed in the reading program were listed on page 80. Check the list against Mr. Cline's lesson and determine which of the creative components of divergent thinking Mr. Cline was developing.

3. Play some of the games suggested in this chapter, keeping the objective for using each game clearly in mind. Is it possible to use games that do not accomplish an objective because they are too involved, too complicated, or poorly presented?

4. Which of the skills mentioned in this chapter are applicable to college (adult) reading and require constant development?

5. Ask someone who teaches a speed reading course to visit your class and tell about his objectives and techniques. Of the material he presents, what is applicable to children?

6. Some men claim to read as many as twenty books a week. How do you think they develop such refined reading skills?

7. Invite someone from a speed-reading course to your adult class to explain the philosophy and strategies used to attain it. Note, especially, the work of Evelyn Wood in this field.[4]

SELECTED BIBLIOGRAPHY

Anderson, Irving H., and Walter F. Dearborn. *The Psychology of Teaching Reading.* New York: The Ronald Press, 1952.

Aukerman, Robert C. *Approaches to Beginning Reading.* New York: John Wiley and Sons, 1971.

Bailey, Mildred Hart. "The Utility of Phonic Generalizations in Grades One through Six." *Reading Teacher* 20 (1967): 413–418.

Byres, Loretta. "Pupils' Interests and the Content of Primary Reading Texts." *Reading Teacher* 17 (1964): 227–233.

Carillo, Lawrence W. *Informal Reading-Readiness Experiences.* San Francisco: Chandler Publishing Co., 1964.

Carlton, Lessie. *Reading, Self-Directive Dramatization, and Self-Concept.* Columbus, O.: Charles E. Merrill Publishing Co., 1968.

4. Christopher T. Cory, "Should You Teach Speed Reading? A Talk with Evelyn Wood," *Learning* 2, no. 1 (March, 1974): 31–34.

Cordts, Anna D. *Phonics for the Reading Teacher.* New York: Holt, Rinehart and Winston, 1965.

Cory, Christopher T. "Should You Teach Speed Reading? A Talk with Evelyn Wood." *Learning* 2, no. 1 (March, 1974): 31–34.

Darrow, Helen Fisher, and Virgil M. Howes. *Approaches to Individualized Reading.* New York: Appleton-Century-Crofts, 1960.

Denby, R. U. "NCTE/ERIC Report on Research in Listening and Listening Skills." *Elementary English* 38 (March 1961): 170–174.

Devine, Thomas G. "Reading and Listening: New Research Findings." *Elementary English* 38 (March 1961):296.

Duker, Sam. *Individualized Reading: Readings.* Metuchen, N.J.: Scarecrow Press, 1969.

Gunderson, Doris V. *Research in Reading at the Primary Level.* Washington, D.C.: Superintendent of Documents, U.S. Government Printing Office, 1963.

Hall, Edward. "Listening Behavior: Some Cultural Differences." *Phi Delta Kappan* 50 (March 1969):379–380.

Harris, Theodore L. "Some Issues in Beginning Reading Instruction." *Journal of Educational Research* 56 (1962):5–19.

Heffernan, Helen, and Vivian Edmiston Todd. *The Kindergarten Teacher.* Boston: D. C. Heath, 1960.

Hellman, Arthur W. *Phonics in Proper Perspective.* Columbus, O.: Charles E. Merrill Publishing Co., 1964.

Herr, Selma E. *Learning Activities for Reading.* 2nd ed. Dubuque, Ia.: William C. Brown Co., 1971.

Herrick, Virgil G., and Marcella Nerbovig. *Using Experience Charts with Children.* Columbus, O.: Charles E. Merrill Publishing Co., 1964.

Howards, Melvin. "How Easy Are 'Easy' Words?" *Journal of Exceptional Education* 32 (1964):377–382.

Jones, Daisy Marvel. *Effective Techniques for Teaching Children to Read.* New York: Harper and Row, 1971.

Kingsly, Bernard. *Reading Skills.* Belmont, Calif.: Fearon Publishers, 1970.

Langdon, Grade, and Irving W. Stout. *Teaching in the Primary Grades.* New York: Macmillan, 1964.

Lee, Doris M., and R. V. Allen. *Learning to Read through Experience.* New York: Appleton-Century-Crofts, 1963.

Mellin, Alta. *Phonics Handbook for the Primary Grades.* Belmont, Calif.: Fearon Publishers, 1970.

Mountain, Lee Harrison. *How to Teach Reading before First*

Grade. Highland Park, N.J.: Drier Educational Systems, 1972.

Reddin, Estoy. "Characteristics of Good Listeners and Poor Listeners." *The Journal of the Reading Specialist* 7 (March 1968):109–113.

Rudolph, Marguerita, and Dorothy H. Cohen. *Kindergarten: A Year of Learning.* New York: Appleton-Century-Crofts, 1964.

Russel, David, and Etta E. Karp. *Reading Aids through the Grades.* New York: Columbia University, Bureau of Publications, 1951.

Safier, Dan. *The Listening Book.* Caldwell, O.: Caxton, 1954.

Schell, Robert E. *Letters and Sounds: A Manual for Reading Instruction.* Englewood Cliffs, N.J.: Prentice-Hall, 1972.

Taylor, Sanford. *What Research Says to the Teacher: Teaching Listening.* Washington, D.C.: National Education Association, 1964.

Wann, Kenneth. *Beginning Reading Instruction in the Kindergarten.* Washington, D.C.: American Association of Elementary, Kindergarten, Nursery Education, 1966.

Wilson, Robert, and Mary Anne Hall. *Programmed Word Attack for Teachers.* Columbus, O.: Charles E. Merrill Publishing Co., 1968.

CHAPTER VI

The Creative Teaching
of Reading Skills
in the Primary Grades

. . . For what I myself learned during these years I have mainly my children to thank. They were my teachers as I was theirs, and the basis of our relationship was sincerity, without which, I am convinced, there can be no creative education.[1]

ELWYN S. RICHARDSON

TO THE READER

If you have been under the impression that the teaching of reading skills must be a very conforming, rigid sort of experience, read the following books by John Ciardi: *The Reason for the Pelican*[2] and *I Met a Man*.[3] Then ask yourself this question: How could I teach phonics with these poems? Discuss this with other people and you will begin to see that your impressions were incorrect.

1. Elwyn S. Richardson, *In the Early World* (New York: Pantheon Books, 1964), p. xiii.
2. John Ciardi, *The Reason for the Pelican* (New York: J. P. Lippincott Company, 1959).
3. John Ciardi, *I Met A Man* (Boston: Houghton Mifflin Company, 1961).

DEVELOPING READING SKILLS

Once the act of reading is established and children have a large enough sight vocabulary from which to develop independent reading skills, attention must be focused on their known oral skills in order to develop the printed skills of word attack. Picture clues are natural steps leading to the more complex use of word-form clues and phonics- and structural-analysis skills. Many of these more complex means of developing reading skill can be taught creatively. Creative teaching calls for strong tension-building motivational techniques—convergent and divergent thinking processes must be initiated by the motivation of *content* of high interest, a *technique* of high interest, or a *process* of high interest.

Many of the following illustrations and suggestions for developing convergent (as well as divergent) thinking processes have been included because of their high motivational interest to children. Others enhance specific phases of creative development, such as substitution, expansion, minimization, or elaboration of ideas. Others were included because they develop affiliated skills necessary to creative development, such as making judgments, developing relationships, and evaluating and making decisions, all of which were demonstrated in Mr. Cline's lesson at the beginning of the last chapter.

Verbal Context Clues

The manner in which a word is used in a sentence or phrase often gives the child a clue to its pronunciation and meaning. Each phonics skill he acquires makes him more certain of the word as he works to decipher it. Lacking phonics skills, he will often guess at the meaning and continue reading if his guess makes sense to him. Phonics analysis, structural analysis, and other forms of word attack are taught simultaneously and are meaningful if they are taught in the situation where the child encounters the problem.

Some general suggestions for teaching verbal context clues follow:

1. Choose the best word out of a group of words to best express a thought, or choose the best cluster of words from a sentence.

2. Draw attention to specific words by giving directions such as: Find the word on this page that means *a small house* [cottage].

3. Begin a notebook where new words are listed alphabetically under various classifications such as *travel, music, art,* and *home.*

4. Make charts that classify words for use in creative writing and reading such as emotion words, fun words, and elephant words (See page 252).

5. Find irrelevant words in a story.

6. List descriptive words for creative writing (see the illustrations on pages 157–167).

7. Think of all the possible descriptive words for a certain object, picture, or action.   Put them on a chart.   Also list *clusters* of descriptive words.

8. Find words of opposite meaning and list them.

9. Learn words that have more than one meaning.

> *Example:*   Mother *set* my hair.
> A hen will *set.*
> We have a *set* of dishes.

Note that these words *look* and *sound* the same although they have different meanings.

10. Find irrelevant words in a classified list.

11. Encourage use of unusual words, and note unusual shapes.

12. Rewrite thoughts using different words with the same meaning.

> *Example:*   Mary *got* a letter.
> Mary *received* a letter.

Note the differences in shapes of words.

13. Have children suggest sentences for a group story, thank-you note, invitation, experience charts, and so forth, and then have them select the ones they like best.

14. Make a picture dictionary; correlate with other subjects to enrich the children's vocabulary.

15. Introduce a primary commercial dictionary.

16. Make cards containing sentences or paragraphs that contain a strange word that cannot be determined from the sentence alone.   This puts the child in the position of using whatever skills he has to determine the pronunciation of the word.

> *Examples:*   Peter bought some *bread* at the grocery
> store.
> Mary *ran* the sweeper every Saturday.
> We cut the bread with a *knife.*

17. Put on cards or on the chalkboard sentences that have an obvious word omitted. Children fill in the word demonstrating how the context gives clues to the word.

18. Compare opposites. Write lists of words and have children dictate opposites. These may be put on cards so that children may try independently to "match opposites."

19. Develop the concept of synonyms by using words from children's stories. For example, a child mentions or writes about a *fright*. A synonym may be a *scare*. Collect these on charts or cards.

20. Refer to the materials for developing audio and visual discrimination (pages 179–193) for other suggestions for developing verbal-context skills.

21. Adapt the fishing game on page 193 to context clues by using on the fish phrases containing new words as well as single words.

22. Print or type a simple paragraph using the children's sight vocabulary but omitting the key line. After it is read, have children dictate the key line. This makes an interesting and diverse type of reading chart.

> *Example:*   I am yellow.
> Mr. Ames drives me.
> I go to school every day.
> Boys and girls ride me.

23. Reverse the preceding suggestion by making riddles. These exercises help the children see the need for total comprehension, the importance of context, and the necessity for the correct reading of key words.

24. Make charts or ditto sheets leaving blanks where one word will make sense:

> *Mary had a _____ doll.*
> *She put on its _____ hat.*
> *She put on its _____ coat.*
> *She put it in its _____ carriage.*

The word can be *small, tiny, big, pretty,* or one of several others. Put the same word in each blank, and then try substitutes that will make the story more interesting to read. This is a good way to show the use of synonyms in context.

25. Children enjoy simple games that help them use context to recognize words.

a. *Color Game.* Write a list of objects (such as snow, apple, carrot, grass) on oak tag and leave a space after each one.   Then put a list of color cards in a separate envelope.   The child who matches the greatest number wins.

Example: apple—red; snow—white.

b. *The Stores.*   On oak tag write headings such as grocery store, bakery, hardware, drug store, and furniture store.   Under each store, list several things you could buy in it.   Then cut the lists apart and put the items of each list in an envelope by themselves.   The headings should also be in a separate envelope.   The object is to see if the child can put the right article under the correct store heading.

c. *Phrase Cards.*   On one set of cards (oak tag or shirt cardboards) print phrases such as "I can see my __" or "I have the __"; on another set have illustrations of objects.   The children put them together to make a sentence.   Some number names can be used as they are introduced functionally in the classroom situation.

Word-Form Recognition

Word form clues are developed in many general ways:

1. Look at words—note the length, note tall and short letters, and note letters that go below the line.   A box can be built around the word to highlight its shape as well as similar or dissimilar parts.

2. Word-form clues are used most effectively by children when they learn certain phonics skills.   The children must have the ability to:

a. Look at the beginning letter and recognize the sound or consonant blend.

b. Recognize root words to which prefixes and suffixes have been added (colored chalk appeals to children).

farm	*read*	*slow*
farmer	reread	slowly
farming	rereading	

     c. Recognize long and short vowel sounds.
     d. Use the main rules for sounds of vowels.
        (1) Final *e* is dropped before adding endings (*rope, roping*).
        (2) *E* at the end of a one-syllable word makes the vowel long (*name, cone*).
        (3) When two vowels are found together in a word, the first vowel is long, the second silent (*moan, seat*).
        (4) *R* is a vowel controller.
        (5) In a two- or three-letter word having one vowel, the vowel sound is usually short (*at, can*).
     e. Know and use the main rules for consonants.
        (1) Recognize silent consonants (*pneumonia, knife*).
        (2) The consonant at the end of the word is doubled when certain endings are added (*run, running, hit, hitting*).

(See pages 108–110 for suggestions for teaching these basic phonics attacks and for cautions to be considered in applying them.)

3. Make a page mask. Cut from a discarded book the page that is to be used as a sample. Cut a piece of paper to fit the page. Attach the paper to the page with a hinge of mending tape or gummed labels. Hold the page against a window so that you can see the page through the paper, and draw little boxes on the paper around the words that the children found difficult. Cut out the boxes and expose the words. This is a way to let the children analyze the words that they have been having trouble with. The teacher can work with them on the difficult words using the mask, and then the children can work in groups, helping each other.

4. Play Charades. On the pocket chart are placed action words such as *angry, temper, generous,* and *flying.* A pupil is then chosen to go to a corner of the room and blindfold himself. Then the teacher points to one of the words on the board. Someone in the class is chosen to come to the front of the room and perform the action indicated by the word. The child who is blindfolded then uncovers his eyes. By watching the actions of the person in the front of the room, he tries to guess the word that is being acted out. He must then find the card that gives the word.

5. Play the Lollipop Game.

> *I'm selling lollipops, I'm selling lollipops,*
> *Fresh sugar candy from the candy shop.*
> *I'm selling lollipops, I'm selling lollipops*
> *No one knows where I shall stop.*

The leader says the above words as he walks around the room holding paper lollipops on which are written words. When the leader says "Stop!" he pauses by a child and shows him the word. If the pupil knows the word, he is given one of the paper lollipops. The game continues until many children have lollipops. Pupils then say or write each word that is found on the lollipops. (*Adaptations:* Use with phrases or sentences.) Use objects in keeping with various seasons instead of lollipops.

> *Example:*   Halloween—jack-o'-lanterns; Thanksgiving —pumpkins; Christmas—Santa or toys.

6. To teach the names of colors, make tops from sucker sticks stuck through the centers of milk bottles. Paint them different colors. One child spins his top and calls the name of another child. The child called must name the color of the top before it stops spinning. Later the second child runs to the chalk tray where word cards are and takes up the correct color card.

7. Obtain a spinner device (like a clock face) numbered from one to fifteen or beyond. On chalkboard or oak tag print the same number of phrases or words. When a child is called on, he flicks the hand on the spinner device, sees the number at which it stops, then reads the corresponding printed phrase or word from the chalkboard or oak tag. (*Adaptations:* Sentences may be used as well as words.)

8. Play Dominoes with word cards. Matching is done according to words, word endings, word beginnings, or rhyming words. You play this game exactly as you do the game of dominoes.

9. Special emphasis must often be placed on special words that are difficult for children to remember at the beginning stages of reading. Sometimes games help children to recognize the form of these special words.

> a. To teach the word *it*, print the word on a large cardboard and punch a hole in the top. Put a string through the hole so that the card can be worn around a child's neck. The child chosen to wear the card will be "it" in a game of tag. Have someone chase him around the room.
>
> b. To help children to distinguish *was* from *saw*, make

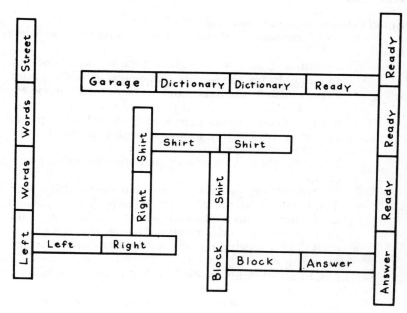

FIGURE 6–1. *Word dominoes.*

folders of sentences in which either word has been omitted. Make small cards with the word *was* or *saw* printed on each. The child is to place the correct word in each blank.

Phonics Analysis

Phonics attack on words begins with the program for developing audio and visual discrimination, and the suggestions on pages 179–193 are appropriate for developing phonics analysis skills. Many of them may be extended to a more direct approach of phonics attack. The ideas suggested in Chapter 2 are also worth reviewing as creative ways to lead children into a phonics consciousness.

Because the creative personality enjoys seeing the order and logic behind life, an understanding of the structure of words can contribute to this aspect of the child's creative development.

Some general suggestions for teaching phonics-analysis skills follow:

Initial Consonant Sounds and Rhyming Endings.
    1. Initial consonant sounds can be developed in several ways:

a. Imitating sounds of objects (trains, bells, and so on) and placing the sounds (*choo-choo, ding-dong*) on a chart to show the importance of sounds as a mode of communication even when these sounds are not really words. Known words can be constructed from these sounds by substituting initial consonant sounds (*ding: sing, ring, king, wing*).

b. Hearing beginning sounds that are alike (*d*og, *d*oor, *d*ump).

c. Finding one word in a group that starts with a different sound than the other words (jump, jar, *cat*).

d. Having children discover what is alike about all words in a series (oral or written)—*r*ug, *r*ake, *r*ing.

e. Matching beginning sounds, both words and pictures.

f. Calling attention to the fact that a new word begins the same as a familiar word.

g. Completing a sentence with a word that begins with the same sound as the first word in the sentence:

Dick has a _____. (*dog*)
                      (*doll*)

h. Changing the first consonant to make new words (*ball, tall, call*).

i. Comparing words with names. "I am thinking of two children whose names begin alike" or "I am thinking of an animal whose name begins like Paul's."

j. Listing words with similar beginnings.

k. Identifying words, objects, and pictures with the same beginning sound.

l. Constructing charts by placing an initial consonant sound at the top of a sheet of poster paper and having the children collect pictures of all the objects they can find that begin with that particular sound. This technique may be extended to speech consonants and consonant blends.

m. Miss Jarmon had her children collect tongue-ticklers to help get across the initial consonant sound.

The children enjoyed chanting "Peter Piper picked a peck of pickled peppers." After a while they made up their own tongue-tickling rhymes. Sally wrote, "Mamma makes much music"; Billy wrote, "Corky the clown can carry a cart," and Jimmy, who could not write many words, dictated, "Gary got a gallon of gas."

n. Asking, "Which one is different? All of these words except one begin with the same sound. Listen carefully. Tell me which word does not begin like the others."

Example: (for initial consonants)

1. sun   soup   ball   six
2. girl   ball   bed   book
3. deer   duck   dinner   bell
4. red   rose   ring   broom
5. fire   apron   fish   frog
6. church   chair   child   goat

o. Telling riddles.
"I am thinking of a word that begins the same as the words *sun, see,* and *sew.* It is the name of a number [*six, seven*]."
"I am thinking of a word that begins like the words *cook, cut,* and *camp.* It hangs at the window [*curtain*]."

2. *Rhyming words* may be introduced by:
a. Having children hear and recognize rhyming words (*jump, bump, thump*).
b. Using nursery rhymes and poems to help children discover rhyming words.
c. Saying words in series and having the children discover the one that sounds different because it doesn't rhyme (sun, *cat*, run).
d. Having the children memorize and repeat jingles.
e. Having children give a rhyming word for one the teacher gives (*joy, toy,* ___).
f. Making a scrapbook of rhyming words (pictures and/or words).
g. Making up short rhymes. (Jack and Jill went up the _____ .)
h. Using the children's creative writing for a study of rhyming words.
i. Collect several sets of large pictures of objects (about three to a set) whose names rhyme. Place two or three

sets on the chalk ledge or on a flannel board and say, "Some of these things have names that rhyme." You may ask other questions: "Who can find pictures of two things that rhyme?" "Are there any others that rhyme?" "Can you think of any other things that you know that would also rhyme?"

j. Collect a set of small pictures of words that rhyme (*man, fan, can; cat, hat, bat*). Use an egg carton of an attractive color. A child can then sort the pictures and put the rhyming cards into the separate sections. (This exercise may be adapted for beginning and ending sounds.)

k. Play Rhyming Words. Have the children think of two words that rhyme. Allow the children to make up rhymes or dictate one already known.

> *Little Jack Horner*
> *Sat in a corner.*
>
> *Out in the snow*
> *Sat a black crow.*
>
> *Giraffes are tall*
> *But ants are small.*
>
> *Little boat, little boat*
> *All around I see you float.*

l. Have the children name a word that rhymes with a given word.

coat	(boat)	tree	(bee)
car	(star)	eye	(pie)
house	(mouse)		

m. Have the children tell the word that rhymes with the first word.

> Ted, *ball, bed, train*
> play, *say, dead, palace*
> red, *balloon, head, candy*

n. Ask a riddle, and give a word that the answer rhymes with.

Something you eat
(It rhymes with dandy) *(candy)*
Something you wear
(It rhymes with boat) *(coat)*

o. Have the children provide the missing word to make a rhyme.

We went so far
In Daddy's new _____ *(car)*

The snow is falling all around
Floating and sailing to the _____ *(ground)*

Bobby fishing in a brook,
Caught a fish on his _____ *(hook)*

p. Using games that teach rhyming words and initial consonant sounds.
(1) Play Verbal Tennis. The children face each other across the room in two teams. One child gives a word, such as *red*. The child across from him must give a word that rhymes with it, such as *head*. This goes on until no more rhyming words can be given. The team that cannot supply any words gets a point and begins another word. The team with the lowest score wins. The teacher may print the words on the board as they are given and then use time at the end of the game to teach some phonics generalizations with their exceptions. Beginning consonant sounds can also be accented and the consistency of the beginning consonant emphasized. From this experience, Miss Eggers began a chart on which children collected words that sounded alike at the ending but did not look alike (*seed, bead; led, dead; rail, pale*).
(2) The teacher opens the game with this riddle: "I rhyme with sled. You sleep in me. What am I?" The child who answers correctly may make up the next riddle.
(3) Shopping at the Supermarket is an adaptation of the game described on page 182. Prepare word cards using the names of items that may be obtained at a supermarket (*bag, book, bottle, cake,*

can, corn). Duplicates are all right. Choose a leader to distribute several cards to each player. The leader may say, "Who has bought something that rhymes with the word *bees*?" The players whose cards answer the question will read them aloud and then give their cards to the leader. For more fun, the leader may hold a grocery bag into which the children can deposit their "purchases."

(4) Play Bingo and Lotto. Match pictures or words with same ending sounds.

(5) Play Rhyming Endings. The leader says, "I end with 'ook.' Can you guess who I am?" A player may take one guess in turn and say, "Are you *look*?" "No, I am not *look*," answers the leader if his word is, say, *book*. The player who guesses correctly becomes the next leader.

(6) Play Bounce-a-Rhyme. Let children try bouncing a ball to a chant consisting of rhyming words. Give a child a one-syllable "starter" word like *will*, which rhymes with many others: *bill, hill, sill, till, spill, fill, Jill*. The youngster continues to bounce the ball as long as he can say a rhyming word each time he bounces it. Other good starters are *can, and, old, it, day, red.*

q. Use choral speaking to develop a consciousness to rhyming words (see Chapter 5 of *Creative Teaching of the Language Arts in the Elementary School*, 2nd ed.).

3. Emphasis from rhyming endings and beginning consonant sounds can be extended by:

a. Finding the same sounds in consonants at the end of a word that were noted in consonants at the beginning of a word (*d*ark, pai*d*).

b. Noting likenesses and differences in beginnings (*c*an, *r*an) and endings of words (ma*n*, ma*t*).

c. Finding a known word in a longer word (*some*-thing).

d. Recognizing the same word whether it begins with a capital or a lowercase letter (Jump, jump).

e. Framing words to show length and form

f. Recognizing plural and possessive forms made by adding *s* or *'s.*

g. Finding similarities and differences in words such as *stop, spot; Dick,* and *duck.*

h. Noting configuration of words.

i. Noting word endings (*car, cars* [*s*]; *box, boxes* [*es*]; *small, smallest* [*est*]; *like, liked* [*d*]; *call, called* [*ed*]; *sweet, sweetly* [*ly*]; *sing, singing* [*ing*]).

j. Noting the same sound regardless of placement in words (*get*, be*g*in, pi*g*).

4. Study letters having more than one sound by:
   a. Recognizing that *x* and *k-s* sound alike.

   Example: boo*x*s, fo*x.*

   b. Listing words that show how the same letter sometimes has a different sound.

   Example: Sally, busy.

   c. Learning the hard and soft sounds of *c* and *g.*

   Example: country, city; grass, ginger.

   d. Recognizing the vowel sounds with *r*, such as *or, ir, er*, and *ur.*

5. Mr. Markin used the book *Ounce, Dice, Trice* to help him develop a consciousness to sounds in his room.   As a result of their experience with that book, children made charts for various purposes: "Words That Are the Same Coming or Going" (*noon, Dad, gag, Nan, pop, pep, sees, toot*); "Words That Are Quiet in Spots" (*knife, beat, angle, wren*); "Words That Grow from One Word" (*all, ball, tall, fall*); "Words That Mean the Same Thing" (*stand, rise; push, shove; box, carton*); "Words That Go Together" (*kiss, love, hug, dear, warm*); "Words That Sound Alike But Aren't" (*hair, hare; see, sea; hear, here; buy, by*).

6. Children can be made aware of the many times they use the vowel and consonant sounds they are learning by:
   a. Underlining words or similar sounds each time they are used in the daily plans the children write together on the chalkboard, in experience charts, or in news bulletins.
   b. Underlining words that are alike from several sentences on the chalkboard, using the same color of chalk.
   c. Matching word cards with words on a chart.

d. Matching word cards with words printed on the chalkboard.

e. Finding and underlining the word in a row of words that is like the beginning word in the row.

f. Playing a recognition game. Put a word on the board or show a word card and then ask, "Where can you see this word somewhere else in the room?" (The word—for example, *one*—may be a word chart, on the bulletin board, in the number center, in the daily news, and so on.)

7. Literature and the development of phonics may be blended when books such as *I Met a Man* and *The Reason for a Pelican,* by John Ciardi, are used by the teacher as springboards for fun with sounds.

8. Motivation for practice in sounds may be developed with a few interesting games: For example, the clapping game. Children clap when they hear a certain blend or letter sound at the beginning of a word, when they hear a certain variant ending, or when they hear a long or short vowel.

9. Children find pictures of words beginning with various sounds, blends, and such, and paste them on the appropriate page of a book or on a chart.

10. Dictate a word such as *parrot,* and have the children circle the word in a list that begins with the same consonant (*doctor, fireman, policeman*). Or dictate a word and have the children circle a word that has the same ending consonant. Again, dictate a word and have the children circle a word that has the same beginning and ending consonants.

Example: foot: *people, forget, lawn.*

Speech Consonants and Consonant Blends. After children have mastered many consonant sounds they can be led to discover that in combination, consonants lose their identity and produce a different single speech sound, such as /ch/, /sh/, /th/, /wh/, /ck/, /gh/, /ph/, /qu/, and /ng/. These are the speech consonants. They will also be aware that some letter combinations consist of two or more letters, each of which has its own distinct sound (/bl/, /br/, /cl/, /cr/, /dr/, /dw/, /fl/, /fr/, /gl/, /gr/, /pl/, /pr/, /sci/, /scr/, /shr/, /sk/, /sl/, /sm/, /sn/, /sp/, /spl/, /spr/, /st/, /str/, /thr/, /tr/, and /tw/) and these are the consonant blends.

Like beginning consonants and initial vowel sounds, speech consonants and consonant blends are best understood when they develop from the oral vocabulary of the child. His spoken language, and the symbol language he already can read, should be the foundation for an understanding of the use of speech consonants and consonant blends as an attack on new words.

Once again, putting his "sounds" into printed form can be a good beginning for recognizing blends and speech consonants. The dog says "grr" (a blend). The train goes "chug-chug" (a speech consonant). Transferral of these discoveries to other words is a simple matter.

1. Many of the techniques used to introduce consonant sounds can be applied to the teaching of blends and speech consonants.

a. Changing beginnings and endings of words to make new words.

Example: eat, meat; meal, squeal.

b. Making a list of new words with a part of a familiar word.   Children say the words.

Example: rain, train, brain, chain.

c. Having children underline beginning blends in a group of words.

Example: cl: clouds, clams, climb.

d. Making large charts of pictures illustrating words that begin with consonant blends (*train, truck*).

e. Listening for and listing words that begin with the same consonant blends.

f. Using riddles ("I am thinking of a word that begins with the same sound as *ch*air.   It is where people pray on Sunday.   What is it?" [*church*]).

g. Collecting words that begin and end with the same speech consonant or consonant blends: *church, shush.*

2. Motivation for individual practice with speech consonants and consonant blends may be provided with some simple games, such as Circle Wheels.   Make one big wheel and attach a smaller one to it with a paper fastener.   On the smaller wheel may be blends such as *ch, wh,* and *st.*   On the larger wheel the word endings may be placed (*op, ip, ick,* and so forth). Children can make these from oak tag.   By turning the small wheel inside the bigger one, new words are formed which children can sound out.   Some of the words will be nonsense words, but careful planning will result in many recognizable words.

3. Increase skill in blending an initial consonant with the familiar part of a word (*rain, train*) by:

   a. Applying results of word-building activities in attacking new words in context (*cat, catch*).

   b. Listing words with initial consonants and blends.

   c. Writing *br, tr, dr, fr,* and so forth on board and having children point to and name the sound they hear at the beginning of such words as *drink, trip, cream,* and *frog.*

   d. Having children name words that begin or end with certain blends *cl, bl.*

4. Increase skill in identifying hard and soft sounds by:

   a. Recognizing hard and soft *c* and *g*: (*Example: car, cent; girl, large.*) Make chart collections of these contrasts.

   b. Asking the children to listen to first sounds in words pronounced. In a natural tone of voice pronounce words like *chilly, cheese,* and *chicken.* Elicit from the children the sound /ch/. The children give other words with the same sound. As the list of blends increases, children may draw from a box cards on which are printed words beginning with blends they know. The child who draws a card gives another word beginning with the same blend as the word he draws.

   Staple a consonant blend or speech consonant to each pocket of a shoe bag and pass out word cards. Children say their word cards and place them in the correct pocket.

   Put consonant blends (*br, cr, st,* and so on) on large pieces of paper or on pages in a booklet. Put a different blend on each sheet. Cut out pictures whose names begin with the blend and paste them on the page.

   c. Finding endings. A child is given an envelope containing sentences such as: Sally is play_____ with her doll. Dick ride_____ the horse. This tree is big_____ than the house. An envelope containing endings accompanies the card. The child is to select the proper endings for the unfinished words.

Vowel Sounds. While most consonant sounds are stable, the vowels can have many sounds. It is the vowels that give language the greater part of its tonal quality. This can be demonstrated by having children sing *America* by singing only the

vowel sounds.   The tune is unimpaired, but it is not possible to
sing the consonants and maintain the tune.

Discovery of the many differences in vowel sounds may be
promoted by using the children's names.   Jane and James have
similar vowel sounds in their names, but Jack and Mary have different sounds.   If the teacher has the children write their names
on the chalkboard and pronounce them, the children can be led
to see the differences in vowel sounds.   The teacher may use this
opportunity to help them establish some of the generalizations of
phonics attack.

1. While Clymer's study shows that only nine of the forty-
five phonic generalizations are applicable 100 percent of the time
and that seventeen of these generalizations are not applicable
even 50 percent of the time, this does not mean that generalizations should not be used to help children.   It does mean that
they should be carefully reviewed and *some* should not be used—
especially the seventeen that do not work 50 percent of the time.
To be a generalization, a rule should work most of the time.   All
generalizations should be taught as clues to unlocking the pronunciations of words—not as rules.   Children may become even
more sensitive to these generalizations if they are challenged to
hunt for the exceptions.   In Mr. Parker's second grade this chart
indicated how he was using the generalizations in phonics attack:

Clue: WHEN TWO VOWELS APPEAR IN
A WORD, THE FIRST ONE SAYS ITS OWN
NAME AND THE SECOND ONE IS SILENT.

Places where it works:

beat	lean
meat	bead
hear	tear
fair	road

Places where it doesn't work:

chief	tough
veil	sweat
soup	loin
cough	

Mr. Parker often used the chart to introduce a new generalization, as in the words *loin, cough,* and *bough,* each of which introduces a new phonics sound.   Children started another chart on
which they placed all the double vowels that made new sounds.
These charts created an exciting word hunt for the children, and

PART 2   The Nurture of Creativity Through Reading and Literature

any child could add a word to the chart when he found one that rightfully belonged there.

As soon as children are aware of differences in vowel sounds and have had many experiences with the different sounds, the teacher can concentrate on the different sounds for each specific vowel, provided, of course, she does so in a meaningful context rising out of the children's needs. Children can hunt for vowels in their words and sentences and learn to mark them. Words from their sight vocabulary should be heavily used during this discovery stage because the children already know the sounds of the vowels in their sight vocabulary and will see how generalizations fit or do not fit these known words.

2. Miss Horton used the color concept mentioned in Chapter 3 to help children understand the difference in vowel sounds. Long vowels were printed on her charts in red, short vowels in blue, and so on. Children quickly figured out strange words under this system, and then Miss Horton had them tell her what generalization had dictated the color she would use. This "color" reading was used to establish the generalizations, after which the children were exposed to new words in sentences without the color but with the commonly accepted vowel markings. This provided for a smooth transition into regular reading material.

3. Common ways of teaching vowel sounds are:
a. Substituting medial vowels to stress sound changes.

Example: bad, bed.

b. Having children tell the vowel sound they hear in a word that the teacher pronounces.

Example: bit, bite.

c. Detecting silent letters in words.

Example: cream.

d. Perceiving how final *e* changes the sound and meaning of such words as *cap* and *cape.*
e. Listing words under vowel headings (long or short sound of same vowel).
f. Having children mark the long and short vowel sounds in their spelling words.
g. Showing the difference in meaning and sound of words when a double vowel is substituted for a single vowel.

Example: met, meet; bet, beet.

h. Having each child try to find the most words with either long or short vowels in a given length of time in one verse of a poem, writing the complete word and marking its vowels in the proper way on paper. When the time is completed, the vowels marked are checked and verified.

4. Increase skill in hearing beginning and medial vowels, with recognition of both short and long vowels, by:

a. Making separate charts for each vowel sound and finding pictures to illustrate each.

b. Listening to two words and designating which has the short *i* (*hit, hat*); the long /*a*/ (*hide, hate*), and so on.

c. Listing words on the board to illustrate the effect of changing the vowel, or inserting an additional vowel in certain short words such as *rug, rag; bat, bit;* and *met, meat.*

d. Showing the child how a final *e* changes the vowel sound and thus the meaning of words: *cap, cape; can, cane; hop, hope.* Collect such words on charts.

e. Showing the child the difference in the meaning and sound of words when a double vowel is substituted for a single vowel: *bet, beet; met, meet.*

f. Showing the effect of *r* on the vowels *a* (*cart*), *e* (*sister*), *i* (*bird*), *o* (*color*), *u* (*hurt*).

g. Showing the differences in diphthongs represented by two letters: *ou* (*ground*), *ow* (*cow*), *o* (*noise*), *oy* (*boy*).

h. Comparing sounds of homonyms (*sow, sew; road, rode*).

5. Well-chosen games such as the following provide interesting practice for phonics development. On three-by-five-inch cards print words with different vowel sounds, such as *pig, hat, wig, can, ran, sat,* and *big.* Shuffle the cards and give four to each child. A small pack should be left face down on the table. The first player reads a word from any of his four cards. If another player holds a card that contains a rhyming word, he must give the card to the player calling for it. The next player receives a chance to call any of his words. When a player fails to get a card from any of the others, he may draw from the pack on the table. If he still fails to get a rhyming word, or if he cannot read the card he has chosen, he must discard the card he called. The player with the most cards at the end is the winner.

Structural Analysis

The teaching of structural analysis begins in the development of visual discrimination. Many of the suggestions on the preceding pages help to develop visual discrimination and structural analysis skills such as:

1. Making word wheels.
2. Naming root words.
3. Observing word endings.
4. Making new words from root words.
5. Knowing and using basic rules about consonants.
6. Making larger words out of smaller words (*and, stand*).
7. Recognizing compound words such as *football.*
8. Recognizing contractions.
9. Knowing and using the main rules for syllables.
   a. If double consonants come together, divide the consonants (*sum-mer, lit-tle*).
   b. If the first vowel is followed by one consonant, divide the word after the vowel (*li-lac, lo-cate*).
   c. If the ending syllable is *le,* the first syllable ends after the vowel (*ta-ble*).
   d. When two consonants come between two vowels, we usually divide the word between the two consonants (*fif-ty*).
10. Using the dictionary as a helping device.

The activities suggested on pages 228–229 are appropriate for the introduction of word structure. Other ways by which children can become sensitive to the structure of words include the following.

1. Mastering *sight* vocabulary words (to the point where they can be spotted in varying content) by:
   a. Finding little words in compound words (*afternoon*).
   b. Taking off beginning and ending prefixes and suffixes to locate root word.
   c. Finding words in a group that are exactly alike.
   d. Determining parts of words that are alike and parts that are different.
   e. Recognizing familiar words in compound or hyphenated words.
   f. Distinguishing common prefixes and suffixes from root words.
   g. Scanning to find answers to questions, descriptive terms, names, and so forth.

h. Dividing words into syllables and marking the accent.

i. Presenting new words in written sentences and discussing meanings.

j. Recognizing compound words.

k. Listing words that are alike except at the beginning (*bell, fell, tell*).

l. Making a dictionary of words to use when writing stories or poems.

m. Developing the ability to recognize derivations formed by adding the suffix *y* to a known root word (*sleep, sleepy*).

n. Developing the ability to attack words when the final consonant is doubled before the ending (*sit, sitting*).

o. Recognizing and understanding the final *e* being dropped before an ending and the changing of *y* to *i*.

2. Seeing how many words can be built from *one* root word and noticing how the new words are all related to the root word in meaning.

Examples: Root word *law*. Words built by adding suffixes, prefixes, and compounds: *lawyer, lawless, lawsuit, lawful, unlawful*. Root word *rain*. Built words: *raincoat, rainy, raindrop, raincheck, raining, rains*.

3. Making collections of compound words and noting whether the meaning of each word is obvious or not. Mrs. Marr's third grade produced the following two contrasting charts:

Words That Tell Us Their Own Meanings	Words That Do Not Tell Us Their Meanings
evergreen	tidbit
shoelace	shamrock
scarecrow	slipshod
teabag	fanfare
boxcar	ketchup
sidewalk	horse-radish
tiptoe	iceberg
sandman	handsome
airplane	nightmare
seashore	
tattletale	

4. Making collections of words that go together but are not written as one word. Mrs. Farr's list looked like this:

*Words We Say Together But
Do Not Put Together*

tie tack
mince pie
candy cane
state fair
hope chest
ice cream
ferris wheel
fish pole
golf ball

5. Increasing skill in identifying the following endings on nouns whose base forms do not change.
   a. The endings *s*, *'s*, and *s'*, which do not add an extra syllable to the word (*boats, uncle's, girls'*).
   b. The endings *s* and *es*, which add an extra syllable to the word (*pieces, watches*).
6. Increasing skill in forming compound words.
   a. Making "solid" compounds (*today, another*).
   b. Building hyphenated compounds (*make-believe, far-off*).
7. Increasing skill in forming contractions by substituting an apostrophe for one or more letters (*I'm, can't*).
8. Increasing skill in identifying *s, es, est, ed, er*, and *ly* as forms of familiar words by:
   a. Naming the root word.
   b. Using the root word to make new words.
   c. Looking through a story or book to find words that were made by adding an ending to a known word.
9. Studying word endings by:
   a. Observing word endings *s, es, est, er, d, ed, ly*, and *ing*.
   b. Identifying root word in attacking new words (*open, opening*).
   c. Making new words from a root word (*want, wants, wanted, wanting*).
   d. Choosing correct word ending to complete sentences. Jane (*play, plays*) with her doll.
10. Playing games and using gimmicks that help develop structure awareness:
    a. Play Word Pyramid. Start at the top of the pyramid with the word *A*. The players take turns adding another letter to form a new and longer word and to

build the pyramid. If the first player adds *t,* the pyramid may develop as follows: *a, at, eat, meat, steam, steamer, teamster.* The pyramid may be built on the chalkboard.

b. Keeping Prefixes in a Box. The child draws out a prefix and makes a new word by adding the prefix.

Example: Using *like,* take *dis* out of box and make *dislike.*

SUMMARY

Every day of a child's life he uses hundreds of words in multiple situations. Creative children have the particular characteristics of wanting to create order out of chaos, of wanting to be independent, and of being able to initiate their own learning. Creative children are flexible and unique; they have original ideas, are sensitive to problems, are individualists, have a fluency of ideas, like to redefine and rearrange, like to produce, and have keen visual discrimination, keen intuition, and strong identification ability. The creative child's preferred learning techniques are actually the natural, healthy ways by which all children learn, if freed to do so—or if conditions have been properly set. If the teacher herself can be flexible enough, observant enough, and creative enough, she can use the hundreds of words she hears the children use to develop the above traits, all of which are necessary to the development of reading and creative skills. In this chapter and the next are many suggestions for teaching reading through the development of each of these skills.

TO THE COLLEGE STUDENT

1. Many commercial reading series contain exercises and workbooks to develop the skills in children mentioned in this chapter. Secure some of these materials. Apply the criteria of creative teaching to the exercises and note which ones develop some aspect of creativity and which are busy work.

2. Discuss the adjustments you might have to make in teaching reading in culturally different schools. For instance: a slum school, a class for retarded children, a bright group of children in a wealthy suburban school, a group of deaf children, a group of blind children. Could the basic principles of teaching

reading discussed in Chapter 2 and in this chapter be applied in all cases?

3. Go to a children's library and spend an afternoon reading contemporary children's books.   Note particularly how these books are different from those you knew when you were a child.

TO THE CLASSROOM TEACHER

1. Look at the next lesson you plan to teach in developing reading skills and see if you can do it with stronger, more creative, motivational power by applying some of the ideas in this chapter.
2. Think of as many ideas as you can to check the comprehension ability of your children without using the workbook exercises.
3. Look at the words below and sound them out.   Check your pronunciation with the dictionary.   Often when children sound out words they encounter the same problem you just did. Knowing this, can you be more patient with children's experimentation with words?   Of what value is phonetic analysis in this instance?   Might not it be as practical to drill on the memorization of the word?
    tapetum, iatrophysical, erythrocyte
4. Check the reading materials you are using in your classroom. Which of them violates the basic principles of creativity by tracing, unimaginative direction-giving, nontension-producing motivation, and so on?   How many ideas can you substitute for some of these uncreative ones?

TO THE COLLEGE STUDENT
AND THE CLASSROOM TEACHER

1. Search through children's literature books and make lists of all those that might serve as a springboard for teaching phonetic analysis or structural analysis.
2. Parties are a natural part of a child's heritage.   Yet in some schools parties have been deleted from the curriculum because they are fun and not educational.   Challenge this idea by planning a party where you would develop the following reading skills: the ability to follow directions, audience-type reading situations, the ability to develop audio and visual acuity, comprehension abilities, organizational skills, the ability to understand ideas in sequence, the ability to dramatize, and the ability to summarize and evaluate.

5. Patty came home crying from first grade about a week after the opening of school. She was clutching a paper on which was printed an apple, a small *a*, and a large *A*. When her mother asked her why she was crying, Patty pointed to a red check mark on the paper and said, "I did this wrong—the teacher said it was wrong." "What were you supposed to do?" asked her mother. "I had to tell her that *A* is for apple—and this is a big *A* and this was a small *a* and that *a* says 'm-m-m.'" "But, darling," her mother said, "*A* doesn't say '*m-m-m*.'" "Oh, yes it does," said Patty. "Apples are good —m-m-m," and she patted her tummy with her hand.

What was Patty trying to do? Was the teacher helping her conceptualize? Of what value was the lesson? Of what value are "marks" on papers at this stage of a child's development? Would you say Patty's teacher was creative? How would you introduce vowel sounds?

SELECTED BIBLIOGRAPHY

Austin, Mary C., Helen J. Kenney, Ann R. Gutmann, and Madeleine Fraggos. *The Torch Lighters*. Cambridge: Harvard University Press, 1961.

Barbe, Walter B. *Educator's Guide to Personalized Reading Instruction*. Englewood Cliffs, N.J.: Prentice-Hall, 1961.

Beery, Althea, Thomas C. Barrett, and William R. Powell, eds. *Elementary Reading Instruction: Selected Materials*. 2nd ed. Boston: Allyn and Bacon, 1974.

Brogan, Peggy, and Lorene Fox. *Helping Children Read*. New York: Holt, Rinehart and Winston, 1961.

Chall, Jeanne S. *Learning to Read: The Great Debate*. New York: McGraw-Hill, 1967.

Clymer, Theodore. "The Utility of Phonic Generalizations in the Primary Grades." *The Reading Teacher* 16 (January 1963): 252–258.

Cordts, Anna D. *Phonics for the Reading Teacher*. New York: Holt, Rinehart and Winston, 1965.

Cutts, Warren G. *Modern Reading Instruction*. Washington, D.C.: Center for Applied Research in Education, 1964.

Dawson, Mildred A., and Henry A. Bamman. *Fundamentals of Basic Reading Instruction*. New York: David McKay Co., 1963.

DeBoer, John, Martha Dallman, and Walter J. Moore. *The Teaching of Reading*. 3rd ed. New York: Holt, Rinehart and Winston, 1970.

Duffy, Gerald G., and George B. Sherman. *Systematic Reading Instruction.* New York: Harper and Row, 1972.

Durkin, Dolores. *Teaching Them to Read.* 2nd ed. Boston: Allyn and Bacon, 1974.

Durrell, Donald D. *Improving Reading Instruction.* New York: Harcourt, Brace and World, 1966.

Fitzgerald, James A., and Patricia G. Fitzgerald. *Teaching Reading and the Language Arts.* New York: Macmillan, 1967.

Gans, Roma. *An Educator Looks at Research in Reading.* Washington, D.C.: American Association of Elementary, Kindergarten, Nursery Education, 1970.

Gray, Lillian. *Teaching Children to Read.* New York: The Ronald Press, 1963.

Guszak, Frank J. *Diagnostic Reading Instruction in the Classroom.* New York: Harper and Row, 1972.

Heilman, Arthur W. *Smuggling Language into the Teaching of Reading.* Columbus, Ohio: Charles E. Merrill Publishing Co., 1972.

Hester, Kathleen B. *Teaching Every Child to Read.* New York: Harper and Row, 1964.

Johnson, Nancy J. *Teach and Do: A Reading Workbook.* New York: Appleton-Century-Crofts, 1973.

McKee, Paul, and William K. Durr. *Reading: A Program of Instruction for the Elementary School.* Boston: Houghton Mifflin, 1966.

Morrison, Ida E. *Kindergarten Primary Education.* New York: The Ronald Press, 1961.

Motivating Readers: The How and Why. Buffalo, N.Y.: D.O.K. Publishers, 1967.

Niles, Olive Stafford. "Building Success Into a Reading Lesson." Scott, Foresman Monograph. Glenview, Ill.: Scott, Foresman, 1973.

Reid, Alastair. *Ounce, Dice, Trice.* Boston: Little, Brown, 1958.

Silvaroli, Nicholas J. *Classroom Reading Inventory.* Rev. ed. Dubuque, Ia.: William C. Brown Co., 1969.

Smith, Frank. *Understanding Reading: A Psycho-linguistic Analysis of Reading and Learning to Read.* New York: Holt, Rinehart and Winston, 1971.

Spache, Evelyn. *Reading Activities for Child Involvement.* Boston: Allyn and Bacon, 1972.

Wallen, Carl J. *Competency in Teaching Reading.* Palo Alto, Calif.: Science Research Associates, 1972.

————. *Word-Attack Skills in Reading.* Columbus, O.: Charles E. Merrill Publishing Co., 1969.

CHAPTER VII

The Creative Teaching
of Reading in the
Intermediate Grades

*I have learned . . . that the head does not hear any-
thing until the heart has listened, and what the heart
knows today the head will understand tomorrow.*[1]

JAMES STEPHENS

TO THE READER

This chapter is a continuation of Chapter 6. The student will
need to skim it to get a total picture of the reading program. It
will be of most value to him when he is in his student-teaching
situation. The primary teacher will benefit from this chapter in
many ways: (1) there are many ideas here that she may adapt
to her reading program; (2) she will understand how the work
she accomplishes becomes the foundation for the development of
reading skills in the intermediate grades; (3) by knowing this,
she may encourage greater continuity in the reading program
from grade to grade; and (4) the preparation she gives her children may become more meaningful when she understands the
skills required for a good intermediate reading program.

The intermediate-grade teacher will find in this chapter
many ideas that, I hope, will spark her own imagination for designing a creative intermediate reading program.

1. James Stephens, *The Crock of Gold: Irish Fairy Tales* (New York:
The Macmillan Co., 1960).

INTRODUCTION

The following account is a combination of a lesson plan prepared by Mr. Banks, a fourth-grade teacher, and the notes taken by an observer during the lesson.

A Lesson Plan: Objectives

1. To build a reading vocabulary through the creative approach to teaching
2. To foster creativity in the children in terms of creative thinking and creative writing
3. To develop the following reading skills:
   a. Selecting the main idea of a communication medium
   b. Extending reading vocabulary through the oral vocabulary
   c. Audience-type reading
   d. Word study—the importance of using the most effective word in a special place
   e. Good oral reading expression
   f. Sequence of ideas
   g. Sight reading
   h. Structural analysis
   i. Phonics analysis
   j. Ability to classify
   k. Choral-speaking ability
4. To diagnose some reading problems
5. To apply reading skills as a tool and integrate them with art, language arts, and social studies material

Motivation

Discussion of purposes of lesson.

Procedure

1. *Discussion: the importance of words.*   Mr. Banks placed a series of cards on the chalkboard that said:

   1. Words Are Important
   2. Words Take Us Far Away
   3. Words Work For Us

4. Words Make Us Feel
5. Words Help Us
6. The Right Word Is Important in the Right Place

The children discussed the cards and explained what each meant to them. Then they played the Adjective Game (see page 198) to show how important it was to get the right word in the right place.

2. *A survey of the children's oral vocabulary and a check on the children's ability to classify words.* Mr. Banks held up some nine-by-twelve-inch pieces of construction paper. On the top of each sheet he had printed a topic. Among the topics were World's Fair, Space Age, summer, spring, baseball, beautiful, old-fashioned, a scare, sports, school, home, airplane, travel, hobbies, pets, farm, and city. He asked each child to choose a topic in which he was interested and, with a flo-pen, list on cards all the words he knew that were appropriate to this topic. They could be descriptive words, related words, or action words. The children worked on the cards for five minutes. Then Mr. Banks asked them to exchange cards and make the lists longer by adding to each other's cards. A second exchange was encouraged. The children then stood by rows and read their word lists, which were then placed on the chalkboard ledge. Mr. Banks suggested some new words for each chart. Soon twenty-two charts of classified words appeared before the class.

3. *Some creative writing.* The children were then encouraged to select one topic on which to work together, and they chose Space Age. Mr. Banks had them work with him and write a poem, using the words on the card and any others they could think of. Soon the poem was composed, and the children put it on the tape recorder as a choral poem. They listened to the tape, evaluated it, made some changes, and recorded it again.

4. *Preparing individual reading materials.* Mr. Banks then encouraged the children to get their own charts from the chalkboard and to write a poem, a story, a description, or a joke, using all the words they could from the list on the chart. Those who finished first could either take another card or illustrate their own writing. As soon as each child finished, he was given a large sheet of chart paper, and he printed his story on the paper with a flo-pen so that all the children could see it. They were encouraged to give their writing titles.

When they were done, the children brought their writings to the front of the room and put them between two large colored cardboards that served as the covers of a "Big Book" of twenty-two original stories.   One child decorated the cover while waiting for the others to finish and gave it a name: "The Big Little Book of Big Ideas."

5. *Audience-type situation.*   While two children held the book open to the proper page, the author of each creative bit of writing shared his work with the class by reading it.   In some instances, the children read each other's work.   Each story or poem was evaluated.

6. *Sight-reading: new material.*   Mr. Banks had dittoed a choral play called *America Today.*   He had anticipated the many words that might arise in it.   The play, about America in the Space Age, was to be read by both groups and solos.   Mr. Banks assigned readings and allowed the children to read the material through once to learn any words they did not know.   In his notebook, Mr. Banks recorded the words that gave group members trouble.   After the dry run, he introduced a recording of "The Battle Hymn of the Republic" and played it as musical background while the children read the choral play once more.   This time it was recorded.   After the playback, the children evaluated their work.

7. *Building reading skills.*   Mr. Banks then told the children he had some notes that he felt would help them.   He spent time reviewing some vowel generalizations that they had had trouble reading aloud, and he introduced some work in structural analysis, using words from the children's charts to show how suffixes and prefixes changed meanings.   He introduced the prefixes *un*, *re*, and *dis*.   Children applied them to words from their charts and changed meanings as follows:

un (to make opposite)		*from chart on:*
happy	unhappy	(spring)
exciting	unexciting	(World's Fair)
comfortable	uncomfortable	(summer)
afraid	unafraid	(airplanes)
related	unrelated	(home)
necessary	unnecessary	(school)

re (to do again)		*from chart on:*
visit	revisit	(World's Fair)
make	remake	(World's Fair)
shape	reshape	(World's Fair)
strict	restrict	(old-fashioned)
pay	repay	(World's Fair)
call	recall	(home)

dis (*to make opposite*)		*from chart on:*
enchanted	disenchanted	(World's Fair)
engage	disengage	(travel)
order	disorder	(school)
interested	disinterested	(baseball)
organize	disorganize	(school)

The children also made lists of words that had opposite meanings to the ones on their charts but were *not* obtained by adding the prefix *un* or *dis* to the original word. Their list included some of the following:

fragile	strong
beautiful	ugly
colorful	drab
pretty	homely
rural	urban
love	hate

8. *Evaluation.* Mr. Banks asked the children to review what they had learned about words, about the prefixes studied, and about oral reading. He asked them, too, if they had enjoyed the afternoon. He told them the "Big Little Book of Big Ideas" would be left in the reading center and he expected them to read each other's stories some time during the week and to ask each other for help with troublesome words. He also put three pieces of chart paper on the chalkboard with the prefixes *un, re,* and *dis* printed at the top and asked that each child add a word to these charts any time they found one in their reading.

Mr. Banks met his objectives well. He also is a creative teacher. Almost all of the principles set up in Chapter 1 of this book were used in his plan.

In developing reading skills, Mr. Banks was also developing creative skills—flexibility of thinking, ability to generalize, ability to abstract and conceptualize, fluency of ideas, originality and individualism, visual and audio discrimination, the ability to discern differences and likenesses, ability to rearrange, ability to produce reactions, retention ability, and the ability to adapt and elaborate. Training children in these skills is fostering creative development as well as reading efficiency.

The creative teaching of reading is enhanced as children learn more and more words and more reading skills, for they are better equipped to put their reading abilities to new uses and new experiences and to create new products. Reading in the inter-

FIGURE 7–1. *A teacher has accomplished her goals when reading becomes a hobby.*

mediate grades should be a powerful tool in the development of creativity.

The instructional jobs of the intermediate-grade teacher, as listed on page 63, will be reviewed below with frequent illustrations of creative teaching. In the lesson above, Mr. Banks taught many of these skills in a meaningful and creative way.

CONTINUED DEVELOPMENT AND EXPANSION OF PRIMARY READING SKILLS

Most of the skills to be discussed in this chapter have been introduced in the primary grades. Work in developing visual perception, oral vocabulary, sight vocabulary, phonic and word analysis skills, word-attack skills, and the use of various context clues continues throughout the child's reading instruction program.

CONTINUED INDEPENDENT READING

Power in reading at the intermediate grade-level comes from many experiences including the following:

1. *The mastery of word-attack skills* as described in Chapter 5. It must be remembered that word-attack skills only aid a child in pronouncing a word; they give no clue to its meaning. Consequently, new words should be introduced for the first time at the meaningful-experience level, which can be either a direct or a vicarious experience.

2. *The careful building of a meaningful oral vocabulary* as each child is exposed to many topics in his science, social studies, arithmetic, and other studies.

FIGURE 7–2. *Reading for information in order to synthesize and make an interesting report.*

3. *The continued development of a sight vocabulary.* Many words can be learned all through life simply by remembering the shape of each word.   The continuous building of a sight vocabulary provides the teacher with a backlog of known words on which she can build phonic generalizations and exceptions, and on which she can develop reading skills such as those demonstrated by Mr. Banks in the reading lesson above.

Mrs. Ames used a homemade tachistoscope for quick recognition of many words.   She cut a piece of oak tag about five by eight inches and folded it back one-half inch along each of the long sides.   This served as a tray to hold her printed materials. She cut an opening in the center of the oak tag strip wide enough to allow for the usual size printed material and fastened another piece of oak tag over this opening with a piece of masking tape to make a hinged shutter.   Printed words on slips of paper cards were slipped into the folds on the back of the oak tag and the shutter was flipped for a second to see if the children could recognize new words at a glance.   Children used this device in drilling each other.

4. *A workable group plan.*   Various plans for grouping were outlined in Chapter 3, and the merits of each were discussed. Rigid ability grouping at the upper elementary grade level is hardly justified (see page 102).   At this age children have a variety of reading problems, and the grouping should be centered around their *problems* rather than their *ability.*   Very slow children will need to be handled separately much of the time, but those within the average range (and this will constitute 84 percent of the class) can be grouped in a variety of ways to work on a variety of problems.   Children should have many opportunities to read together as a total class in lessons similar to the ones described on pages 22 and 78 and at the beginning of this chapter. An independent reading program that is highly individualized is the most logical grouping plan for children of this age and can best foster creative teaching and learning.

5. *Many books and materials on all levels of reading and about many topics.*   This is essential if all reading abilities and problems are to be met.   The materials for the upper elementary reading program should include copies of many text books, many commercial trade books, SRA materials, reading machines, some workbooks for individual practice, and programmed reading materials for some children.   A school library is a *must* for a good intermediate-grade reading program.   Three or four sample books from many sets of social studies, science, and arithmetic books are a wiser choice in stocking room libraries than are twenty-five

books from one series that are all alike.   At least one newspaper and several magazines should be available to children.

6. *A strong program in children's literature.* The skill of writing and the joy of reading should be shared daily as a motivation for reading and as a practical way to help boys and girls apply their reading skills.   Chapter 8 deals with this subject in detail.

7. *Individual records of reading growth and power.* Careful records must be kept of each child's reading power.   At this age record-keeping is possible because children can keep their own records.   The SRA materials offer help in this direction. Teachers and children can devise check sheets and record sheets that keep a record of each child's problems, the books he has read, his reading power, and the areas where he needs help.

8. *Strong incentives for reading.* Some creative teachers have used the following gimmicks with success in motivating children for independent reading.

> a. Keep records of books read on cards or book-jackets. Use the card file to which each child contributes as a master file for the class.   In selecting books, children read the file cards to guide them in choosing books classmates have enjoyed.

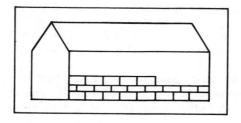

> b. Build a reading house of bricks.   Each brick represents a book read by a student.   On a large cardboard, draw an outline of a house.   When a student finishes a book, he draws a brick on the house.   On the brick he writes the name of the book and his own name.   The children start building the house from the bottom and can see it grow as their reading progresses.
> c. Build a resource file to help children select books for independent reading.   At the first part of the school year, as the students read books from the room library, they write the name of the books, the authors, and one

or two sentences about the books on six-by-nine-inch cards, which are placed in a box in front of the library books. The cards are in constant use. The students seem to select books after reading the cards.

d. Children can make a "bookworm" bulletin board. Cut circles from colored construction paper. Each child makes one to resemble a worm's head, then on assorted colored circles they write the name and author of each book they read. The circles are pinned, overlapping slightly, on the bulletin board to make the "bookworm."

e. For children who cannot read well, yet who crave stories and biographies, there are many new commercial materials on the market that can be of great assistance to the classroom teacher. These include the Scholastic Record and Book Companion Series. In these sets such old favorites as *Caps for Sale, Curious George, Jack and the Beanstalk, Stone Soup,* and *Lentil* have been put on a recording or on a cassette tape by an excellent storyteller. Children may follow the story on the accompanying illustrated text. This makes possible another aspect of individualized reading instruction and does not deny children the joy of hearing literary classics that they cannot read well.

In addition to recording stories, expert readers have recorded a wealth of poetry. *Selections from the Arrow Book of Poetry* includes the work of Carl Sandburg, John Masefield, Langston Hughes, and others.

Information is also imparted to children through such devices. Some tapes and records bear such titles as *The Life and Words of Martin Luther King, Jr., The Moon Explorers, Runaway Slave,* and *The Story of Harriet Tubman.* All children can enjoy these recordings, but they are of special value to the slow reader because he must use other methods than reading to glean information for use in class reports and discussions.

Most of the companies who manufacture such materials also produce the machines on which to play them. The Scholastic Listening Post, for instance, contains a four-speed record player, a student listening center with eight complete headsets, and special packages of supplementary materials. Such units make possible a good listening experience in the classroom for any particular group while the teacher works with no noise distraction. Much creative classroom organization and creative teaching can take place when a teacher has these helpers.

DEVELOPMENT OF OTHER MIDDLE-GRADE SKILLS

Expanding the Vocabulary and Range of Materials

In the intermediate grades, the child is often introduced to a world of new words through the social studies program of the school and through the expanding, varied number of activities in which he finds himself.   Up to this time, most children have been reading familiar material in their social studies books.   They have studied their own community, contrasting communities, and then the history of communities.   In each instance, the children have added unique words to their base oral and reading vocabularies, but the bulk of the words were learned in studying their own communities.   These vocabularies were developed with meaning, since most of them were derived from the child's common, local, everyday experiences.   These base vocabularies made it possible for him to transfer meanings into a study of other communities because all communities are alike to a degree.

In the area of science, especially in topics related to the Space Age, children have acquired a unique vocabulary by the time they reach the fourth grade.   Through television, newspapers, movies, and other forms of mass media, children at this age have often integrated a larger vocabulary in some of these areas than their teachers.   In selecting and constructing reading and instructional materials, teachers need to recognize this fact, threatening though it may be to some of them.

Also, by the time the child reaches the fourth grade he has learned many things from reading.   He is now capable of living many experiences in his mind; that is, word symbols suggest experiences about other people that he can visualize and that he no longer has to experience directly or vicariously in order to understand.   His own vast background has given meaning to word symbols to the degree that he can now use them in new thought patterns and imagine the experience being described on the printed page.   This ability makes it possible for children of this age to learn a great deal more from books than the early primary child who can only read with understanding about those experiences that are much like his own.

One precaution should be taken in order to avoid reading disability at this time, however; *new* words should still be introduced at the experience level.   Social studies books, at best, are a collection of important concepts, and any one page may contain several concepts outside the realm of the child's comprehension.   One of the first jobs of the teacher is to be sure that the vocabulary to be introduced for any social studies unit is taught at the experience level.   For instance, a group of children who are going to study Mexico will need to understand a vocabulary unique to that country in order to be able to use these words with meaning as the unit develops.   Such a list might contain such words as *adobe, sombrero, serape, fiesta, siesta, tortilla, frijole,* and *burro.*   All of these words can be meaningfully introduced by showing a good film that illustrates each word, stopping the film to discuss with the children those parts that give meaning to the words.   A word is assigned to an object or an experience in meaningful context so that it has equal meaning when read later in the context of the social studies book.

In addition to social studies, there are several other experiences for which the children need to build new vocabulary— current events, regional experiences, introduction to new heroes, sports and political events, and family travels.   Reading power can be developed most logically if the child is helped to acquire the meaningful oral vocabulary first, then is shown the words he is speaking in print as suggested by language sequence development.

A creative teacher will recognize that learning words is a social and academic skill that children of this age must develop and will find many ways to continue to develop the oral and reading vocabulary of every child.

Ideas for building vocabulary in the intermediate grade child include the following:

1. Reread the section on vocabulary development in the chapter on oral vocabulary.

2. At the front of the room, keep a vocabulary chart to which all new words discovered or experienced by the class or by individuals are added.   Remember that the *sight* of the word will help the child to read it and that children still learn words most quickly this way even though they now possess many phonic and word analysis skills.

3. Introduce units by films, filmstrips, trips, and so forth, so that the oral vocabulary of the material to be developed in the unit is acquired in a meaningful way at the *beginning* of the unit.

4. Refer to Chapter 8 (page 296) for ways of using bulletin boards, puppet shows, and such, to develop reading vocabulary.

5. Have children make individual card files of the new words they find.   Each child can make a box for his own words and keep them filed alphabetically in his desk.

6. Make individual scrapbooks of words.

7. Play descriptive games. Take a word such as *tree*. List all the words that could be used to describe a tree—*green, tall, stately, rough, smooth, leafy, majestic, twisted*.

8. Print sentences or phrases on strips of paper; leave out descriptive words and then print on the chalkboard all the words that would fill the space. Some examples are:

The _____ house stood in the woods.
I like to see the _____ light in children's eyes at Christmas.
The _____ smell of the pine trees.
The _____ odor of smoke.

9. Make a matching game with new words in one column and meanings in the other.

10. Have each child make his own dictionary of new words. Illustrate dictionaries with verbal descriptions or pictures.

11. Have children make up descriptive riddles.

12. Play guessing games, such as: I am thinking of a word that means a large tank or well in which water is kept. It begins with a /c/ and ends with a /d/. (Be sure the word is printed on the chalkboard after it is guessed.)

13. Use picture cards with word cards to match. A child who has a picture must find the child with the matching word. Then they sit together to study spelling words or for some other paired activity.

14. The feltboard and stickboard can help to develop new words and new word skills.

15. Flash cards can be used effectively to check reading vocabulary—especially with difficult words.

16. Make word trees. Bring in a branch and set it in a container. Print a key word on a piece of brightly colored construction paper. Children tie on related words as they discover them. One tree may contain words unique to Alaska, one may contain words describing Canada, one may be built around a new science unit.

17. Print individual stories of each child on shelf paper. Have the child draw an illustration for his story. Make a roll movie of it, and each child can read his story to the class as it comes into view.

18. Use games to develop vocabulary, such as:
   a. *Word Lightning.* The object is to name in one minute as many English words beginning with the letter being worked on as you can. The one who can

think of the most will be the score-keeper next round. This would be very helpful in stimulating reading and vocabulary study.

b. *Word Parchesi.* A parchesi board may be made or drawn on the chalkboard. The spaces will contain words from the vocabulary of the class. The child must give the word definition before he goes on. This can be worked in teams also.

19. Put several or all of the vocabulary words on slips of paper and/or on the board. Divide the class into groups and have them create original stories around these words. Read the stories to the class or have the children exchange stories and read them in groups. This can stimulate the imagination, reinforce the vocabulary, and give practice in oral expression.

Developing More Refined Techniques of Effective Comprehension

Reading without comprehension is not reading. Throughout the primary grades reading comprehension is checked with each day's reading lesson in a variety of ways. Comprehension will be no problem if the child's reading is based on material within his own experience. When he begins to read widely and independently, however, he meets many words he has not experienced, or his experience is limited, and the word does not make sense as applied in a new situation, so comprehension often breaks down. More frequent checks on comprehension are needed, and skills in helping children obtain the meaning of new words and old words used in new situations need to be taught.

Checking Comprehension. Comprehension may be checked in many interesting ways in these grades, as in the following:

1. Listen to children tell stories they have read.

2. Encourage children to give interesting and unusual book reports.

3. Refer to the many good exercises listed in the teacher's manual accompanying basic readers.

4. Show children how to select the most helpful facts to answer a specific question.

5. Prepare exercises for children in which they are asked to reorganize a series of closely related thoughts.

a. Have them make up and solve crossword puzzles in subject areas.

b. Have them follow directions for making a diorama, slides, roll movies, and so forth.

c. Have them read dramatizations and write plays of favorite stories.

6. Prepare cards of more difficult directions for children to follow. For example, during a class party have a treasure hunt, with clues planted at various places for children to find.

7. Keep a file of cards on which are printed directions that children can follow independently to prepare materials for the room.

8. Distribute slips of paper with some secret activity to all the children. For example, one might read, "Get out the new book from the top of teacher's closet. Look it over and see what it is about." This will give the children an opportunity to talk about something new and of interest to the class at the end of the activity period.

9. Use many methods of studying to develop study techniques. (See *Creative Teaching of the Social Studies in the Elementary School* for detailed discussion on study techniques for social studies.)[2]

    a. Using guide words to study.
    b. Using outlines to study.
    c. Using dramatization as a study skill.
    d. Setting up questions for study.
    e. Studying by committees.

10. Use outlining as a means of developing comprehension. Outlining is especially useful in helping children to select minor items that are related to a central thought.

11. Use techniques to help children select the central thought in short and long selections.

    a. Collect baby pictures and have children write clever captions for them.
    b. Pictures of animals in various poses may be used the same way.
    c. Read paragraphs or stories together and then make up titles for them.

12. Read a paragraph and draw a picture showing the main idea, *or* read a story and draw many pictures showing a succession of main points. These pictures can be used in a roll movie or a classroom mural.

13. Make a bulletin-board display showing the central idea of a story.

14. Run off a series of paragraphs on a ditto sheet, and at the bottom of the sheet ask a series of questions that point out the

2. James A. Smith, *Creative Teaching of the Social Studies in the Elementary School* (Boston: Allyn and Bacon, 1967), Chapter 10.

main idea of each paragraph.   Children match paragraphs and questions.

15. Have the children write paragraphs with the main idea (or sentence) missing.   Have each child type or print his paragraph on a five-by-eight-inch card.   On another card print the missing sentence that expresses the main idea.   Children will have fun reading each other's paragraphs and matching them to the main ideas.

16. Show children that riddles are often paragraphs without a main idea.   Have them write riddles and allow the rest of the class to guess the answers.   Then rewrite the riddles as a paragraph with a main idea and use these paragraphs to show that clear, uncluttered writing gives the main idea immediately.

17. Give the children paragraphs to read from which the main idea has been omitted so that they will see how the lack of one sentence in a paragraph can render it meaningless.   One such example follows:

> It was a lovely place, full of fun and laughter.   We saw all the characters from the famous moving pictures made by the inventor.   We rode on every sort of ride; for a moment we were Alice in Wonderland and then Peter Pan flying to Never-Never Land.   We went from the underwater world of Atlantis to the depths of the African jungle.   It was an experience we shall never forget.

This paragraph leaves the reader with an odd, unsatisfied feeling.   The sentences are complete, but the explanatory sentence is missing.   Read it again but this time add this sentence at the beginning.

> Last summer we visited Disneyland.

Now the paragraph sounds complete.   Point out to the children that each paragraph and each article they read will have a main idea.   Collect newspaper and magazine articles and underline the main idea in each paragraph.

18. Ask pupils to bring to class colored pictures from calendars, magazines, or advertisements.   Mount and number all pictures.   On worksheets made of sheets of paper numbered to correspond with the pictures, have each child write a caption appropriate to each picture as it is passed along. Later, when the pictures are placed on the bulletin board, the captions are read and the one that best shows the main idea of the picture is printed below it.

19. By writing headlines children have the experience of writing a complete but brief summary of the BIG idea of the story or article. Collect some short newspaper articles. Paste them on white paper for convenience in handling. Number each article for identification and discussion.

Have each child read an article to find the BIG idea. On a worksheet numbered the same as the articles, have them write a brief headline telling what the article is about. After all the children have had the opportunity to read and brief the articles, the headlines each wrote may be shared. Who was able to write the most appropriate headline?

20. Help children to select and judge relevant materials.

a. Have them send for material from various resources by writing letters and then judge the material received.

b. Teach them how to use a film catalogue to select classroom films.

c. Teach them how to select, order, and use filmstrips.

21. Play the Stagecoach Game. Make a list containing parts of a stagecoach, equipment, and passengers, such as *wheel, bridle, harness, springs, cushion, cranky old gentleman, young college girl, maiden lady, young farmer, sacks of apples, newspaper, brake, seat, window, laprobe, white-and-black horse, dashboard, foot warmer, suitcase, cane, parasol, canary bird,* and *hat box.*

Formation: The players are seated on chairs in a circle. One extra player is chosen as Storyteller and gives each player in the circle a word or phrase from a list such as the above. The same word may be given to more than one player if the circle is very large.

The Storyteller makes up a story in which he brings in as many references as possible to the passengers, parts, and equipment. As each word is mentioned, the player who represents that part must stand quickly, whirl around once, and sit down. If the Storyteller should bring in the words "and the stage coach upset" all the players change seats, and the Storyteller tries to get one of the seats. The player who is left without a seat takes up the story and the game continues.

22. Have children study pictures and paintings to answer specific questions, such as: Did the artist use any other color besides white to show snow?

23. Develop skills in reading graphs, charts, and maps.

24. Develop a vocabulary for each unit to be taught in science, social studies, literature, and so forth.

25. Have children keep an individual vocabulary notebook in which many word-comprehension skills are recorded: varied meanings, homonyms, synonyms, antonyms, definitions, pronunciations.

26. Help children to adjust speed to purpose; that is, help them to realize that some assignments require skimming; some, careful reading for details.

a. Teach children to skim by using supplementary reading material printed in columns rather than across pages. Tell children to run their eyes down, selecting key words in each line of print, and to try to reconstruct the story through use of these key words.

b. Collect headlines and guidelines from newspapers and use them to anticipate the story. Check to see how this helps speed comprehension.

c. Scan sports pages to find batting averages, etc.

27. Help children develop skills in rereading for such specific purposes as finding specific facts, selecting general ideas, and drawing conclusions. For example, have children reread to find clues as to what should be included in a mural or in scenery.

28. Provide many books (on all reading levels and on a variety of topics) in the reading center to broaden the scope of the child's leisure reading.

29. Use the teacher's manual of a basic series for ideas for developing comprehension with specific textbook stories.

Comprehension Skills and Questioning. Among the comprehension skills developed above are the following:

1. Reading to find the main idea of a paragraph, a page, or a story
2. Reading to identify a logical sequence of events
3. Reading to answer specific questions
4. Reading to draw attention to important details
5. Reading to develop the ability to summarize facts
6. Reading to develop the ability to make generalizations
7. Reading to locate information
8. Reading to help other people enjoy what you read (audience-type situation)
9. Following a given set of directions
10. Reading to predict outcomes
11. Making critical evaluations of materials
12. Reading for enjoyment
13. Reading to think creatively
14. Reading to think critically

Reading is a thought process. Much can be done to further the development of *thinking* skills while reading is being taught. Various taxonomies are of help to the teacher in developing thinking processes. Bloom's Taxonomy[3] identifies six levels of reading skills.

1. Knowledge
2. Comprehension
3. Application
4. Analysis
5. Synthesis
6. Evaluation

Inasmuch as questions are tools by which teachers teach and without which they cannot teach, careful planning of the questions used with children is essential.

Many basic materials do not attempt to develop all the levels of thinking outlined by Bloom. Very few, if any, list questions that are open-ended and that lead to the development of creativity in children. In light of this fact, teachers need to think carefully about the questions they ask to develop thinking through reading.

Jones has devised an organization of thinking skills intended to clarify and adapt the taxonomy of Bloom in a way that

makes its practical application to the work of the classroom readily understandable. The six categories of Bloom have been altered in light of the goals of reading instruction, and four distinct levels of pupil responses have been identified.[4]

Jones then develops a diagram consisting of four categories that contribute to the total thinking process of the child: literal comprehension, interpretation, critical thinking, and creative thinking. Jones is one of the few authors who place creative thinking in a category by itself. Jones explains her categories as follows:

1. *Literal comprehension:* This is the level where teachers all too often elicit a response requiring the parroting of a fact just

3. Benjamin S. Bloom, Max D. Engelhart, Edward J. Furst, Walter H. Hill and David R. Krathwohl, eds., *Taxonomy of Educational Objectives: Handbook No. 1: The Cognitive Domain* (New York: David McKay, 1956).
4. Virginia W. Jones, "Reading Comprehension and the Development of Thinking Skills" (Lincoln, Neb.: The University Project, Mimeographed Bulletin), p. 3. Used with permission of the author.

read and consider the task concluded. At this level, however, a child needs *intelligence, reading ability,* and *memory* in order to be able to perform the required task. It is a low level of thinking and requires no independent thinking.

2. *Interpretation:* At this level the child does what he could do at Level 1 but in addition he must add two new ingredients. The first is a *background of experience* upon which he can draw. The second is the *ability to relate those experiences* to the task at hand.

3. *Critical thinking:* When a child is capable of performing these five enumerated skills, he can then draw a conclusion, make a generalization, or formulate a judgment. In order to do this he must analyze a given situation. He must not only draw upon his previous experiences, but he must synthesize several experiences, evaluate them, discard extraneous ones, and, on the basis of these procedures, arrive at a conclusion that satisfies him as an answer to the problem. At the stage known as critical thinking, then, the child must exercise *intelligence, reading ability,* and *memory; have a background of experiences; be able to make associations; analyze,* and *synthesize;* and then *make judgments.*

4. *Creative thinking:* Jones, like me, feels that creative thinking is the highest of all levels of human thought and worthy of placement in a separate category. In addition to the eight qualities mentioned above, the creative thinker must add to these one or more of the following: *imagination, emotion,* and *energy.* Jones says,

> If a child has arrived at a judgment or a generalization or a conclusion through his ability to think critically, and if he then can add to this the highly individual ingredient, imagination, he can come up with an original, creative thought. If this original thought is one about which he feels strongly (has emotion), and if in turn his strong feeling overcomes his lethargy and causes him to exert energy in this direction, he produces original thinking.[5]

In developing creative thinking, the questions are open-ended, and there is no right or wrong answer. Each child's answer is original with him and should be accepted.

Jones summarizes her taxonomy as follows:

1. Literal feedback
   a. requires intelligence, reading ability, memory
   b. requires that pupil parrot back words of text

5. Ibid., p. 6.

2. Interpretation
   a. requires literal comprehension
   b. requires background of experiences, plus ability to make associations
3. Critical thinking
   a. requires literal comprehension
   b. requires interpretation
   c. requires the ability to analyze, to synthesize, to make judgments
4. Original thinking
   a. requires literal comprehension
   b. requires interpretation
   c. requires critical thinking
   d. requires imagination, emotion, and energy

The types of thinking stimulated by questioning according to Jones's categories may be illustrated by using a popular children's story, *The Wizard of Oz.*

1. *Literal Comprehension:* Knowledge questions (literal comprehension of material read)
   a. Who went down the yellow-brick road?
   b. Where were they going?
   c. What was the cowardly lion going to Oz for?
   d. What was the tin man going for?
   e. What was the scarecrow going for?
2. *Interpretation* (ability to relate background to a task at hand)
   a. Was the scarecrow unhappy? How do you know?
   b. Did Dorothy, the scarecrow, the tin man, and the cowardly lion go down the yellow-brick road quickly? How do you know?
   c. Is Kansas a temperate or a torrid climate?
3. *Critical Thinking* (ability to draw conclusions, synthesize, make generalizations, and form a judgment)
   a. Why was the lion happy with the diploma?
   b. Why did no one ever see the Wizard?
   c. Did Dorothy's dream help her to be happier?
   d. Does this story teach us a lesson?
4. *Creative Thinking* (ability to imagine and to react with emotion and energy)
   a. What might have happened if the Wizard had been a monster?
   b. Who else might be waiting along the yellow-brick road to go to Oz, and why might they be going?
   c. What happened to Oz after Dorothy left it?
   d. What is happening in the land of the Munchkins right now?

FIGURE 7–3. *Children are highly motivated when they write and print their own books.*

Developing the Skill of Critical Thinking

Critical thinking is problem-solving toward some goal.   It is taking a group of facts, making decisions, and passing judgment consistent with those facts.

Critical thinking can be stimulated by situations in which children find themselves forced to pass judgments or make decisions.   The motivation for critical thinking comes from questions teachers ask, problems at hand in the classroom that must be solved, or problems posed by a textbook.

However, many of the questions asked by teachers and textbooks under the guise of developing critical thinking do not. The answers can be found simply by rereading parts of the text. This is not to be confused with critical thinking.   The exercise is little more than a series of lessons in reading comprehension using a text.

Following are some questions taken from various social studies texts that were listed under the pretense of developing critical thinking but which actually are only comprehension questions:

1. Why did the pioneers often take their stoves west in their wagons when space was so precious?
2. Why did people migrate west?

3. What are the various means of transportation and what goods are shipped by each means?
4. At sixty miles per hour, how long will it take to travel across Texas?
5. Why is Alaska growing in importance?

The following questions were taken from the plans of two teachers who were concerned that their children learn to think critically. The difference between this type of question and the type listed above is obvious.

Questions That Provoke Critical Thinking

1. What effect has the St. Lawrence Seaway had upon our country?
2. What were the desirabilities and undesirabilities of plantation life?
3. Why were a desert state (Nevada) and a swamp state (Florida) the two fastest growing states in 1960?
4. What were some of the differences and similarities of settlers in Virginia in 1607 and in California in 1849?
5. Where would you want to live if you moved to Alaska? Why?
6. Do you suppose Russia is sorry that she sold Alaska to us?
7. What has happened that has made it possible for people to live on the desert now?
8. The coldest and hottest places in the world are in the temperate zone. Why isn't the coldest place in the Frigid Zone and the hottest place in the Torrid Zone?
9. Why do homes in northern Switzerland have such steep-sloping roofs?
10. What has made it possible for homes in the temperate climates of North America where there are severe winters to have flat roofs?

Here are some ways textbooks might set conditions for critical thinking.

Some Problems to Solve

1. In Chapter I you learned much about geography. Geography helps us to understand why the world and the universe are as they are. It helps us to understand why people in some parts of the world are alike and why they are different. You have already seen many still pictures, moving pictures, and television shows of people from other places doing things differently than you do.
   Here is a big problem for you:

Collect all the pictures you can of people who are doing things differently than you do in your town. Also collect pictures of people who dress differently than you do. Make a big bulletin-board display of these pictures. Then see if you can answer these questions about the people in your pictures.

a. If they are working, why are they doing the work they are doing? Is it because the land where they live is different from the land where you live? Is it because the weather or climate is different?

b. Can you tell by your pictures what part of the world these people come from?

c. Can you guess what temperature zone they might live in?

d. Can you tell which places are hot all the time, which are cold all the time, and which are in-between?

e. If people in your pictures are playing, can you tell if the climate and geography determine how they shall play?

f. See if you can make lists of facts that are *sometimes* true of cold countries but not always (such as: There is generally ice there), of hot countries (such as: They generally do not have snow), of temperate countries (such as: They generally have cool or cold winters and warm or hot summers), of high countries (such as: They are generally cooler than low countries), of low countries (such as: They are generally near the seacoast).

2. Here is another problem that will make you think. Arrange a bulletin board or a chalkboard with signs as follows:

Found *only* in hot countries	Found *only* in cold countries	Found *only* in temperate countries

Found *sometimes* in hot countries	Found *sometimes* in cold countries	Found *sometimes* in temperate countries

Never found in hot countries	*Never* found in cold countries	*Never* found in temperate countries

Now take the following list of words and fit them in the proper spaces. After you have done this, make up lists of words of your own and put them in the proper spaces:

mining	palm trees	equatorial forests
roses	westerly winds	hurricanes
whales	the equator	bananas
ice caps	fishing	apple trees
oranges	sponge fishing	evergreen trees
jungles	deserts	lakes
glaciers	snow-capped	lemons
hailstones	mountains	pelicans
cactus	icebergs	pearl divers
bathing beaches	dates and figs	sandy beaches
alligators	snowstorms	polar bears
seaweed	oysters	corn
dairy farming	wheat	sugar cane
bamboo	igloos	pineapples
sailboats	sunburns	rice

3. Ask your mothers and fathers to tell you the answers to these questions and you will see how quickly things change:

a. What was your favorite television program when you were ten years old?

b. What kind of automobile did your father have when you were my age?

c. How long did it take a large passenger airplane to travel from New York to San Francisco when you were ten years old?

d. What materials were used to make your clothes when you were my age?

e. When you were in the fourth grade, what kind of school did you go to and what subjects did you study?

f. What happened to people who had polio when you were young?

Now see if you can figure out why there are so many changes from the time your mother and father were your age up to now.

4. Here are some statements. Using this chapter, see if you can find material that shows these statements are true:

a. People work all the time to bring order in their world.

b. Most people have religious beliefs.

c. People depend on each other for their living.

5. Find passages in this chapter which make these ideas true:

      a. People try to bring order to their world by making laws about living together.
      b. People are always trying to make their lives interesting and happy.
      c. Inventions and discoveries change people's ways of living.
      d. People live as they do because of the world around them.
   6. One of the freedoms we now have is freedom of the press. People can print what they want to.   But do they always print the truth?   Look at the clippings and advertisements in Figure 7–4, taken from a famous newspaper. Is what they say really true?

Developing Techniques for Effective Reading Rate

In a culture where much reading material is available and where the average citizen must read a great deal to remain literate in national and world affairs, speed in reading becomes an essential skill.   But speed in reading is a skill only if the reader comprehends what he reads.   Therefore, the teacher must help the child *think* about what he reads.   The *type of thinking* will determine the speed.   Is he reading to think *critically, evaluatively, imaginatively, appreciatively,* or *analytically*?   The purpose of reading determines the proper speed for reading.   Part of the problem

FIGURE 7–4.   *Is freedom of the press sometimes abused?*

in developing speed for reading, then, is to help the reader recognize material that should be read with speed and material
that must be read slowly.   Parts of the daily newspaper may be
skimmed without losing the essential point of the article, while
other parts must be read with great care in order not to confuse
essential points of any given issue.   Much of the work of the
teacher in developing reading rate is to help children determine
the intensity of speed to be used with any given article.   Children
may make lists of material that should be read carefully and
material that should be skimmed.   One such list in a fifth-grade
classroom looked like this:

Things We Read Carefully

1. Arithmetic problems
2. Directions
3. Science experiments
4. Research material to get facts
5. Things we read for details
6. Charts, graphs, maps, globes

Things We Read Quickly

1. Newspaper articles
2. Stories
3. Articles, when we want the main idea
4. Material in which we are trying to locate something
5. Cartoons
6. Comic papers

Some suggestions for helping children develop speed in
reading follow:
   1. Examine each article or story the children plan to read
together, determine the purpose for reading it, and decide whether
it can be skimmed or should be read carefully.
   2. To help children develop a skimming skill, have them
use their supplementary school reading materials, such as the
Weekly Reader, or any other paper arranged in columns.   Throw
one sample on a screen with the opaque projector.   After one
child has read the column aloud, work with the class in reading
each line separately and have them then select and underline
the main *word* in each line.   Then read the column by reading
the key words *down* the page.   After a while try this with other
news items without reading the whole item first.   After reading
down the page, discuss the article, glean its meaning, then check
by reading it carefully.   Before long, comprehension may be

checked by having children read articles in their school papers, textbooks, or supplementary reading materials in this way, and then giving a comprehension test on it. If children can read this way with 70 percent comprehension or more, they are doing well.

3. Poor reading rate generally means a child has a short eye span. He sees only a few words with each eye fixation as his eyes cross a page. Lengthening the eye span helps his reading rate. This can be done by various drills that train the child's eye to recognize a wider span of material.

Put numbers on cards and flash them before the children or on a screen. Have the children tell you the numbers on the card (for example, 3628). As soon as they can do this easily, add numbers to each end of the series (such as 236289). Work a while with these numbers and then add more. Finally, change all the numbers.

Pictures placed on strips of cardboard will also help the children notice more things in one sweep of the eye. Make the strips longer as the children gain proficiency in recognizing and remembering the number of objects and their names.

4. Use easy material to improve the children's speed. Familiar material (that which has been read before) may also be used if children are remotivated to reading it. Tell them that you are going to try to develop their speed, so you will use something they know. Then check their comprehension by asking general questions—but not the usual ones.

Easy books with good stories that are new to the children provide good material for reading quickly. Mrs. Frank set aside one period each week in her sixth grade for easy books she brought into the classroom from the town library. Each child was to see how many of these books he could read in one half hour. Comprehension was checked by the discussion that followed.

5. Teacher's manuals accompanying the basic series used in the classroom offer excellent suggestions for increasing speed in reading.

6. Anticipation of material helps children read with speed. Use clues (guidelines, headlines, pictures, charts, graphs, or cartoons) to help children get the gist of the article quickly before they begin to read it. The nature of the material helps children anticipate the vocabulary necessary to read it.

7. Time tests can be effective in developing speed when used in situations that are fun. Children are given a selection to read in a book related to their independent reading level. The teacher starts them reading and stops them at the end of three minutes. Children estimate the number of words they have read

and find the number they are reading per minute.   Then they read the same material again to see how much faster familiar material can be read.   The results can be graphed so that each child can see his progress over a period of time.   Frequent comprehension tests should be given along with the reading to be sure the child is getting meaning from his reading.

Developing the Skill of Reading Carefully for Directions and Details

Some reading must be slow to the point of being laborious in order to be effective.   Reading for directions and for details may fall into this category.   In teaching children to read carefully without destroying the speed essential to other kinds of reading, probably the first step again is to help them recognize material that will require slow reading.

In Mrs. Mead's fourth grade, the children made an analysis of their reading over a period of two weeks and listed all the material they had read slowly and carefully.   Their list looked like this:

Things We Read Slowly

1. Directions for our test.
2. Stage directions for our play.
3. John read slowly when he learned how to stock the terrarium.
4. Recipes for making candy for our bake sale.
5. Mary read the new fire drill directions to us slowly.
6. Our daily plans.
7. Mrs. Mead read the new playground rules to us slowly.
8. We read our workbook exercises slowly.
9. We read the directions in our Girl Scout and Boy Scout manuals slowly.
10. Mrs. Mead read "Uncle Remus" slowly to us.

Later these children made lists of times they had seen their parents read slowly at home.

Times Adults Read Slowly

1. Mother reads recipes slowly and carefully.
2. Father reads slowly when he assembles new furniture, the new lawn mower, or a new toy.
3. Mother reads slowly when she makes out the family schedule for the week.

4. Mother reads her grocery list slowly.
5. We read the bulletin board with rules for using the park slowly.
6. Dad reads the road map slowly.
7. We read directions in our erector sets and science sets slowly.
8. We read our school homework assignments slowly.
9. Mother reads the notices we bring home from school slowly.
10. Mother and Dad read the church bulletin slowly.

A summary of such experiences in Mrs. Mead's room resulted in a chart like this:

Materials We Read Carefully and Slowly

1. Directions
2. Rules
3. Recipes
4. Schedules
5. Maps
6. Bulletins and programs
7. New material
8. Our daily plans
9. Dialects

Once a sensitivity has been built up to what should be read slowly, children will learn to identify this kind of material by glancing at it. A word from the teacher will often help act as a guide while children are learning about differences in material.

Many techniques and methods can be employed to help children read for detail.

1. Just as anticipation of the nature of the article helps build speed, it can help the student read for details. Use headlines, guidelines, pictures, and maps to determine the nature of a story or article, then have the children list questions whose answers would fill in the unknown details of the article. Read to find these answers.

2. Unit teaching offers ample opportunity for helping children to find material and read it for detail. In listing and classifying questions at the beginning of a unit, children are setting up realistic conditions for reading for details.

Developing Skill in Oral or Audience-Type Situations

Oral reading is used much less than silent reading in actual life experiences. Consequently, it is not emphasized as heavily in

the reading program as it once was.   Excessive oral reading reduces rate in speed and comprehension.   The use of oral reading
in the classroom should be restricted to those purposes for which
children use oral reading in life.   Intermediates use oral reading:

1. To impart information or background material, such
as reading to a class about a famous scientist.

2. To prove a point or verify information.

a. Have children look up populations of countries in
several books, note differences, and determine which
source is most reliable.

b. Check with original sources when a debatable or
incorrect piece of information is given by a child during a report.

c. Use newspapers to check batting averages, store
prices, etc.

3. To answer questions in a check on content.

4. To read written reports (social studies reports, book
reports, reports from interviews).

5. To read to an audience.   For example, Miss Holmes set
up a Storytelling Bureau at a table in the rear of her room.
Whenever a child finished a story or a book that he liked well
enough to tell it to the rest of the class, he put an ad in the bureau offering the name of his story and his services in telling it.
Time was provided in the daily program for one such story each
day.

6. To give directions

a. One child reads directions for making cake or candy
for a party while others follow them.

b. One child reads directions from the principal's office
for fire drill, air raid drill, or other civil defense drills,
and other children listen.

7. To "walk out" a dramatization that children are reading.   (See section on literature, page 303, Chapter 8.)

8. To read from charts or dittoed sheets that were origi-
nally made by the children, such as plans for studying, plans for
a play, a field trip or an exhibit, and questions or other material
that needs frequent reviewing.

9. To read from minutes or notes for class meetings, book-
club meetings, and so on.

10. For appreciation and fun, such as:

a. Telling stories.

b. Reading a story while the other children watch a
filmstrip (Weston Woods Filmstrips are especially
suited to this).

FIGURE 7–5. *Listening experiences for intermediates include experimentation with different sounds.*

c. Reading captions on filmstrips.

d. Reading for dramatization.

e. Choral reading from books or chalkboard.

f. Reading reports of favorite books to each other.

g. Reading poems aloud.

h. Reading for sociodramas (see *Creative Teaching of the Social Studies*)[6]

i. Reading in role-playing or problem stories.

j. Reading to accompany flannel-board stories or pantomimes.

k. Reading certain verbal games.

11. To read stories to each other or take turns reading parts of the story aloud. (Tape the readings and play them back so the children may hear themselves. This is an excellent way to improve expression and correct gross mistakes.)

6. Smith, *Creative Teaching of the Social Studies*, Chapter 9.

Developing More Skilled Approaches to Word Study

Among the word-attack skills developed in most intermediate grades (if they have not already been developed in the primary grades) are the following. Each child:

1. Gains auditory perception of digraphs and diphthongs, such as *oa, ea, oo, ow, ou, oi,* and *oy.*
    a. Make a list of words containing the above letters.
    b. Play a flashcard game using the above letters in words.
    c. Use telephone books to find words having the above letters.
    d. Use magazines and the *Weekly Reader* to find words containing such letters.

2. Recognizes phonograms useful in attacking new words (*aw, ou, ight, ick, ack, ock, ing, old, ill, all, est, ake, orn,* and *ong.*
    a. Make a list of words containing the above cluster of letters.
    b. Print the phonograms on cards with a flo-pen and construct words from them by adding suffixes and prefixes.

3. Recognizes that *x, k,* and *s* sound alike (boo*k*s, fo*x*).
    a. Pronounce rhyming words (*box, fox*).
    b. Give lists of words and have the children strike out the word that doesn't fit (*box, chair, books*).

4. Recognizes that *s* sometimes sounds like *z* (visit, bu*s*y).
    a. Use flashcards where necessary.
    b. Use lists of such words for pronunciation.

5. Recognizes words with both voiced and unvoiced *th* (*they, their, thin, thought, through*).
    a. List words to pronounce orally.
    b. Make up sentences and underline words having voiced or unvoiced *th.*

6. Knows that *wh* has sound of /w/ in *wh*en, *wh*ere.

7. Knows *wh* has sound of /h/ in *wh*o, *wh*ole.

8. Learns the principle of contractions (apostrophe used in place of one or more letters).

9. Learns meaning and uses of common suffixes and prefixes, such as *ful, less, re,* and *un.*
    A wheel with word roots and prefixes and suffixes can be designed to turn so that the words change when new prefixes and suffixes are added to the root words.

10. Receives continued instruction in using the context to develop meaning in passages read.

11. Learns that words can have more than one meaning, such as "run *fast*," or a "*fast* color."

12. Learns that meanings of words may shift from line to line or page to page. Cards can be made showing this:

It was a *fair* day.   The Joneses were going to the *fair*.

13. Learns that some words have no meaning until they are text, such as the word *cleave*.

Example: The butcher will *cleave* the beef into several parts. The barnacles will *cleave* to the side of the ship.

14. Learns that there are exceptions to all rules.

Example: The prefix *in* often negates a word, as in *destructible* and *indestructible; valid* and *invalid*.
Exception: valuable and invaluable.   The meaning is not negated—both mean *valuable*.

15. Applies the generalizations learned in the primary grades to multisyllabic words.

16. Learns of more sophisticated markings, such as the schwa (ə) (the unstressed vowel sound of the *a* in *about* and the *u* in *circus*).

Developing Reference Techniques

To become independently adequate in applying reading skills to the subject-matter areas, the intermediate-grade child will need to master many reference techniques.   Specific skills he will need are:

1. The ability to locate information easily
2. The ability to take notes
3. The ability to outline
4. The ability to summarize

Developing the Ability to Apply Reading Skills

No reading skills should be taught without direct application of the skill to the particular child's reading program.   For a highly developed teaching program, a few skills must be extracted and taught, and then the learned skill should be applied continually to reading material. Skills are often taught as another part of the language arts program and then applied to reading.

A list of skills to be taught in the intermediate grades (if not developed before) in order to promote independent reading and reading power would include the following:

Dictionary skills: Use the dictionary to—

1. Recognize alphabetical arrangements.
2. Train in the use of guide words.
3. Learn divisions and parts of dictionaries.
4. Learn pronunciations and how to use pronunciation keys.
5. Select suitable meanings for words used in varied context.
6. Understand phonetic spelling and syllabication (using syllables as an aid to spelling and pronunciation).
7. Find single and blended sounds of letters.
8. Interpret diacritical marks.
9. Find and use homonyms, synonyms, and antonyms.
10. Recognize simple parts of speech.
11. Recognize symbols for nouns, verbs, and adjectives.

Book skills: Use various books to learn how to—

1. Use exact title of book in making references.
2. Use author's name in making references to book.
3. Use index and table of contents.
4. Use glossary.
5. Use paragraph headings.
6. Use cross-references.
7. Use preface.
8. Be aware of copyright date.
9. Introduce classification of books and library procedures.
10. Use letter keys of encyclopedia or reference book.
11. Use simple footnotes.

Skills of locating information: This involves the development of—

1. Use of dictionary.
2. Use of encyclopedias.
3. Use of almanacs and similar reference materials.
4. Use of film and filmstrip catalogues.
5. Use of television guides.
6. Use of newspapers.
7. Use of magazines and periodicals.
8. Use of the telephone book with particular emphasis on the yellow pages section.
9. Use of cross-references.
10. Use of indexes of free materials for sending for materials.

FIGURE 7–6. *Adventuring with materials is adventuring in reading: developing spatial concepts.*

11. Use of book skills.
12. Use of school library (call cards, picture files, materials files, and the Dewey Decimal System).
13. Use of periodicals.
14. Use of children's guides to locate materials.
15. Use of room files.
16. Use of reading maps and charts.

Developing Skills in Selecting Main Ideas

1. See suggestions pages 264–272.
2. Refer to teacher's manual of basic reading series for suggestions and ideas.

Developing Skills in Reading Dialects
and Other Levels of Vocabulary

1. Children are constantly exposed to many levels of vocabulary. One such level, often called the homely level, includes regional speech. For many years, textbooks failed to print stories containing dialect because it was considered too difficult for children to master. Many children were deprived of the joy of reading such stories as "Uncle Remus" because of the inability to use this skill.

Yet children *do* learn to read regional speech. Some of the current comics (such as "Snuffy Smith") are written in regional speech. As regional speech becomes more and more a part of our printed literature, children are exposed to it more frequently and should be taught to read it.

Dialect requires phonic reading. Familiar words become unfamiliar because they now appear in different shapes. Teaching dialect reading cannot precede basic training in phonics. As they must with all reading, children must have oral experiences with dialect before they can hope to pronounce it with phonic skills. The teacher can read dialect and explain it to children. Most children are exposed to many forms of dialect on television shows (southern dialect, cowboy, Irish). They are as eager to read it as to hear it, for dialect gives the language its contrasting rhythms and patterns.

Other types of vocabulary should also be taught in the intermediate grades. Classical literature can be introduced as part of a program in literature and creative writing, and at that time children can be taught how to read this level of writing.

One fifth grade was studying the New England States. Kenny brought "The Courtship of Miles Standish" to school because it was about the people they were studying. The teacher realized the reading was above the children's vocabulary level, so she told them the story. She then explained the style in which it was written. She typed and dittoed those parts that she felt the children could read, and they read them first silently, then in an oral audience-type situation. They discussed the beauty of the writing. Many children volunteered to read parts to the class. The entire class enjoyed it so much they decided to dramatize it. Later they included it in a moving-picture film that they made.

At no time during this experience was the beauty of the writing lost to the group. The original was not rewritten or watered down. To do that is to destroy the literary quality of the writing. Instead, the teacher helped the children bridge the gap between their own inadequacies and the skills required to read the poem. If children are unable to read certain pieces of literature they should not be asked to do so without some teaching that gives them the new skills required to enjoy it.

Part of the joy of learning reading skills comes from applying these skills to unexplored areas and making them work. Application of word analysis skills to dialect and classical literature can be a challenging and satisfying experience for intermediate-grade boys and girls.

READING LEVELS

Throughout the reading program the teacher must realize that all children operate on three basic reading levels: the independent, the instructional, and the frustration reading level.

At the independent reading level, the child can read with enjoyment and without help from his classmates and teacher. The material read will generally be below the level of instruction. At this level many easy books are read, and most children enjoy rereading stories they have previously enjoyed. The independent reading level is recognized by the fact that the child can read almost 100 percent of the material selected.

The instructional reading level is that level of reading where the child reads fairly well but needs help in certain reading skills or in the mastery of new vocabulary. It is at this level that actual teaching occurs. The criterion for the instructional level is that the child is reading 80 percent of the selected material independently.

The frustration reading level is that at which the child cannot read well enough to receive enjoyment or understanding from his reading. The criterion is that he reads little of the selected material with comprehension.

EVALUATING THE READING PROGRAM

A teacher can best evaluate her reading program by noting how the children read, their attitudes toward reading, and their selection of reading materials. Many good reading tests are available, although their misuse has frequently spoiled their effectiveness. Standardized tests help teachers find the ability levels of their students and, in many cases, will help the teacher identify the specific problems of each child. When used for this purpose, the tests can be of extreme value, but when teachers spend their time trying to get children up to "grade level" they are defeating the purpose of such tests. They must remember that the tests are based on norms (averages); therefore, half the class must fall above the midpoint and half below. If this is not true, the chances are that the teacher has either a brilliant or a retarded group.

The best readers are those who have a wide background of experience and basic reading skills from which to draw, and who enjoy reading immensely. The most effective way of evaluating a reading program is through the use of individual check sheets that show each child's abilities and needs in reading and indicate clearly his frustration level, his independent level, and his instructional level. Such charts used over a period of time will clearly show the child's progress and will remove threatening grade-level classifications and useless grade indicators. Children can help teachers keep these charts, which can be used to diagnose the children's difficulties, plan their instruction, and evaluate their growth. Many excellent charts and scales are available commercially, but children and teachers can do some creative thinking in making their own. The activity of constructing such a chart helps the children understand the teacher's objectives for the entire reading program and creates a high motivational interest in their own reading progress—the first step in the creative process.

The most useful of all the tests in teaching reading are those that may be used for diagnostic purposes. National achievement tests indicate a child's reading ability in relation to that of his peers. Because recent trends in the teaching of reading are toward individualized instruction, this information has become fairly irrelevant. What is important is that the teacher can identify those facts or skills that she has not taught or those that the children have not learned. A frequent diagnosis of the child's reading ability, along with the charts and records mentioned above, gives her this information and enables her to plan individualized instruction for each child.

SUMMARY

Reading is a skill that develops as a result of a mixture of instruction and the many components making up the personality of the child.   Basic to all reading instruction is the child's awareness that, through reading, he may find the answers to many of his problems and curiosities and experience adventures far removed from his own life.   To each child, reading is a personal thing—it serves to round out the knowledge, experience, and concepts his own living cannot afford him.   It is a skill he must acquire in order to live effectively in his society.

The teaching of reading must, above all, be exciting, practical, and individual.   No child should be hindered in his reading by being forced to wait for a poorer reader.   Nor should any child be pushed into material that does not communicate to him.   No child should waste time learning skills he already knows.   Nor should he be handicapped in his reading ability through lack of adequate materials that are on his level and interesting to him.

The basic purpose of teaching reading is to refine the skills to communicate.   The development of these skills gives the child the ability to do new things with his life.   Reading, for many children, can unlock the doors to creativity.   Most of the skills needed for the good reader are the skills necessary to develop creative people.   Teaching reading can contribute substantially to creative development.

TO THE COLLEGE STUDENT

1. Have one class member make a report on "The Individualized Reading Program" from the following viewpoint: The Individualized Reading Program is the most creative approach to the teaching of reading.

2. Work out a series of grouping plans for a reading period of one hour in any intermediate grade of thirty-two students when the following conditions are present:

   a. There are five different ability levels, and on this particular day the teacher is grouping by ability.   She has two readers who are two years above grade level, four who are a year above grade level, eight who are reading at the top of the grade, ten who are average, six who are a year or more below grade level, and two who are reading almost nothing.

   b. A particular teacher has discovered through the use of a diagnostic reading test that half of her class of thirty children does not comprehend at the 60 percent level, six others are very slow readers, and the remaining nine all have difficulty making generalizations.

In planning this one-hour period, be sure to plan work for all groups so that they may work independently when you are not working with them directly, and *be sure each group is creatively occupied, not just engaged in busy work.*

3. Divide your class into groups and assign each group the job of demonstrating the development of one of the skills listed in this chapter. Try to create an idea of your own, but, if you have difficulty, demonstrate one of the techniques suggested in this chapter.

4. In a fifth-grade classroom a teacher recently said, "I follow the reading manual religiously. After all, the men who write it are experts in their field and know a lot more about reading than I do."

   What is the fallacy in this teacher's reasoning?

5. Discuss this statement: Reading can be taught creatively without knowing all the things about reading presented in this chapter. What part does knowledge play in creative teaching?

6. Check Mr. Banks's lesson against the objectives listed at the beginning of the chapter. Did he accomplish each? If so, how?

7. Ask someone from your reading clinic or from a neighboring public school to give your class a demonstration in administering a reading diagnostic test and a readiness test.

8. Using the situations described in (2) above, plan how you would handle each group's reading levels in an open-classroom situation. What equipment might you have in the reading centers?

TO THE CLASSROOM TEACHER

1. Make a chart of the skills listed in this chapter so that you can check each pupil's name against it. Then ask yourself what you are doing to develop these skills in each child. If you are not doing much, plan a program that will start you working in the skills-building direction.

2. Do your children know *why* they are reading *every* time you have a reading lesson? Try informing them and see if it makes any difference in their attitude. Reading is a tool and is put to use for a reason. Let the children know the reason.

3. What program do you have for your slowest and poorest readers? Try meeting with them once a day and printing individual stories, which they dictate, for them to read. Perhaps a good reader who also prints well may do this for you. Allow the slow reader to make as many stories as possible just as

fast as he can read them.   Spring a surprise story on him once in a while using the same words he is using.   Encourage him to bind his stories in book form.   Check his speed, comprehension, and vocabulary development over a period of weeks.   Is this creative, open-ended learning and teaching?

4. Most reading manuals give lists of questions that can be answered by the children after they have read a specific selection in a reader.   This is closed, uncreative learning, for it does not put knowledge to new use.   Look over some of the lessons you plan to teach within the next few days and decide on ways you can change them to open-ended lessons where the new knowledge acquired is put to use.   For example: The children may be reading about a great invention, such as the telephone.   Instead of asking many uninteresting questions, why not start your lesson with this approach: "Today we are going to read about an invention that did a great deal for the world but also created many problems.   Let's read to see how that invention came to be and what good it did.   Then you will have to think about the problems it could and did create."

TO THE COLLEGE STUDENT
AND THE CLASSROOM TEACHER

1. Look at the list of instructional tasks of the intermediate teacher on page 63.   Plan a lesson for developing each task that will be creative in that it places children in a situation where they use old skills to develop some new ones.

2. Here are two questions taken from two different sixth-grade reading books:

    1. Why was the Battle of New Orleans fought after the War of 1812?
    2. Why did Vermont lose population in 1961 while a desert state, Nevada, and a swamp state, Florida, became the two fastest growing states in the United States?

    Which of these two questions is more likely to result in a lesson of critical thinking?   Why?

3. Think of five ways you might increase your own reading rate and reading comprehension.   If your college has a reading clinic, check to see what methods are used to increase reading speed and comprehension in adults.   Are any of these methods applicable to children?

4. Analyze your own study habits.   In what ways are you weak?   In taking notes, outlining, selecting main ideas from a lecture,

taking exams? Try to remember whether you were ever *taught* these skills or whether you just picked them up as you went along through school. How many of these deficiencies are due to improper reading habits? Do you see the value of teaching these skills in the elementary school? Try to work out a plan to help you remove your deficiencies. One resource that will help is *Effective Study*, 4th ed., by Francis P. Robinson (New York: Harper & Row, 1970).

5. Review the lesson Mr. Banks taught, which is presented at the beginning of this chapter. Check the skills described in this chapter against his lesson. Note how subtly he taught the skills in his presentation. Discuss these statements:
   a. An integrated language arts program is more meaningful than isolated periods of reading, spelling, and so on.
   b. Mr. Banks spent too much time (a whole afternoon) on teaching reading.
   c. Mr. Banks' lesson was a good example of the language-experience method approach described in Chapter 3.
   d. Mr. Banks met individual needs well without stratifying the children.

6. Review the lesson described at the beginning of this chapter and notice how many objectives Mr. Banks attempted to accomplish in his work. It is more customary for small reading groups to meet and work at one or two objectives. In terms of the philosophy of creative teaching summarized in Chapter 1, which of the two approaches sets conditions more conducive for teaching creative reading and developing creative potential?

SELECTED BIBLIOGRAPHY

Braun, Jean S. "Relationship between Concept Formation Ability and Reading Achievement at Three Developmental Levels." *Child Development* 34 (1963):675–682.

Cleland, Donald T., and Isabella Touissant. "The Interrelationships of Reading, Listening, Arithmetic, Computation, and Intelligence." *Reading Teacher* 15 (1962):228–231.

Cohen, S. Alan. *Teach Them All to Read: Theory, Methods, and Materials for Teaching the Disadvantaged.* New York: Random House, 1969.

Dechant, Emerald. *Detection and Correction of Reading Difficulties.* New York: Appleton-Century-Crofts, 1971.

Edwards, John L., and Nicholas J. Silvaroli. *Reading Improvement Program.* Dubuque, Ia.: William C. Brown Co., 1969.

Fallon, Berlie J., and Dorothy Filgo. *Forty States Innovate to*

Improve Reading Programs. Bloomington, Ind.: Phi Delta Kappan, 1970.

Harris, Albert J., ed. *Casebook on Reading Disability.* New York: David McKay Co., 1970.

Henderson, Richard L., and Donald R. Green. *Reading for Meaning in the Elementary School.* Englewood Cliffs, N.J.: Prentice-Hall, 1969.

Herber, Harold L. *Teaching Reading in Content Areas.* Englewood Cliffs, N.J.: Prentice-Hall, 1970.

Hunt, Lyman. *Learning to Read: The Great Debate.* Washington, D.C.: American Association of Elementary, Kindergarten, Nursery Education, 1968.

Mazurkiewicz, Albert J. *New Perspectives in Reading Instruction.* 2nd ed. New York: Pitman Publishing Corp., 1968.

Otto, Wayne, and Richard McMenemy. *Corrective and Remedial Teaching.* Boston: Houghton Mifflin, 1963.

Peltola, Bette J. "A Study of Child's Book Choices." *Elementary English* 40 (1963):690–695, 702.

Plessas, Gus, and Peggy A. Dison. "Spelling Performances of Good Readers. *California Journal of Educational Research* 16 (1965):14–22.

Potter, Thomas and Gwenneth Rae. *Informal Reading Diagnosis: A Practical Guide for the Classroom Teacher.* Englewood Cliffs, N.J.: Prentice-Hall, 1972.

Robinson, H. Alan, and Sidney J. Rauch. *Guiding the Reading Program.* Palo Alto, Calif.: Science Research Associates, 1965.

Schubert, Delwyn G., and Theodore Togerson. *Improving Reading Through Individualized Correction.* 2nd ed. Dubuque, Ia.: William C. Brown Co., Publishers, 1968.

Sebesta, Sam Leaton, and Carl J. Wallen. *The First R: Readings on Teaching Reading.* Palo Alto, Calif.: Science Research Associates, 1972.

Spache, G. P. "Contributions of Allied Fields to the Teaching of Reading." *Innovation and Change in Reading Instruction, Sixty-seventh Yearbook of the National Society for the Study of Education,* edited by Helen M. Robinson, pp. 237–290. Chicago: National Society for the Study of Education, 1968.

Stahl, Stanley S., Jr. *Teaching of Reading in the Intermediate Grades.* Dubuque, Ia.: William C. Brown Company Publishers, 1965.

Stauffer, Russell G. *Directing Reading Maturity as a Cognitive Process.* New York: Harper and Row, 1972.

————. *Teaching Reading as a Thinking Process.* New York: Harper and Row, 1971.

Stern, Catherine, and Toni S. Gould. *Children Discover Reading: An Introduction to Structural Reading.* New York: Random House, 1965.

Trela, Thaddeus M. *Fourteen Remedial Reading Methods.* Belmont, Calif.: Fearon Publishers, 1970.

Umans, Shelley. *New Trends In Reading Instruction.* New York: Bureau of Publications, Teachers College, Columbia University, 1963.

Wallen, Carl J. *Word-Attack Skills in Reading.* Columbus, O.: Charles E. Merrill Publishing Co., 1969.

CHAPTER VIII

The Creative Teaching
of Literature and Poetry

*Books are no substitute for living, but they can add
immeasurably to its richness. While life is absorbing,
books can enhance our sense of significance. When
life is difficult, they can give us momentary release
from trouble or a new insight into our problems, or
provide the rest and refreshment we need. Books
have always been a source of information, comfort,
and pleasure for people who know how to use them.
This is as true for children as for adults. Indeed, it is
particularly true for children.*[1]

MAY HILL ARBUTHNOT

TO THE READER

The above quotation bears special significance for teachers, for
they may enter the world of children through reading children's
books. Last year in this country there were as many children's
books as adult books published. If you have not read any children's books lately, read several before you read this chapter. It
will take on more meaning for you if you do.

INTRODUCTION

Miss Wilson typed the story of "The Elephant's Child" on ditto
paper for her fourth grade and numbered each paragraph. The

1. May Hill Arbuthnot, *Children and Books* (Chicago: Scott, Foresman
and Co., 1957), p. 2.

day's reading lesson was to be a combination of teaching new words in meaningful context and enjoying a good piece of literature. And it was to be a period when *all* children might enjoy reading together for a change rather than in small reading groups. Miss Wilson planned one such period each week, and the children always looked forward to it.

Miss Wilson knew her children well. She was well aware of their reading skills and abilities. She knew which of those numbered paragraphs Sammy and Julia could read and which they could not. She knew which words would be new to the entire group and which would be new to certain children.

She had many objectives in mind in planning her lesson. First, she intended to use it as an audience-type situation in order to check the children's oral expression in reading. Second, she planned to use the lesson as a means of developing certain word analysis and phonics skills. She also intended to build a picturesque vocabulary among all the children while realizing that some children would learn more words than others. She planned to use the whole of Friday afternoon to integrate literature, oral expression, reading, music, and art.

The children had been studying jungle life and jungle animals. This accounted for Miss Wilson's choice of "The Elephant's Child." Miss Wilson planned to do a great deal with Kipling's work and this was to be the children's introduction to him.

When school began, she asked all the children to take their seats. She told them she had a story about some animals who lived in the jungle and she wanted to read it to them. The children were ready at once, and Miss Wilson read the story with all the expression and drama she could muster. A discussion followed—and then a hunt for new words, which were placed on the board.

"I knew you would enjoy this story," said Miss Wilson, "and I ran off some copies for you so that we might read it together. While I am passing out these copies, will you think of someone to choose in this room who can make a voice like a baby elephant—like the elephant's child?"

Soon five names were suggested, and each of the five children was asked to read a selection from the dittoed papers, speaking like the elephant's child. After each had tried out for the part, they were asked to leave the room, and the children voted for the one they thought was best. Mark was chosen, and the children returned to the classroom.

Miss Wilson asked the children to take the dittoed sheets and find a paragraph that they could read well. While they were scanning the sheets, she walked around the room and assigned certain paragraphs to her slower or poorer readers.

When all the numbered paragraphs had been assigned, Miss Wilson suggested that the children read the story through once so she could help in the pronunciation of new words and they could all "feel" their voices. Mark, of course, read each time the elephant's child spoke.

"Now," said Miss Wilson, "I have here several records and I am going to play a small part of each one. While I'm playing them, will each of you think of the one you feel goes best with this story because it has the same rhythm, the feeling of the jungle, and seems to make a good background—just as they have a musical background in the movies."

She played excerpts from five different records. The children chose "The Elephant Walk" as the one they felt to be most appropriate.

Miss Wilson then suggested that the children think of a way they might announce the story if they were to read it and put it on tape while the music played in the background. The ideas were written on the chalkboard; the class finally agreed on this one:

Miss Wilson's Fourth Grade Class
Presents
THE ELEPHANT'S CHILD
by
Rudyard Kipling

Mark was asked to read it. The children then read the story into the tape recorder (while the music played in the background) passing the mike from one child to another.

"Before we hear how the story sounds on tape," said Miss Wilson, "I have something else here that I know you will enjoy doing. Here are some frosted and plain pieces of glass, which will fit into our lantern slide. Now, I want you to think about what will happen if we draw pictures on these slides and put them in the projector. Remember our science unit on light? How might we make colored pictures on these glass slides which will show up as colored on the screen in the front of the room?"

The children discussed this problem. Many new words were introduced and placed on the vocabulary chart at the front of the room—words like *transparent, translucent,* and *projection.* Some experimentation took place; they tried different media on the slides and tested to see whether the color would project onto the screen. The children found out that ordinary wax crayon cast only a shadow on the screen and that the color was lost. At this point, Miss Wilson introduced transparent Eastman crayons, which do project color. Soon a list of media that project color appeared at the front of the room, including the following: flo-pen ink, water colors, colored cellophane, Eastman crayons, colored ball-point pens, and regular ink. The children also discovered that some media could be applied directly to the frosted glass while others, such as the cellophane, had to be arranged and held in place with two pieces of clear glass, taped together with masking tape.

Each child then decided how he would make a slide to go with the paragraph he read—he could use any medium from the box of materials that Miss Wilson had placed in the front of the room. After each child had selected his materials and was working at his desk, Miss Wilson again played the music from "The Elephant Walk" to help the children keep the mood of the story. Each child was instructed to number his picture in the left-hand corner to correspond with the number on his paragraph. Children who finished early were set to work making and decorating title slides and one that said "The End." As each drawing was completed, the children brought it to the front of the room and put it in a box in the proper order.

Soon the production was ready. Miss Wilson chose two capable children to run the slides with the tape, and the children saw their own interpretation of "The Elephant's Child" in a combination of music, picture, color, and voice. They were so delighted with the project that they burst into applause at the end. Immediately they proposed showing it to other children in the school. So a list of the classes that might enjoy it was made on the chalkboard. A date was set to show it and a committee dispatched to the principal's office to sign up for the auditorium on the chosen date. Invitations were written and delivered, and, before the children went home, they had to see the story once more.

In the above account we have an excellent example of the creative teaching of literature and reading. In her lesson, Miss Wilson employed all the basic principles of creative teaching discussed in Chapter 1. On subsequent days the children used their vocabulary chart to discuss word structure and phonic structure. They were asked to show their project at a PTA meeting, and this resulted in poster-making and the study of the writing of announcements and letters of thanks. The basic "conforming" skills were learned by every child while all kinds of creative, individual products were being produced. Creative teaching accomplishes so much more than traditional teaching in the same length of time.

The following suggestions and illustrations are ideas that creative teachers have used to develop an enthusiasm and love for reading, literature, and poetry among children while at the same time developing their own creative powers.

GENERAL CONDITIONS THAT BUILD APPRECIATIONS AND STANDARDS IN LITERATURE

1. Have a library corner with good books easily available.
2. Keep a bulletin board of good books before the class. Discarded book jackets, posters, and pictures of favorite authors will help make these bulletin boards attractive.
3. Read a poem or story to the class at least once a day.
4. Encourage children to share the good books they have read by providing time during "sharing" periods.
5. Provide time every day for children to choose favorite books and to read silently.
6. Encourage the children to tell and write stories, poems, and books.
7. Take the class to good motion pictures of great pieces of literature or show these films in the classroom.
8. Use filmstrips, such as those of the Weston Woods, to create an interest in new books.
9. Use creative book reports for children to share each other's literature experiences.
10. Draw or paint pictures of favorite poems, books, or characters.
11. Encourage children to share their home libraries with the class. Ask them to bring three or four books from home and tell the others about them while they show the pictures.
12. Encourage frequent trips to the town library or the school library.
13. Reserve time occasionally for the school librarian to come into the room and show new books from the library or tell a story.
14. Encourage children to take advantage of local children's theater groups or traveling companies that do a notable adaptation of some piece of children's literature.
15. Watch the paper for good commercial television dramatizations of great children's literature.

16. Play some of the better commercial recordings of dramatizations of children's stories, such as *Hansel and Gretel, The Littlest Angel, Peter and the Wolf, Little House on the Prairie*.

17. Organize a Book Club that meets once a week in your classroom.

18. Have children make their own book jackets for their favorite books.

19. Make up good-book lists for parents and have them dittoed to be sent home. This may be done around Thanksgiving time as a guide for parents in purchasing children's books for Christmas gifts.

20. Watch for radio programs that dramatize children's literature.

21. In art class, have the children make posters of books they like. When made in three dimensions these posters add interest to book exhibits, library displays, and bulletin board exhibits.

22. Devote a few assemblies each year to programs about books. If each grade would take responsibility for putting on one assembly program during the year, to which other classes were invited, the children would be constantly exposed to books on all reading levels and all topics.

23. Celebrate Book Week with assemblies, exhibits, visits from authors, library trips, story hours, displays, and special programs. Be sure all children have a part in preparing for Book Week. (Many ideas for Book Week programs may be found on the following pages.)

24. Hold at least one or two Book Fairs a year where the materials made by the children may be exhibited. However, a fair should expose children to hundreds of new and exciting books. It will be necessary to arrange for traveling commercial exhibits. The books should be covered with strong plastic covers so that they may be handled and skimmed by children.

25. Correlate literature with all your classroom work. Every aspect of the school curriculum may be correlated with some great children's story or poem.

a. In social studies, read great books to help children understand the life of any given country. *Heidi* correlates well with a study of Switzerland, *The Secret Garden* with England. Kipling's stories relate well to India, and *The White Stag* is perfect reading when studying the countries of central Europe. Many books provide excellent material for dealing with social problems and may be used in bibliotherapy (see *Creative Teaching of the Social Studies*).

b. In grammar classes, study styles of writing by reading from various authors.

c. Much literature has been set to music, such as "The Lord's Prayer," "The Owl and the Pussycat," "Little Boy Blue," "A Nautical Ballad," "Cradle Hymn," and "The Nutcracker." Less notable but nonetheless, part of the children's rightful heritage are "A Visit from St. Nicholas," nursery rhymes, and folk ballads of the west, the mountains, and the plains. Music and literature can be closely correlated by singing some of the great poems set to music or by hearing them sung by great artists on high fidelity recordings.

26. Art work is a close companion to literature. Correlations in art have already been suggested in bulletin-board displays; creative book reports; drawings and paintings of stories, books and poems; posters, and, Book Week exhibits and displays. Other ways art and literature may be correlated include the following:

a. Use cut-out illustrations for children's favorite selections.

b. Use crayon sketches.

c. Use prints (potato prints, cork prints, block prints, and linoleum prints) to make book covers, program covers, and invitations to Book Week programs.

d. Have the children fingerpaint pictures of the literature they read.

e. Use spatter-paint designs as variety in illustration.

f. Make silhouette designs of favorite scenes from children's readings.

g. Use colored chalk to lend variety to illustrations, especially in covering large surfaces such as murals or backdrops for dramatizations.

h. Depict favorite characters with soap carvings.

i. Construct sand-table scenes of favorite stories.

j. Construct wood models.

k. Dress dolls to represent storybook characters (real and paper dolls).

27. Development of good oral expression can be closely allied with the development of an appreciation of good literature. In reading stories to the class, the goals of good oral presentation —poise before the group, clear enunciation, correct pronunciation of words, correct phrasing, a pleasant and interesting speaking

voice, and the ability to read with expression—can be developed.

28. In addition to the many activities suggested in *Creative Teaching of the Language Arts* that may be correlated with literature, children will enjoy making tape recordings of their favorite selections or stories; making up storybook quizzes; reading favorite selections to each other; telling the saddest part or the most humorous part of the story; holding a tall-tale contest; reading or quoting favorite poems; showing and telling about illustrations; and holding round-table discussions of favorite books, stories, characters, incidents and authors.

29. We have already seen how written expression can be correlated with literature in many ways. When the children create their own literature they will appreciate that of the writers. Some activities to develop written expression are writing plays and radio or TV scripts, writing character sketches, making dictionaries or reference books containing new or strange terms, collecting sayings, making riddles, keeping individual records of books read, writing short reviews for a local or school newspaper, making and working crossword puzzles, writing letters to friends about books, making animated book lists for children in another grade or of another age, and writing biographies of authors.

30. Keep a good, up-to-date anthology of children's literature on your desk so that you have a story or poem to use on any occasion.

CONTRIVED CONDITIONS THAT BUILD APPRECIATIONS AND STANDARDS IN LITERATURE

Dramatization. Most obvious of all the ways to live literature is through dramatization, which helps the children get the feel of the characters and sense the mood of the story. Many stories and poems lend themselves well to dramatization. The dramatizing of a poem or story can be creative in itself if children are encouraged to interpret characters, improvise props, and develop moods.

If we apply the principles of the creative situation to dramatization, however, we must go beyond a simple dramatization of a story in order to build up those qualities that make for creative and critical thinking. Mr. Brooks, a sixth-grade teacher, read *The Adventures of Tom Sawyer* to his children. They then chose to dramatize the fence-painting scene. Many children volunteered to play the parts. Mr. Brooks chose a cast and gave

them a few minutes to get simple props and to establish a crude
setting.   Then the group dramatized the scene.   When they had
finished, Mr. Brooks and the rest of the sixth grade told what they
had liked about the scene and also suggested how it could be im-
proved.
    Then another cast depicted the scene.   In the discussion
that followed, Mr. Brooks pointed out that the differences in the
interpretation were good, since different characters could be por-
trayed different ways without spoiling the plot of the story.   The
children also noted that the character of Aunt Polly lent itself
least to a varied interpretation.
    Through evaluation of this sort, children come to under-
stand characterization very well.   They also use words that describe the characters they are portraying, thus developing a good
oral vocabulary for later use in their own writing.
    Dramatization does not always have to be a story.   Little
children dramatize freely—they will mimic ducks, chickens, and
pigs as easily as they mimic people.   Intermediate-grade teachers
might well make use of this technique to build up the idea of
character.   Here are some suggestions for dramatizations, other
than stories, that teachers may use.

1. Pretend you are an animal.   Act like the animal you choose
   and let the class guess what you are.
2. The next time you go to a shopping center watch one person
   closely.   Then dramatize this person for us and we will see
   if we can tell what he was doing.
3. Show anger, pain, hunger, fear, joy.
4. Working in groups, dramatize a scene you saw during the
   past week at home or in school.   Use no voice, just pantomime.
5. Dramatize a holiday using no sound, only action.
6. Dramatize a day and have the class guess what the weather
   is like on that particular day.
7. Dramatize such words as *airy, beauty, hopeful, tremble, pain-
   ful, exciting.*
8. Dramatize your spelling words.
9. Dramatize one line of poetry.
10. Pretend you are in a circus.   Show us what you do.

    Poetry also lends itself well to dramatization.   Mr. Palm-
er's sixth grade dramatized "Casey at the Bat"; Miss Hobart's
third grade did "The Elf and the Dormouse."   In both instances
the children came to understand the drama and humor in the
poems.

Some books lend themselves to other kinds of dramatizations, such as pageants, shadow plays, or puppet plays. A discussion of some of these forms of dramatizations appears in *Creative Teaching of the Social Studies in the Elementary School,* Chapter 9.

Telling and Reading Stories. Both telling and reading stories have a place in presenting good literature to children. Some stories, poems, and plays are written in such a way that to tell them would be to spoil them. This is especially true of books where the script rhymes or where especially beautiful words are used to set a specific tone for the story. Dr. Seuss's rhyming books need to be read (unless the teacher can memorize the script). Robert McCluskey's *Time of Wonder* is a book that needs to be read because of the way he uses the soft sounds of *s* and *c* to give the impression of the softness of fog and rain, and the way he uses other sounds to develop an audio atmosphere for his story.

Other books should be read because of the close relationship between the story and the pictures. Many primary books are written in such a way that the pictures help tell the story. McCluskey's *Blueberries for Sal* and *Make Way for Ducklings* are good examples of such books. When books of this nature are

FIGURE 8–1.   *Children put the finishing touches on a scroll movie of* Island of the Blue Dolphins, *by Scott O'Dell.*

read, it is essential that the teacher set proper physical conditions so that all children can easily see the pictures.

When the teacher *tells* a story, something different happens. When reading, the book is the focus of attention for both teacher and children; but when a story is told the focus of attention is the teacher's face. Her voice inflections, her expression, her degree of animation, and her own enthusiasm play the major parts in putting the story across. The art of storytelling has almost become a lost one. It is due for a revival. Children gain something unique and special from this kind of experience with literature.

In telling stories the teacher need not memorize the entire story; this often makes for a stilted and wooden performance. In general, she only needs to know the story well, with the logical sequence of events carefully organized in her mind. But she must memorize the words, lines, or phrases that give the story its personality and charm—and repeat them in exactly the right places.

Because folk tales have always been passed along orally, they lend themselves especially well to telling. Such stories as "The King of the Golden River," "The Man Who Kept House," "The Gingerbread Boy," "East of the Sun and West of the Moon," and "The Princess of the Glass Hill" are especially suitable for telling. Legends and fairy tales fall into the same category.

Proper physical conditions are essential in storytelling. All distractions should be removed. Children should probably sit facing the quietest wall in the classroom. The teacher should stand if children are seated—at any rate she must be easily seen. Her voice must be sure and clear. Her face must show the animation and expression necessary to project the story as well as the mode or feeling of the words. She must see herself as the author, telling the story directly to the audience for which it was written.

Storytelling becomes highly personal in that it is person-to-person, with no barriers or distractions. It is communication in its most elementary and most beautiful form. The great literature of the past was all passed along this way before man could read and write. All children should experience the joy of hearing their teachers tell stories, since this is the way young children will communicate at home before *they* can read and write. Storytelling is an art children should be encouraged to practice throughout their lives, and teachers can set conditions for this art to develop in their classrooms.

Making Films. Film-making is less expensive today than it used to be, and children can have many worthwhile experiences making a real movie and showing it to other children.   Actually, making a moving picture is not much different from making a play —only much more permanent!   An 8mm camera can be used with black-and-white or colored film.   Taking movies is so simple with modern built-in viewfinders that children can be taught quickly how to do it.

Book Reports. There are many ways of giving book reports so that they are creative and challenging to children.   Too often, books are read for the primary purpose of making a report on Book Report Day, which makes the literature secondary.   Book reports assigned in this manner often make a child hate a book. If he has liked the book he will *want* to tell others about it!   The inventive teacher will find many ways to encourage the child to *tell* about his book.

Field Trips. Mr. Caldwell took a group of children to a museum. The children were well prepared for the trip and enjoyed the experience very much.   In a discussion following the trip, Mr. Caldwell talked about bigger museums and various other types of

FIGURE 8–2. *A dramatization of* Charlie Brown *is given as a book report by a group of slow learners.*

307

museums found in large towns.   He read the introductory chapter of E. L. Konigsburg's *From the Mixed-Up Files of Mrs. Basil Frankweiler,* that delightful story of the two children who run away from home and hide in the New York Metropolitan Museum.   Almost all the children then checked out the book in order to finish the story.

Bulletin Boards.   Bulletin boards can be exciting condition-setters for experiences with good literature.   Throughout this book frequent mention has been made of the bulletin board as an instructional device.   Bulletin boards may be arranged for a variety of objectives; in the realm of children's literature some of them are:

1. To interest children in new books or poems.
2. To have the children share their writing and reading with their classmates.
3. To summarize an experience in literature.
4. To impart information.
5. To provide individual instruction or individual work for the children.
6. To share beautiful passages, phrases, or words.

FIGURE 8–3.   *A clever bulletin board in the Glendale library.   Fixing your eye to the holes in the glasses assures you of a peep show glimpse of a scene from a favorite story.*

7. To encourage children to write creatively.
8. To advertise or announce new books and events about books.
9. To display first editions, unusual books, or illustrations in books.

Bulletin boards can be very creative and helpful in setting conditions for the enjoyment of literature. To be creative they must be ingenious, fresh, and interesting. They provide an outlet for the teacher's and the children's creative expression, much as a painting or a clay model will. Here are a few suggestions that should be considered in making bulletin boards that place no restrictions on the creator.

1. The overall effect of the completed bulletin board should be as good in design and as pleasing to the eye as a painting. Too much material can make bulletin boards confusing and cluttered.
2. Any lettering should be as much a part of the total design as the other material on the bulletin board. It should not be tacked on as an afterthought.
3. Bulletin boards are more attractive if material is grouped according to related ideas rather than simply spread out in any manner. Rest spaces for the eye help the purpose of the bulletin board to become more apparent.
4. Every bulletin board should be centered around an idea or purpose and that idea or purpose should be outstanding enough both to be immediately recognizable and to be conveyed across the room. The main idea should attract the children so that they are drawn to the bulletin board to read or see the subtopics. Importance can be obtained for the outstanding idea by having it larger, brighter, or more prominent than any other idea on the bulletin board.

Displays and Exhibits. Displays and exhibits can help children develop a love of books. During Book Week, many schools have Book Fairs where all the grades display the creations they have made that relate to good children's books. Often, assembly programs are given to stimulate an interest in stories and poems. Displays of commercial books, original sketches for various books, and bulletin boards about the authors' lives can add a great deal of interest to a Book Fair exhibit. To make the exhibit even more meaningful and "live," films may be scheduled at various times. Many schools invite an author to be present to tell stories or an illustrator to sketch for the children.

Commercial publishing houses will supply catalogues for

such exhibits.   Children should have the opportunity to handle books and help select those that are to be purchased for the school library.   Good children's magazines and periodicals should constitute a portion of book exhibits.

Often the neighborhood library advertises a children's book exhibit.   School personnel should take children to see it.

The value of displays and exhibits is enhanced when children have a part in setting them up.   This involves careful planning, however.   Haphazard exhibits are often so confusing that they become ineffective.   Material should be grouped topically, by authors or by reading level.   When tables are used, they should be elevated at the back in some way so that all books are readily exposed to view and some are not hidden behind others.   Books that are to be handled should be on tables low enough for the children to see them easily.   Often a theme for the exhibit (such as "A Book Is Like a Ship" or "Adventures through Books") makes it possible to organize the exhibit more logically and interestingly.

Although a large exhibit once a year is a worthy activity for any school, smaller exhibits and displays should be used constantly.   The school library should always have displays of new books and bulletin boards that excite an interest in reading.   A showcase near the main entrance of the school building can provide notice of the new books in the library as well as develop an interest in a special gem recently acquired.   Such a showcase or bulletin board can also keep children informed of the worthwhile television shows built around children's literature.   It can draw attention to fine films in town based on great writing.   The showcase can be used to announce unusual events, such as the Book Fair, special noon-hour film showings, and current neighborhood library displays.   Such announcements and displays create even more interest among children when they have had a part in creating them.

Pegboard Displays.   Pegboard is invaluable in the modern classroom.   It is adaptable to many uses and purposes, especially in the promotion of children's literature.   With the variety of hooks, metal pockets, and bars manufactured for the pegboard, the teacher is able to display three-dimensional objects very effectively as part of her bulletin-board display.   The books themselves can be placed in the pockets; through the use of the adjustable wires, they can be displayed open to selected passages.   Pegs help to hold pictures in place.   Bars make it possible to construct simple shelves where clay modeling or other three-dimensional objects may be displayed.

Contacts with Authors. It is thrilling for a child to become acquainted with an author through his writings and then to correspond with that author or, to see him. Teachers can develop a great love for literature, and for reading, by writing to live poets and authors, or by influencing a local organization to bring one to visit the children during Book Week or any other appropriate time. Writers of children's books love children and are most gracious with them. Acquaintance with these fine people is a constructive and inspiring experience for children.

Dioramas. Dioramas provide children with a three-dimensional picture of the images created in their minds by the stories and poems they read. Similar to a shadow box in construction, the diorama provides an opportunity for the creative use of materials in group or individual projects. They can be made from cardboard cartons or can be constructed as a real art form with heavy cardboard and wood.

Dioramas are especially effective at book fairs and exhibits. A series of them can show scenes from several stories or poems, or can show several scenes from the same story. Sometimes dioramas can be made in various forms to add uniqueness to an exhibit.

Puppet Shows. Puppet shows sustain the quality of make-believe that permeates much of children's literature; therefore, they are very well suited to dramatizing children's stories and poems. Children who use puppets a great deal to interpret literature soon become skilled in using them creatively.

Box Theaters. Box theaters provide another form of dramatization that can be adapted to many different uses in presenting children's literature. Box theaters are actually dioramas with some sort of movement added. Sometimes the movement comes simply from slits in the bottom of the box through which stick figures make their appearance on the stage. Larger box theaters can be used with hand puppets.

One group of children who were studying magnets used a box with a thin cardboard bottom and made their characters move about the stage through the use of magnets. This was done by making cardboard figures and inserting a paper clip in the base that held each figure upright. The powerful magnet, when touched to the cardboard floor, attracted the paper clip. By moving the magnet about on the underside of the floor, the figures in

FIGURE 8–4. *Dioramas made by children of their favorite books.*

the box theater moved about also. To stop them in a particular place, the magnet was simply pulled away from the cardboard floor. One group of children used this technique very effectively in dramatizing *Hans Brinker and the Silver Skates*. The magnet was especially effective in making the skaters glide.

Shadow Plays. A quick way to make a shadow play is to hang a sheet before the class but far enough away from the front wall so that an overhead projector may be placed along the wall. The projector must cast a large enough square of light to fill the sheet. Very effective shadow scenery can be made by cutting small trees, houses, porches, and pillars from chipboard or cardboard and simply laying them on the lighted surface of the overhead projector. The shadows cast can then be focused sharply to create the illusion of the intended scene. Characters play the scene standing near the sheet so that they cast sharp shadows and the illusion continues. Exciting effects can be obtained by adding colored cellophane to change the lighting or by adding

FIGURE 8–5. *John and David prepare a marionette show of* The Painted Pig.

moving color to create psychedelic effects.   The scenery can be
changed in a few seconds simply by turning out the overhead
light, removing the cardboards, and setting up the next scene.

One group of middle schoolers who loved the story and
illustrations of *A Story, A Story,* by Gail E. Haley, were able to
capture the color and excitement of the book illustrations by using
colored cellophane for scenic backgrounds and cardboard figures
to make shadows for the main characters.   The story was then
narrated on a tape recorder with an appropriate musical background and shown at a school assembly.

Shadow Boxes.   A large shallow box can be made into a shadow
box that will serve as a focal point for arousing interest in good
literature in the classroom.   The front of the box can be cut out,
leaving a frame which is then painted and hung on the wall.   Because of the depth of the box, three-dimensional objects may be
displayed in a variety of ways to obtain many interesting effects.
A feeling of greater depth may be obtained by painting heavy
cardboards to represent various aspects of a scene and placing
them one behind the other.   Sometimes lights (the Christmas
tree variety) can be added to gain more realistic effects.

The Lap Story.   Lap stories are very effective in helping children
become involved in a piece of literature, and many variations are
possible.   Lap stories serve as another way to make interesting
book reports.   They may be planned by individuals or by groups
of children.

Commercial materials are often well adapted to the lap-
story technique.   Miss Ames found the characters of Red Riding
Hood printed on a Post Toasties box.   She punched them out and
used them for a lap story.   The paper dolls were designed in such
a way that Miss Ames could insert two fingers in the holes near
the base of the figures and thus, by moving her fingers, make
them walk.   "Dr. Seuss" figures, purchased at the department
store, also served as the core for a good lap story.   Paper dolls
can also be used for this purpose.

Felt-o-grams and Flannel Boards.   Felt-o-grams and flannel
boards are especially effective for stories that are developed by
adding a character or two as the story progresses (such as "The
Gingerbread Boy") or for those stories where there are not many
scene changes but there is a building up of one or two scenes
(such as "The Duchess Bakes a Cake").

Stories with several scenes can be effectively depicted by

tacking several layers of flannel along the top of a board and drawing a simple scene on the flannel with crayon.   The pieces of flannel can then be flipped as the scenes unfold, and the characters and scenes can be added in their logical sequence.

Many creative effects can be developed with the flannel board if children are encouraged to find all materials that might adhere to the flannel.   Colored pipe cleaners can be bent quickly into many shapes and they will stick readily to felt or flannel. Blotters will also stick to felt and flannel, and many figures and objects can easily be cut from them.   Decorative materials, such as glitter or Christmas snow, also adhere to flannel and can create interesting illusions.

Peep Boxes.   Peep boxes are constructed much like shadow boxes. They allow the children to put into visual form the images that words from their favorite stories create in their minds.   They are

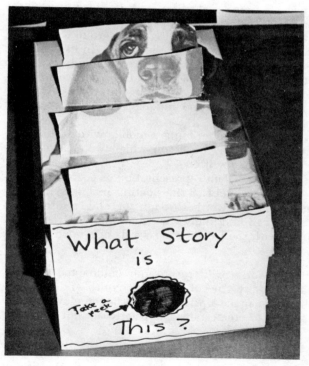

FIGURE 8–6.   *A creative use of materials: an old shoe box becomes a peep show of a child's favorite book. Slits in top admit light.*

especially useful for individual projects. The element of mystery added by "peeking" at the scenes is high motivation for children. Peep boxes can be used effectively in school book exhibits, at book fairs, and for book reports.

Clay Modeling. Children enjoy using clay or plasticine to model their favorite characters or scenes. Clay modeling helps the child capture the feeling of the character he is depicting. Sometimes this can be done by a facial expression, a stance, a posture, or a gesture.

Mobiles. Mobiles are especially fascinating when units on literature are being taught. Miss French's second grade was reading Dr. Seuss. The children and the teacher read all the Dr. Seuss books they could find. They also read and collected material about Dr. Seuss as an author.

Their five favorite Dr. Seuss stories were listed on charts. Each child signed his name under the story he liked best of the five. Then the children met by groups and planned what they would like to put on a Dr. Seuss mobile. Each group worked out its mobile, which was suspended from the ceiling, in its own way. One group used a tree branch, which they painted white. From it, suspended by threads, were Horton, Maizie, the two hunters, an egg, a circus tent, and a ship. Another group crossed sticks and balanced many grotesque and unique animals to represent *If I Ran the Zoo.*

In the center of the room hung a mobile with a picture of Dr. Seuss surrounded by tiny books on which were printed the names of every book he had written.

Mobiles are an excellent representation of poetry and well-written prose. The movement of the floating mobile symbolizes the flow of characters and words through the child's mind. An imaginative teacher can find many ways to match the free, fluent action of a mobile with the free-flowing words of a good poem or story.

Fingerplays. Many works of literature may be adapted to finger plays. This is especially true of nursery rhymes and counting poems. Children can make up rhymes for finger plays or they can use their fingers to create table puppets to act out stories or selections.

Games. Certain games, such as charades, can help children to develop an interest in literature. A child can act out the title of a book while the rest of the class tries to guess what it is. Games such as "Who Am I" or "What Am I" encourage descriptive word usage.

Often the games that children play regularly in gym periods can be adapted to a game dramatization. Bombardment is an excellent game to play along with the reading of *The Adventures of Robin Hood* or "The Charge of the Light Brigade."

Creating Ballads. Another way that music and literature can be correlated is to help the children put their favorite stories into ballads. They can pretend they are singing the story just as the old minstrels did long ago. The story can be retold in free or rhyming verse. Atmosphere can often be added if someone in the room strums a guitar or the teacher plays a recording of guitar or string music. Often one child begins the story and points to another to continue. Children who cannot make rhymes are not pressured to do so; they just tell their portions of the story in their own ways. The musical background will help to determine the tempo and rhythm with which they tell it.

Impersonations. One very effective way of creating interest in an author's ability to describe characters is to encourage the children to impersonate characters from the books they have read together while the rest of the class guesses who the character is. These impersonations can be done in many ways. Children can dress in costume and tell about themselves; they may act out a character silently; or they may use the "I Was There" technique, where they sit before the class and pretend they were eyewitnesses to a particular scene of the story in which the character they are depicting took an active part. Some primary teachers have encouraged this sort of activity by using a large cardboard box as a television set on which children tell about themselves.

Dance Interpretations. Many poems and stories lend themselves well to dance interpretation.

After the children in the second grade had read "The Elf and the Dormouse," Miss Bradford asked them if they would like to dance the story. A large umbrella, used as the toadstool, was set in the middle of the room. Some of the children then made up "elf" steps. Others made up "mouse" steps. The children selected the two interpretations they liked best, and then Miss Bradford composed music to go with their steps. After one group had danced the story, another group gave their interpretation.

In Miss Harmon's fourth grade the children made up a dance for "A Visit from St. Nicholas." There were many step patterns to be planned—the prancing reindeer steps, the heavy, plodding "Ho-ho-ho" steps of Santa Claus, the airy steps of the sugar plums dancing through the children's heads, and the fast steps of the wind and the leaves that "before the hurricane fly." Miss Harmon used a Fred Waring recording as a background for this dance.   At another time her children dramatized "The Elves and the Shoemaker," and she composed music for the dance.

For their Book Week Assembly program, a group of fifth-grade girls and boys created a dance from "Snow White and the Seven Dwarfs."

Whenever possible, children should have the opportunity to see literature translated into dance interpretations; for example, a corps de ballet dancing the *Nutcracker Suite, The Red*

FIGURE 8–7.   *A dance interpretation of Eleanor Estes'* The Hundred Dresses.

Shoes, Peter and the Wolf, Hansel and Gretel, Cinderella, or *Robin Hood.*

Setting a Mood for a Story. Since literature often creates a mood, teachers should be conscious of the mood, or tone, of stories and should set conditions for the full enjoyment of these stories.

Some, such as ghost or mystery stories, are effectively told with the lights out in the classroom and the shades drawn. One candle burning on a table in the center or at the front of the room often lends additional mystery to the situation.

Some stories are told most effectively against a background of soft music. This is especially true of poetry, which lends itself to mood very well. Interesting combinations of voice and music can be developed, both when the teacher reads to the children and when they read to each other.

Roll Movies. Roll movies can be an excellent way to introduce stories and poems, to develop the sequence of a story, or to use the author's language to translate words into visual imagery.

FIGURE 8–8. *A scroll movie of* John J. Plenty and Fiddler Dan, *by John Ciardi.*

Miss Fry's class made a roll movie of trees as a result of reading "A Tree Is Nice." Almost all stories lend themselves to roll movies, which provide a fine opportunity for children to express themselves creatively in a group project. (A roll movie is shown in Fig. 8–1.)

Radio and Television Shows. Almost all children these days have the opportunity of putting on a live television or radio performance. But too often the "showy" aspects of a school program are exploited in such presentations. Children's literature could be used much more than it is for these programs. This would not only help educate parent viewers to good literature for children but would also motivate child viewers to watch better television shows. Simple or elaborate props can be used for such programs. It is important for the teacher to remember that it is the beauty of the words that makes good literature, so the author's words should be used as much as possible. Many of the suggestions in this chapter are well-suited to television programming: choral speaking, puppet shows, shadow plays, dramatizations, reading with music, dance interpretations, pantomimes, book reports, displays and exhibits, dioramas, interviews with authors, flannel boards, pictorial maps, and impersonations.

It is well to remember that although most of this material should grow out of regular classroom work, the class is justified in striving for a polished performance when it is to be presented before the public.

Choral Speaking. Poems and many prose selections lend themselves well to choral reading or choral speaking exercises. Many illustrations of the effective use of choral speaking were given in *Creative Teaching of the Language Arts,* 2nd ed. Choral speaking can enrich children's enjoyment of literature by giving them a method of using the words of the author in beautiful and varied ways. It can often be used *with* many of the other activities for promoting children's literature that have been mentioned in this chapter. Choral speaking provides an excellent background for shadow plays, puppet shows, and pantomime. Probably no other device is as effective in enriching a child's oral vocabulary.

Booklets. All kinds of booklets can be made as a result of experiences in children's literature. These range from simple booklets containing book reports and illustrations to very highly developed scrapbooks of collections of all kinds.

Book-binding can be taught to children so that they can

make their own scrapbooks or booklets. Attractive covers dealing with themes built around their favorite characters will enhance the value of these booklets. Booklets and scrapbooks can contain many interesting materials relating to children's literature.

Murals. Literature can be expressed very well in mural painting. Tempera paint, cut-out construction paper, and colored chalk lend themselves well to the creation of brightly colored murals for the classroom, the school corridors, or the school library.

Murals can grow out of one story or poem, or they may be a composite of many of the works of literature that the children have read.

POETRY IS FUN

A special word must be said about the teaching of poetry. So few children above the primary grades seem to love and know poetry that it seems essential to give poetry some extra attention and explore ways of reviving an interest in it.

Poetry is part of a child. It exists in the rhythm of his walking, his speech, his dancing, his movements, and his singing. By setting the proper conditions for learning, teachers can encourage the child to express his poetry in written form. Once a child writes his own poetry he needs little motivation for enjoying the poetry of others. However, teachers should constantly present poetry in new and exciting ways so that the children may gain deeper appreciations and skills in using it as a creative outlet. Much of the tension in children can be positively released if they can put their feelings down on paper in a creative form. A revival of interest in poetry is a must in a world full of the tensions of the Space Age.

All of the ideas suggested in the preceding pages are applicable to setting conditions for the creative teaching of poetry. Because poetry is a unique form of written expression, however, some additional suggestions are entered here.

1. Use choral speaking for the teaching of many poems.

2. Write a poem on the chalkboard and divide the class into groups. Encourage each group to think of a different way to present the poem through choral speaking.

3. Print a rhyming poem on a large sheet of paper. Cut the poem into rhyming strips and pass out the strips. Allow the children who have the strips to go to the front of the room and

reassemble the poem by rhyming it.   Then allow them to do the poem in choral speaking.

4. Create special moods by reading such poems as these to the children:

> "The Song of Hiawatha," by Henry Wadsworth Longfellow (with drum beats) (A)[2]
> "The Bells," by Edgar Allan Poe (with bells) (I)
> "Gerald McBoing-Boing" (with "boings" and other sounds suggested by the story) (P)
> "The Monotony Song," by Theodore Roethke (with clapping patterns) (P)
> "An Easy Decision," by Kenneth Patchen (with a whistling tune) (I)
> "The Song of the Jellicles," by T. S. Eliot (with a phonograph record in the background softly playing "Buffalo Girl, Won't You Come Out Tonight") (A)

Special moods may also be created simply by reading poetry that is beautifully written.   Discuss with the children the mood created by such poems as these:

> "Flight," by Steve Allen (I)
> "The Coming Star," by Juan Ramón (A)
> "The Prayer of a Butterfly," by Carmen Bernos de Gosztold (A)
> "Loneliness," by Haskin (A)
> "Youth," by Langston Hughes (I)
> "Within A Word," by Karla Kuskin (A)

5. Read action poems and then have the children create sounds or actions to go with them.

6. Encourage the children to find as many poems as they can on one topic, such as *The City*, and discuss the many interpretations and feelings people can have of the same place.   For instance, a comparison of David Budbell's "New York in the Spring," Quandra Prettyman's "Still Life: Lady with Birds," and John Updike's "Scenic" can show children dramatically that much beauty is in the eye of the beholder.

7. Find a mood picture and place it on the bulletin board. Under it place a placard saying, "What poems tell how these people feel?" or "What poems describe the feeling of this picture?"

---

2. In these lists, (A) indicates "any grade," (I) indicates "intermediate," and (P) indicates "primary."

Help children find appropriate poems by providing anthologies of children's poems.

Poetry, like all literature, must be a source of enjoyment to children in order to be appreciated. The study of the structure of poetry has little place in the elementary school except as it relates to helping children structure their own poems.

In selecting poems for children, certain criteria can be kept in mind. A poem should do one or more of these things:

> . . . it should catch moments of beauty; it should penetrate the honest feelings of the author and the reader; it should picture interesting people; it should release hearty laughter or it should tell appealing stories.[3]

Teachers should be very skeptical of poems that attempt to teach lessons, contain remote adult ideas, or drip with sentimental doggerel.

Poetry can be *lived* by children and *loved* by children.

SUMMARY

Literature is the record of man's living that contains his feelings as well as his way of life. Children can capture the spirit of literature because they have inherited the same feelings as other men even though they live in a different age. Literature is a common bond of communication of feelings across the continents, across the countries, and across the years. The beauty of living in all times is captured in it. It is the rightful heritage of all children everywhere. Teachers can help children relive and re-feel the history of the world by helping them read and experience their great literary heritage.

TO THE COLLEGE STUDENT

1. One of the most valuable references you can have in your teaching is a file of children's literature. Explore children's

3. Leland B. Jacobs, "Children's Experiences in Literature," *Children and the Langauge Arts*, Virgil E. Herrick and Leland B. Jacobs, eds. (Englewood Cliffs, N.J.: Prentice-Hall, Inc., 1955), p. 195.

books by having each member of your class bring one to class each day to read. Have each member find out something about the author and the other books he has written. Each class member can take notes on these readings on 3 x 5 cards and can begin to build such a file.

2. Also start to collect magazine articles and pictures of children's books and build a file of these for use in your student teaching.

3. There is a great deal of trash sold as children's literature today. Have each member of the class bring a book of recent publication to class. Using the criteria for selecting children's literature defined in this chapter, evaluate the books brought in by the class members.

4. There are many children's magazines on the market. Some are excellent, others are tawdry. Collect copies of various kinds of children's magazines and assess their literary value.

TO THE CLASSROOM TEACHER

1. The best way to use children's literature as a part of the reading program is through an individualized reading program. Note the books listed on individualized reading at the ends of Chapters 7 and 8. If you have not tried such a program, read these books and try to individualize your top group as a starter, allowing the children to select their own materials and keep their own records. Later you can try it on your other reading groups.

2. One way to help children become interested in literature is to afford them the opportunity to share books through creative book reports. Take one reading period a week and devote it to this kind of activity rather than to skills reading. Watch to see if it pays dividends. Do children become more interested in books? Is the library frequented more often? Do the children carry books home more often?

3. In planning your next unit, use the *Elementary School Library Collection* to see how many ways literature can be used in correlation with social studies, science, arithmetic, and the creative arts.

TO THE COLLEGE STUDENT
AND THE CLASSROOM TEACHER

1. Make a list of all the current television shows that are based on children's literature. View some and discuss them in class with the following aspects in mind:

    a. Did the presentation catch the flavor of the story?

    b. What justifiable changes were made for television presentation?

    c. How creative was the producer in transferring the book to the television screen?

    d. Do you think television programs of this sort encourage or discourage the children from reading good literature?

2. Obtain a copy of the report of the American Library Association's Annual Conference and look for these facts:

    a. How many children's books were published in the past year?

    b. How many children's books were published in 1940?

    c. Note the books that were the most popular with children. How many of them do you remember as being translated into television shows?

    d. From these observations, can you tell whether children are reading more or less than they did twenty years ago and can you make some conclusions about the effect of television on children's reading?

3. Many children's stories have been made into motion pictures or cartoons. Among the many popular ones are: *Snow White and the Seven Dwarfs, Bambi, Peter Pan, Treasure Island, Hansel and Gretel, Cinderella, Pinocchio, Lassie Come Home, Sounder, Pippi Longstocking, Charlotte's Web, Ivanhoe,* and *Mary Poppins.* In translating these classics to the screen, were the producers justified in taking liberties with the original manuscript? Do you feel the interpretation for any particular one was creative or commercial? Do you think films of great literature endear the writing to children or just make it easy for them to get the idea of the book? Discuss this.

4. The next time a children's classic is being shown at a local theater, call the manager and ask for an approximate attendance figure. Then call the local library and check on the circulation record of the particular book being shown in the film. Also check with your school library. Check other evidence to determine whether or not films encourage or discourage the reading of the book.

5. The *New York Times* publishes a Sunday supplement of children's books once a year. This is a very valuable resource. Watch for it and add it to your files.

6. Which are your favorite children's stories? Can you determine why they remain so dear to you after all these years? Think about the situation under which you were first introduced to these stories and of succeeding experiences with them. How much did the content of the story contribute to your liking it. The mood? The circumstances under which

it was first read?   Are conditions important in introducing literature to children?

7. A description of bibliotherapy is given in *Creative Teaching of the Social Studies*.   Discuss this question: Is bibliotherapy a creative way of using children's literature?

8. List all the ways that Miss Wilson's lesson (see p. 296) developed creativity in the children and followed the principles of creative teaching.

9. Many creative thinking skills can be developed through the use of children's literature in the classroom.   Select some well-known children's book and study it for answers to the following questions:
   a. What creative thinking skills does the author develop— does he appeal to the imagination? display clever use of words? challenge the reader's ability to use empathy?
   b. What kind of personality characteristics are encouraged or discouraged by the story?
   c. Does the author tell a story, moralize, develop a "cautionary" tale, set a mood, or combine any of these?   If so, does the work ring true?

10. Can you select enough children's trade books that are of literary value to form a logical base for a reading instruction program beginning with Easy-to-Read books and continuing through books that could be used to develop word attack skills?   Try to do this using the resources of a children's library.

SELECTED BIBLIOGRAPHY

Adams, Bess Porter.   *About Books and Children*.   New York: Henry Holt, 1953.

Allen, Arthur T.   "Literature for Children: An Engagement with Life."   *The Horn Book Magazine* (December 1967), pp. 732–737.

Anderson, Paul.   *Flannelboard Stories for Primary Grades*.   Minneapolis: T. S. Denison & Co., 1962.

Bacon, Wallace A., and Robert S. Breen.   *Literature as Experience*.   New York: McGraw-Hill, 1959.

Baker, Augusta, comp.   *Books about Negro Life for Children*.   3rd ed.   New York: New York Public Library, 1963.

Bamman, Henry J., Mildred A. Dawson, and Robert J. Whitehead.   *Oral Interpretation of Children's Literature*.   Dubuque, Ia.: William C. Brown Co., 1964.

Barnet, Sylvan, Morton Berman, and William Burto. *The Study of Literature*. Boston: Little, Brown, 1960.

Batchelder, Marjorie H., and Virginia Comer. *Puppets and Plays: A Creative Approach*. New York: Harper and Row, 1956.

Burger, Isabel B. *Creative Play Acting: Learning through Drama*. New York: Ronald Press, 1966.

Cameron, Eleanor. *The Green and Burning Tree: On the Writing and Enjoyment of Children's Books*. Boston: Little, Brown, 1969.

Carlson, Ruth Kearney. *Literature for Children: Enrichment Ideas*. Dubuque, Ia.: William C. Brown Co., 1970.

Chambers, Dewey W. *Literature for Children: Storytelling and Creative Drama*. Dubuque, Ia.: William C. Brown Co., 1970.

Cianciolo, Patricia. *Literature for Children: Illustrations in Children's Books*. Dubuque, Ia.: William C. Brown Co., 1970.

Clark, Margaret. *Keeping Up with Children and Books, 1963–1965*. Dallas: Scott, Foresman, 1966.

Crosscut, Richard. *Children and Dramatics*. New York: Charles Scribner's Sons, 1966.

Cullinan, Bernice E. *Literature for Children: Its Discipline and Content*. Dubuque, Ia.: William C. Brown Co., 1971.

Eakin, Mary K. *Good Books for Children, 1948–1961*. Chicago: University of Chicago Press, 1962.

Early, Margaret, and Norine Odland. "Literature in the Elementary and Secondary Schools." *Review of Educational Research* 37 (April 1967):178–185.

Ellis, Alec. *How to Find Out about Children's Literature*. New York: Pergamon, 1966.

Fenner, Phyllis, ed. *Something Shared: Children and Books*. New York: Day Publishing Co., 1959.

Fenwick, Sara Innis. *A Critical Approach to Children's Literature*. Chicago: University of Chicago Press, 1967.

Fitzgerald, Burdette S. *World Tales for Creative Dramatics and Storytelling*. Englewood Cliffs, N.J.: Prentice-Hall, 1962.

Gaven, Mary V., ed. *The Elementary School Library Collection* (A Guide to Children's Books and other Media). 7th ed. Phases 1–2–3. Newark, N.J.: Bro-Dart Foundation, 1973.

Georgiou, Constantine. *Children and their Literature*. Englewood Cliffs, N.J.: Prentice-Hall, 1969.

Greene, Ellin, and Madalynne Schoenfeld. *Multimedia Approach to Children's Literature: A Selective List of Films, Filmstrips and Recordings Based on Children's Books*. Chicago: American Library Association, 1972.

Gruenberg, Sidonie M. *More Favorite Stories Old and New for Boys and Girls.* Garden City, N.Y.: Doubleday, 1948.

Haviland, Virginia. *Children's Literature, A Guide to Reference Sources.* Washington, D.C.: U.S. Government Printing Office, 1966.

Hinman, Dorothy, and Ruth Zimmerman. *Reading for Boys and Girls* (a subject index and annotated bibliography for the Illinois State Library). Chicago: American Library Association, 1970.

Hodges, Elizabeth D. *Books for Elementary School Libraries: An Initial Collection.* Chicago: American Library Association, 1969.

Hoffman, Miriam, comp. *Authors and Illustrators of Children's Books: Writings on their Lives and Works.* New York: Bowker, 1972.

Kingman, Lee, ed. *Newbery and Caldecott Medal Books: 1956–1965.* Boston: Horn Book Co., 1965.

Larrick, Nancy. *A Teacher's Guide to Children's Books.* Columbus, O.: Charles E. Merrill Publishing Co., 1963.

Lonsdale, Bernard, and Helen K. Mackintosh. *Children Experience Literature.* New York: Random House, 1972.

McCaslin, Nellie. *Creative Dramatics in the Classroom.* New York: David McKay Co., 1968.

Nunnally, Nancy. *Guide to Children's Magazines, Newspapers, Reference Books.* Rev. ed. Washington, D.C.: Association Childhood Education International, 1966.

Palovic, Lora, and Elizabeth B. Goodman. *The Elementary School Library in Action.* Englewood Cliffs, N.J.: Prentice-Hall, 1968.

Pearson, Mary D. *Recordings in the Public Library.* Chicago: American Library Association, 1963.

Pellowski, Anne. *The World of Children's Literature.* New York: Bowker, 1968.

Saunders, Jacqueline. "Psychological Significance of Children's Literature." In *A Critique Approach to Children's Literature,* edited by Sara Inis Fenwick, p. 15. Chicago: The University of Chicago Press, 1967.

Sawyer, Ruth. *The Way of the Storyteller.* Rev. ed. New York: Viking Press, 1962.

Siks, Geraldine B. *Children's Literature for Dramatization.* New York: Harper and Row, 1964.

Tooze, Ruth, and Beatrice Perham Krone. *Literature and Music as Resources for Social Studies.* Englewood Cliffs, N.J.: Prentice-Hall, 1955.

Viguers, Ruth Hill. *Story-Telling and the Teacher.* Washington, D.C.: American Association of Elementary, Kindergarten, Nursery Education, 1967.

Woods, Margaret. *Creative Dramatics.* Washington, D.C.: American Association of Elementary, Kindergarten, Nursery Education, 1967.

CHAPTER IX

Conclusion

My book and heart
Shall never part.

—THE NEW ENGLAND PRIMER

There is no one approach to reading that works with all children.
Many teachers today use the best of each of many suggested
methods, and this is as it should be. Research on which one of
several systems of teaching reading is best is plentiful but not
conclusive. Together, all the systems emerge as one of two basic
approaches: the analytic (which is a words-to-reading approach)
and the synthetic (a letters-to-words approach). Children actually need both analytic and synthetic skills in order to be effective readers. They need to observe both the whole words and
the characteristics that individualize words.

In reviewing the countless hours I have spent in the past
ten years observing the teaching of reading to children, I must
admit to a great sense of boredom and lethargy as the lessons
moved along. I have empathized with the children with all my
heart. Even when the lessons were challenging or unusual, they
soon lost their excitement because the teacher, sensing she had
hit on something good, began to repeat her motivation techniques
day after day and soon the freshness and excitement were gone.
I have seen children subjected to boring lessons taught from
manuals, from workbooks, with machines, and with audio-visual
materials. I have seen children plunged day after day into reading experiences with little motivation other than a phrase such
as, "Come on, it's time for reading." The number of teachers
who really made reading exciting to the point where I sat on the

edge of my chair and listened and participated in rapt attention have been very few.

Yet these were conscientious teachers doing what they had been told to do according to manuals and systems and principals and experts. In most cases, after a few weeks, they became as bored with their teaching as the children had become bored with their learning. I have watched and over and over I have felt, "There must be a better way!"

Children and teachers are human beings; they were not meant to be robots and middlemen.

From my own teaching experiences in the elementary school, where I have been privileged to teach all grades, I have learned one lesson: Reading must be fun for children. *All learning must be fun in order for it to be learning.* For having fun to children does not mean the opposite of *work* as adults are prone to define it. It means having a great sense of achievement, of having taken your part comfortably in a congenial group, of having contributed to the work of the group, of feeling happy and contented because you are a better person for being with the group. It means having a feeling of being accepted, being important, and being wanted. It means you pass your time in a way that is meaningful to you so you are satisfied with yourself. And having fun is hard work. I have seen intermediate grade boys dripping with perspiration while building scenery for a play, which they thought was great fun. I have seen primary children concentrate to the degree that I thought their knotted and furrowed brows would crack open with the intensity of their thinking over a word game only to jump up and down two minutes later clapping their hands and laughing, because they had mastered the task and it was fun!

"Cook-book" teaching is playing too great a part in today's education, and that is not as it should be.

Teachers today are well-trained. They are the experts of children. A teacher who is not has no business being a teacher.

And experts of children are needed to teach reading successfully. They are, indeed, needed before the experts in reading.

Our elementary teachers spend large amounts of time studying how to teach reading. Courses in the teaching of reading are mandatory by law in several states. Many conscientious teachers continue to take reading courses as part of their master's degree program because they want help with the reading problems they find in their classrooms. Yet, after they prepare themselves and secure teaching positions, they are often told that they must follow a certain system, or plan, or basal series, or workbook series, and their children must reach certain grade standards by the end of the year. It is a paradox that some school systems ridicule or practically ignore the training teachers receive in their colleges of education by insisting that they follow prescribed systems or programs. Many of my graduate students have sat in my office with me over a cup of coffee and have told me how their administrators (who often have never had a course in the teaching of reading) will not allow them to use creative approaches to reading but insist that they follow a prescribed set of books. One student recently said, "My principal said to me at our first faculty meeting, 'Now that you're really teaching forget all that junk you learned at the college. It's all theory. This is the real thing and you'll find it's all different.' " Yet, that same principal wanted to reimburse me handsomely for coming to his school for a week's workshop on the teaching of reading.

When all is said and done, the one great variable in the teaching of reading, as in all teaching, is the teacher. No system will work if the teacher is not behind it, but the chances are strong that any system will work if the teacher considers the children first and then is creative enough in her approach to make reading a stimulating, exciting experience and pastime for every child every day, regardless of his ability level.

The one thing that impressed me most in the schools I studied in England where I met Charlie (who opens this book) was the eagerness, the joy, and the excitement of learning that was apparent on the faces of all the children. These children were with creative teachers who considered and knew the children before they prescribed any method of teaching.

Creative teaching, I believe, can make any system work with children; but not by following the prescribed words of a manual or a programmed course in reading. It will work when the teacher starts with her own students whom she knows, loves, and wants to help, and when she knows the materials that are available in the school and understands the objectives they were designed to meet. She will then be able to adapt the materials to each individual child to help him to learn according to his own learning patterns by using her own creative ideas and making each lesson (both group and individual) so challenging and stimulating that children will *want* to learn, will have fun learning, and will be confident in their own ability and success.

The teaching of reading can be a creative act. Moreover, there is a type of reading that can justifiably be labeled *creative reading*. For it, certain skills and methods of teaching are needed in order to develop divergent thinking processes in children. This type of reading has been greatly neglected in reading programs to date, although many current reading systems incorporate several of the components necessary for the development of creative reading.

Teachers can be trained to be creative teachers of reading and creativity can be developed in children through the creative teaching of reading. That is the message of this book.

TO THE READER

1. The following chart lists some films that you may wish to view. They may be used with children to develop reading skills.

Name of Film	Length	Color or B&W	Com- pany	Level
Choosing Books to Read	13½ min.	B&W	Coronet	JH*
Reading for Beginners: Using Context Clues	11 min.	C	Coronet	P
Reading for Beginners: Words and Word Parts	11 min.	C	Coronet	P
Reading for Beginners: Word Shapes	11 min.	B&W	Coronet	P
Reading for Beginners: Word Sounds	11 min.	C	Coronet	P
Reading Growth: Adjusting Your Reading Speeds	13½ min.	B&W	Coronet	I
Reading Growth: Basic Skills	13½ min.	C	Coronet	I
Reading Growth: Getting the Big Ideas	13½ min.	B&W	Coronet	I
Reading Growth: Reading Creatively	13½ min.	B&W	Coronet	I
Reading Growth: Under- standing Word Meanings	13½ min.	B&W	Coronet	I
Reading Signs Is Fun	11 min.	C	Coronet	K–P
Reading Stories: Characters and Settings	11 min.	C	Coronet	I
Reading Stories: Plots and Themes	13½ min.	B&W	Coronet	I
Reading with a Purpose	11 min.	C	Coronet	I

* To indicate level, the following code is used: P, Primary; I, Intermediate; JH, Junior High.

2. There are many resources to help teach reading creatively that you may wish to explore. A few are listed below:

Material	Description	Company
Alphabet Blocks	Thirty multicolored plastic blocks, grouped by color into fifteen identical pairs. Each pair is devoted to two letters of the alphabet and has on the sides capital and small forms of each letter and a labeled picture for each letter.	Scott, Foresman Co.
Alphabet Cards	Each nine-by-twelve-inch card shows a color picture and the capital and small forms of one letter of the alphabet.	Scott, Foresman Co.
Basic Phonics Charts	Thirty-five six-by-nine-inch cards with large type and colored pictures introducing sounds, word lists, and a sentence repeating the sound.	Educational Aids
Magic Vowel Cards	Forty flash cards. One side of each card contains a word with a short vowel sound; on the other side, the sound is changed to the long vowel sound by the addition of one or more letters.	Educational Aids
Match-and-Check	Five two-sided boards (12¾″ x 6½″) with a disc to turn at each end allow children to match pictures, colors, shapes, or words.	Scott, Foresman Co.
Match the Vowel Cards	Two sets of fifty cards. The yellow deck has short and long vowels; the blue deck contains vowel digraphs.	Educational Aids
Picture Alphabet Cards	Set of twenty-six cards (11″ x 14″) show attractive illustrations of well-known animals and other objects.	Educational Aids
Third Syllable Game Cards	Fifty-four flash cards give practice in attacking big words one syllable at a time.	Educational Aids

SELECTED BIBLIOGRAPHY

Arbuthnot, May Hill. "Developing Life Values through Reading." *Elementary English*, 43 (January 1966):10–16.

Betts, Emmett A. *Foundations of Reading Instruction*, Part IV. New York: American Book Co., 1957.

Carroll, J. B. "Linguistics and the Psychology of Language." *Review of Educational Research* 34 (April 1964):119–126.

Fries, Charles Carpenter. *Linguistics and Reading*. New York: Holt, Rinehart and Winston, 1963.

Glass, Gerald, and Muriel Walzer Klein. *From Plays into Reading*. Boston: Allyn and Bacon, 1969.

Goodman, Kenneth S. "The Linguistics of Reading." *Elementary School Journal* 64 (April 1964):172–178.

Guilford, J. P. "The Structure of Intellect." *Psychological Bulletin* 52 (1956):277–295.

Henderson, Richard L., and Donald Ross Green. *Reading for Meaning in the Elementary School*. Englewood Cliffs, N.J.: Prentice-Hall, 1969.

Hildreth, Gertrude. *Teaching Reading*. New York: Holt, Rinehart and Winston, 1968.

Kennedy, Eddie C. *Classroom Approaches to Remedial Reading*. Itasca, Ill.: F. E. Peacock Publishers, 1971.

MacCampbell, James E., ed. *Readings in the Language Arts in the Elementary School*. Part 7, Reading Instruction, pp. 283–331. Boston: D. C. Heath, 1964.

McKee, Paul, and William K. Durr. *Reading: A Program of Instruction for the Elementary Grades*. Boston: Houghton Mifflin, 1966.

Mathews, Mitford. *Teaching to Read: Historically Considered*. Chicago: University of Chicago Press, 1966.

Sartain, Harry. *Individualized Reading: An Annotated Bibliography*. Newark, Del.: International Reading Association, 1964.

Schonell, Fred J. *The Psychology and Teaching of Reading*. New York: Philosophical Library, 1962.

Smith, Henry, and Emerald Dechant. *Psychology in Teaching Reading*. Englewood Cliffs, N.J.: Prentice-Hall, 1961.

Smith, Nila Banton. *American Reading Instruction*. Newark, Del.: International Reading Association, 1965.

Spache, George D. *Toward Better Reading*. Rev. ed. Champaign, Ill.: Garrard Press, 1968.

——— and Evelyn B. Spache. *Reading in the Elementary School*. 2nd ed. Boston: Allyn and Bacon, 1972.

Spitzer, Lillian K., comp. *Selected Materials on the Language-Experience Approach to Reading Instruction.* Newark, Del.: International Reading Association, 1967.

Stauffer, Russell G. *Directing Reading Maturity as a Cognitive Process.* New York: Harper and Row, 1969.

———. *Teaching Reading as a Thinking Process.* New York: Harper and Row, 1972.

Strang, Ruth. *Helping Your Child Improve His Reading.* New York: E. P. Dutton, 1962.

——— and Donald M. Lindquist. *The Administration and the Improvement of Reading.* New York: Appleton-Century-Crofts, 1960.

———, Constance M. McCullough, and Arthur Traxler. *The Improvement of Reading.* 4th ed. New York: McGraw-Hill, 1967.

Tinker, Miles A. *Bases for Effective Reading.* Minneapolis: University of Minnesota Press, 1965.

Wardaugh, Ronald. *Reading: A Linguistic Perspective.* New York: Harcourt, Brace and World, 1969.

Wilson, Robert M. *Diagnostic and Remedial Reading for Classroom and Clinic.* Columbus, O.: Charles E. Merrill Publishing Co., 1967.

Zimet, Sara Goodman. *What Children Read in School.* New York: Grune and Stratton, 1972.

Zintz, Miles V. *Corrective Reading.* Dubuque, Ia.: William C. Brown Co., 1966.

INDEX